Open Boat
CANOEING

by Bob Wirth

PARKER PUBLISHING COMPANY, INC.
West Nyack, New York

Special thanks to the following people . . . . .

Audrey Baiett
Carol Behl
Joel Burris
Aaron Hathaway
Glen Hathaway
LiAnn Hathaway
Ross Hathaway
Chris Grove
Katherine (KC) King
Carl Metelits
Cathy Miller
Jill Pressman
Sharon Rose
Phil Schwartz
Janet Simpson
Dan Suthers

for help with the photographs.

© 1985, by

PARKER PUBLISHING COMPANY, INC.

West Nyack, N.Y.

Library of Congress Cataloging in Publication Data

Wirth, Bob,
  Open boat canoeing.

  Includes index.
  1. Canoes and canoeing. 2. Canoes and canoeing—
United States. I. Title.
GV783.W54 1984   797.1'22'0973   84-14907

ISBN 0-13-637596-0

ISBN 0-13-637547-2 {PBK}

Printed in the United States of America

HOW THIS BOOK
CAN HELP YOU

Welcome to the world of canoeing! The thrill of whitewater, the comforts of solitude, the companionship of friends, the challenge of a wilderness expedition, the freedom of mobility and self-sufficiency . . . these are the joys of canoeing. There's a world of sunshine and water and fishing and swimming and tradition and adventure out there along our waterways and it's all yours for the price of a song. As you'll soon find out, almost everyone in North America is within a short drive of canoeable water, and while advanced canoeing techniques require some time to master, anyone can get started in the sport with little effort and often even less expense.

If you aren't familiar with canoeing, it may seem like there's so much gear to collect and so many techniques to learn before you can really begin. Just the size and apparent complexity of this book may frighten you. When it comes right down to it though, canoeing is a relatively simple sport. Though whitewater techniques take a while to learn, you can be out there paddling on a calm river or secluded lake in almost no time at all. For your first canoeing experiences, almost any equipment will do, and you don't even need to know the proper way to launch a canoe or paddle it to have fun.

Sooner or later, however, you'll get the urge to really master the sport instead of ignorantly poking around in a canoe. Maybe you've gotten tired of watching other canoes glide effortlessly along while your rental boats seem to handle like sunken battleships. Maybe you've decided that you'd like the thrill of paddling through rapids or would like to extend your backpacking and camping experiences to canoe camping as well. Maybe a friend convinced you that canoeing is an excellent way to escape a high pressure, fast-paced lifestyle. In any case, you have an interest in learning more about the sport.

Canoeing has changed dramatically over the last few years. Computer design simulations, the invention of space-age materials, and new construction techniques have drastically affected the development of canoeing equipment. There's no need to invest in a floating bathtub anymore. In addition, advanced racing techniques have refined canoeing strokes to give you maximum power with minimum effort, and with the invention of substances such as Goretex and Thinsulate, outdoor clothing has undergone profound changes. Nowadays, experienced paddlers don't even consider wearing wool instead of pile for warmth or paddling in a vinyl rainsuit.

While canoeing, kayaking, rafting, and closed boat canoeing (C1's and C2's) have much in common with each other, the refined techniques of each sport are quite different. You can't learn to canoe from a kayaking book, for example. Due to restricted publishing space and limited authors' experiences, "all-inclusive" books about those sports blur their differences instead of highlight them. This book, on the other hand, is only about open boat canoeing. Its content is focused, direct, and complete. While parts of it are useful for kayakers and rafters, it's written exclusively for open boat paddlers. *Open Boat Canoeing* is a complete, up-to-date, "how-to" book describing everything you need to know about the sport of canoeing. General topics include buying equipment, reading a river, poling, and water safety. No-impact canoeing is stressed throughout the book, because unfortunately, the outdoor world is too small and too crowded for us to travel the way we please anymore.

Like my previous book, *Backpacking in the 80's*, *Open Boat Canoeing* is written in a clear, simple style. As you read it you'll get the feeling that I'm talking directly with you and that I'm explaining technical terms in a down-to-earth, easy-to-understand fashion. However, don't be misled by this book's comfortable writing style. There are no filler words, off-the-track stories, or gaps of information in it. *Open Boat Canoeing* is clear in reading, concise in its presentation, and complete in content.

This book is organized in an easily referenced manner. If you're new to canoeing, simply read it from cover to cover to get a feel for the sport. Then, read sections of it as needed when buying equipment, and use other sections of it as a reference guide when perfecting your canoeing techniques. If you're an experienced paddler, use this book when buying additional equipment or teaching friends how to paddle a canoe or read a river. Enjoy!

Bob Wirth

Contents

Other Books by the Author:

Backpacking in the '80s

PROLOGUE

"We've had many crazy experiences canoeing here, but today had to be one of the best days!"

"Yeah, man, that sun was superb! No rain, no pinned canoes, no blizzards, no capsizes, no wet sleeping bags . . ."

"John, you forgot that water battle we had just before the Barryville Rapids. Everyone went overboard in that one."

"Yeah, you're right."

"Water battles don't count as capsizes. We got too many of them to count."

"We've seen some spectacular capsizes here, though."

"Yeah, I think one of the best was when Lou and Bob, the 'experienced ones' among us . . ." Several campers interrupt with laughter. ". . . the experienced ones," Ed continues, "had their first capsize in a riffle in a snowstorm!"

". . . and they didn't pack their packs right. All their stuff got wet! Remember what Bob looked like when he finally crawled out of that river!"

"I'm glad they built that Laundromat at Barryville. It was worth the hike to have a dry sleeping bag that night."

"I think all of you used that Laundromat more than Bob or I ever did," Lou said defensively. "In fact, I remember the time Mark got so cold he crawled into a dryer to warm up."

"I missed that trip."

"That was the time Kip threw our chicken dinner into the river. I guess he didn't like the way I cooked it."

"It wasn't cooked. It was on fire!" Kip quickly added. "Who wants to eat burned chicken?"

"Yeah, and that's when we all ganged up on you and tied you to a tree!"

"Hey, you guys, we need more wood," a voice with a spatula said.

"Speaking of capsizes, I remember the time the two Ralphs were paddling near Port Jervis. They pinned their boat on the only rock in that whole section of river!"

"It was a funny sight, alright! Both of them were standing up in their boat to keep dry, while the Delaware poured in over the side. Finally the boat slid off the rock and left them neck deep in the river!"

"And Ralph still had his cigar in his mouth!"

"Hey, you guys, the fire's going out. We need more wood," the voice with the spatula interrupted.

"I think John had to be the funniest person I ever paddled with," Mark said. "Once we were paddling around somewhere in Quebec when he stuck his paddle into a lake to see how deep it was and he lost it! He lost his paddle!! It just sank into the lake!''

"We all know about John. He does more ruddering than paddling. He probably didn't need the paddle anyway.''

"You guys want dinner?'' the voice with the spatula said. "Then you better get more wood. Fire's going out!''

Silence. Then laughter.

"You want wood, then you get it.''

"I'm cooking. You guys get the wood.''

"I'll cook for you while you get the wood.''

"Jeff, you don't know how to cook!''

"Maybe not, but I can hold the spatula as well as you've done for the last 20 minutes or so.''

"I'm waiting for the burgers to cook.''

"I can wait as well as you've waited for the last 20 minutes. I'll do the waiting. You get the wood.''

"Why don't we all get wood?'' the leader suggested. "The sun's going down.''

"So what?''

"You guys want a campfire tonight or not?''

"Yeah, I'll order a campfire, medium well done. Side order of wood too . . .''

"Food'll be ready as soon as the fire gets going again. We gotta get wood or we'll starve.''

"We don't have to starve. We could eat raw burgers.''

"Raw burgers or burned burgers. Not a big selection. Tom's cooking again . . .''

"Mark, who's doing the dirty dishes that Mark should have cleaned because it was Mark's turn to wash the dishes this morning, huh, Mark? Even if we got wood, how can we eat with all these dirty dishes?''

"Same way we always do.''

"Why don't a couple of you wash dishes, a couple of others get wood, and the rest of you set up the tents?'' the leader suggested.

"Set up the tents? Ralph, you crazy? The weather report said it'll be clear all weekend . . .''

Early that next morning, while Noah sailed his ark down the Delaware and before dawn cracked the eastern skies, ten hungry weekend warriors began the long, cold, rainy, slippery hike to the Barryville Laundromat. "Driest, warmest place around,'' they muttered to each other. And so it came to pass, through rainstorms and blizzards and campfires and cookouts, they learned about canoeing, learned about life, and learned the rivers' song.

To Ed, Tom, John, Lou, Mark B., Mark C., Kip, Jeff, the Ralphs, and the rest of the gang for a bunch of crazy years. And to the Delaware, where it all began so far away and so long ago . . .

EQUIPMENT

1

CANOES

THIS chapter may seem unnecessarily long and complicated for those of you just getting started in canoeing, but it's important that you understand the information in it so you can get the best possible canoe for your needs. Hopefully after reading it, you'll have a much better understanding of the boating world in general and the confusing array of canoes and canoe design features available.

KINDS OF PADDLE BOATS

The next few paragraphs describe and compare the kinds of self-propelled paddling boats available. Don't be concerned if you don't understand the underlying concepts like maneuverability or the terms like rocker discussed here. They're explained in detail later in the book. At this point, just try to get a feeling for the various kinds of paddle boats that exist and for how open boat canoes compare with other self-propelled boats on the market.

Canoes

There are several kinds of canoes available (Example 1-1). *Open boat canoes* are the kind of boats that an average man off the street would identify simply as a canoe. They are called "open" because they have no permanent cover over them to keep out water. These canoes are by far the most popular paddle boats in use and are the focus of this book. In fact, over 100,000 paddle boats are sold in North America each year and the vast majority of them are open canoes.

Open boat canoes are very versatile crafts. Because of their large capacity, they're ideal for long expeditions, carrying passengers, boating with small children, hauling freight, hunting, and fishing. You can easily store and access gear in them because of their open hull design. They handle up to class III (moderately difficult) whitewater with dignity, yet are as much at home on lakes as on rivers. Furthermore, open canoes are easy to learn how to use, offer a host of sitting and kneeling positions for comfort on long trips, and are easily rigged for sailing, rowing, and motoring. The major disadvantages of open canoes are their comparatively sluggish maneuverability in rough whitewater, their tendency to swamp in rapids and waves, their high profile which catches the wind, and the relatively inefficient single blade paddling stroke used to propel them.

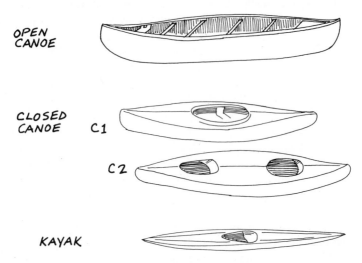

Example 1-1: Comparison of an open canoe with two closed canoes and a kayak.

Closed canoes are canoes that have a permanent, rigid cover across their top to keep out water. They are often designed specifically for paddling in rough whitewater where there's a great chance of capsizing or swamping an open boat. When closed canoes capsize, you can immediately perform a technique called an *Eskimo roll* which rights them so you can continue paddling without interruption. Because closed canoes are often designed for rough whitewater, involve complicated maneuvers like the Eskimo roll, and require specialized equipment like helmets, canoeists in closed canoes are almost always experienced paddlers. Closed canoes are called C-1s if they have one paddler in them and C-2s if they have two paddlers. C-1s are about 12 to 13 feet long while C-2s are usually 14 to 16 feet long. Large C-2s occasionally have a third cockpit for easier access to stored gear and for carrying a passenger.

Kayaks

Kayaks are sleek, graceful, maneuverable, fast closed boats almost always designed for one paddler. While open boat canoes could be characterized as dependable but not overly responsive work horses and rafts as lumbering elephants, kayaks resemble quick and agile butterflies. Kayaks are ideal in rough whitewater because of their closed top and quick maneuverability and are quite satisfactory in flatwater because of their efficient double-blade paddling stroke.

Kayakers are pleased with their boats' advantages. Kayakers and closed boat canoeists can often linger and "play" in rapids where open boat canoes can't maneuver or would swamp. The double-bladed paddling stroke typical of kayaks is extremely efficient and powerful. After each stroke, no energy is wasted returning the paddle blade to its starting position, and almost no effort is expended making sideways course corrections when paddled properly. Kayak paddling strokes are transmitted directly to the water because the paddler is locked into the boat with a form-fitting seat and knee and foot braces. A kayak's low center of gravity is ideal for maintaining balance in the boat, for leaning it during complicated whitewater maneuvers, and for "feeling the water" through it. While canoeists ride *on* the water, kayakers ride *in* it—a subtle but significant difference.

There are disadvantages with kayaking, however. Because you ride so low in the water in them, it's hard to gain a good perspective of safe routes through upcoming rapids. All the features of a rapids look the same from their just-above-waterline vantage point. The "locked in" kayak sitting position is often uncomfortable at best. It's not uncommon for kayakers to have stiff backs, numb legs, and a sore butt after only an hour or two in their boats. Kayaks have limited storage space for gear, and it's difficult to access that gear when secured because of their permanent top covering. Finally, you must master the Eskimo roll technique and be a good swimmer before paddling unsupervised in a kayak.

Rafts

Rafts are generally large, round, inflatable boats that are cumbersome in rapids and hard to paddle in flatwater. They either are rowed with oars like a rowboat or are paddled with single-blade paddles like a canoe. Because of their large size and great stability, rafts are popular on larger rivers containing difficult rapids like those in the Grand Canyon, on extended river trips where you must carry plenty of gear, and on social outings. Disadvantages include their lack of maneuverability, their slow speed, the tendency to clutter them with too much gear, and the hard work required to propel them on flatwater.

Inflatable and "Folding" Boats

Inflatable boats are relatively inexpensive, stable, roomy, lightweight canoes, kayaks, and rafts. Generally, unless made of a durable, thick outer fabric, inflatable boats are too fragile for long term use and for running intricate rapids. Instead, they're best used on rivers with high volumes of water and for casual flatwater float trips. Many inflatable boats are not suited for long distance or high speed travel because of their excessive hull flexibility.

"Folding" or "suitcase" boats are rigid-hulled canoes and kayaks you put together each time you want to use them. While their portable nature is ideal for people with no room to transport or store a standard, rigid boat, they're designed more for occasional recreational boating than for specific kinds of technical

paddling. It takes about 20 minutes to rig a folding boat, assuming you haven't lost any pieces. You can, of course, leave them set up for long periods of time, but that negates their portability advantage.

KINDS OF OPEN BOAT CANOES

There are several kinds of open boat canoes. *Tandem canoes* are designed for two paddlers. They're somewhat longer, wider, and heavier than *solo canoes*, which are made for a single canoeist. *Square-ended canoes* are built for use with a motor. All three kinds of boats are designed for recreational, flatwater/touring, racing, or whitewater use or for a combination of those uses.

Recreational canoes are general purpose boats suitable for use under a wide range of conditions but not designed to be the optimum boat for any one situation. This is the kind of boat you'd buy if you needed a canoe for a variety of uses such as running rapids, canoe camping, family lake paddling, and fishing. *Flatwater/touring canoes* are designed primarily for paddling on flatwater and for use on long expeditions involving only mild rapids. They have more room for carrying gear than other kinds of canoes and emphasize traveling in a straight line rather than maneuvering in rapids. *Racing canoes* vary widely in design from *slalom* boats built with great maneuverability to *downriver* models designed entirely for straight ahead speed. Specialized gear like built-in foot braces, toe straps, and adjustable seats are common on both slalom and downriver models. *Whitewater canoes* are strong, durable canoes made for running rapids. They emphasize maneuverability at the expense of traveling in a straight line.

In addition, canoes can be categorized as comfort models, high performance models, or combinations of both. *Comfort or utility canoes* are preferred by novice and carefree boaters. In general, they offer greater initial stability, a larger size, and more personal comfort features (like seats, for example). They handle satisfactorily under a wide range of conditions, but aren't the best possible canoe to use for one specific condition. *Performance canoes*, on the other hand, sacrifice personal comfort for any number of specifications such as speed, light weight, maneuverability, and strength. They tend to be expensive, higher quality models designed to give the best possible performance under the specified conditions. Downriver racing canoes, for example, sacrifice stability, strength, and personal comfort for speed. Touring canoes sacrifice speed for greater carrying capacity.

Finally, two special categories of canoes exist. *Freight canoes* are designed primarily for hauling cargo, and *ceremonial canoes* are very large boats used mostly at camp ceremonies. Neither are common on waterways or popular among serious canoeists.

BASIC TERMS

Become familiar with the terms explained below as soon as possible, since they're used extensively throughout the rest of this book and in the canoeing world as well. Using them incorrectly is an indication that you're an inexperienced boater.

Nautical Terms

The general nautical terms related to canoeing are (see also Example 1-2):

abeam	to the side
ahead	in front of
astern	behind
bow	the front
stern	the back
amidships	the middle
fore	towards the front
aft	towards the rear
starboard	the right side
port	the left side. An easy way to remember the difference between starboard and port is that both port and left contain four letters.
windward	the side closest to the wind or the direction of travel into the wind
leeward	the side sheltered from the wind or the direction of travel away from the wind
whitewater	turbulent water caused by obstructions or sudden changes in a river's flow
flatwater	water with no apparent current

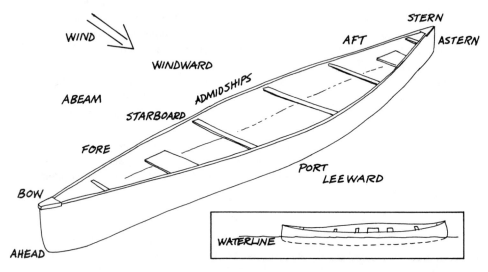

Example 1-2: General nautical terms that relate to canoeing.

whitecaps	the white tops of large waves. This term refers to wind-blown waves and not to waves caused by obstructions in a river's flow.
waterline	the imaginary line around a boat that marks the boundary between air and water
solo	one, single, or alone
tandem	two

Canoe Dimensions

The following terms describe common canoe measurements. They are illustrated in Example 1-3.

beam	the width of a canoe at its widest point
draft	the minimum depth of water needed to float a canoe
depth	the vertical height of a canoe from its keel to a designated point along its gunwales. Usually depth is measured at the bow, stern, and amidships.
freeboard	the distance from the lowest point along a gunwale to the waterline. This is measured with the canoe fully loaded (people and gear) and resting level in calm water.
length	the distance from the farthest front part of the bow to the most distant part of the stern
rocker	the degree of upward curvature from amidships to the bow and stern
width	the horizontal distance across a boat at a designated point

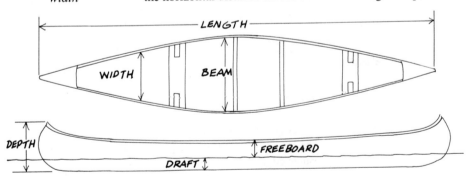

Example 1-3: Canoe dimensions.

Parts of a Canoe

The terms outlined in the following list and illustrated in Example 1-4 are the typical parts of a canoe. They're listed below for quick reference and explained in detail in the text that follows.

bang plate	a piece of material that reinforces the bottom front of a canoe when paddling through rapids
bilge	the place of greatest curvature between the bottom of a canoe and its sides
bow cap	the piece of bow material sealing the place where the hull, deckplate, gunwales, and stem meet
bulkhead	the partition between the flotation compartment and the interior of a canoe
decks	the flat upper surfaces covering the flotation compartments at the bow and stern
flotation	lightweight material usually stored in the bow and stern to prevent a boat from sinking when swamped
grab loops	short loops of rope secured at the bow and stern used for carrying a canoe

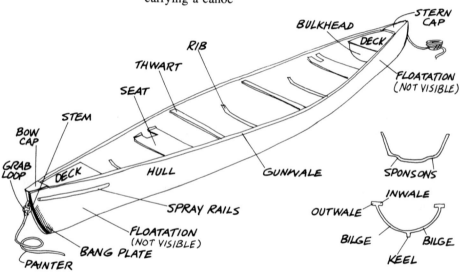

Example 1-4: Parts of a canoe.

gunwale	the edge running around the top of a canoe. The *inwale* is the lip on the inside of the gunwale and the *outwale* is its outer edge.
hull	a general term describing the entire outer part of a canoe
keel	the ridge running along the bottom, outside, center of a canoe
painters	10- to 15-foot sections of rope attached to the bow and stern used to secure a canoe to shore, to a vehicle, and to a lining or rescue rope

ribs	lateral, internal supports that stiffen the hull
seats	specially built thwarts you can sit on
skin	the outer covering of a canoe. In effect, it's the outer-most "layer" of the hull.
sponsons	bulges in a hull at the waterline that increase a canoe's initial stability
spray rails	strips of material attached to the outer hull to keep splashed water out of a boat
stem	the strip of material running up the outside of the bow and stern
stern cap	the piece of stern material sealing the corner where the hull, gunwales, deckplate, and stem meet
thwarts	reinforcing bars placed across the opening of a canoe from gunwale to gunwale
trim	any component including thwarts, gunwales, ribs, deck plates, and seats not composing the hull itself

CANOE CONSTRUCTION

The *hull* is the main part of a canoe. Manufacturers construct it with different materials and vary its shape to achieve any number of performance criteria (see page 19). Desirable hull material qualities are strength, durability, low cost, light weight, aesthetic appeal, and ease of manufacturing. These qualities and the materials used to construct the hull are explained in the next section.

A *keel* is a strip of material running down the bottom, outside length of a canoe that reinforces the hull and aids in tracking. Better keels taper into the stem at the bow and the stern so they don't snag on obstacles in the water and overlap it for greater strength. For maximum durability keels should be constructed from one and not several pieces of material. Some canoes designed almost exclusively for flatwater use have several additional keels in their bilge area. Keels are discussed in greater detail on page 28.

The *stem* is a narrow strip of protective material running up the outside of the bow and the stern. Because this is the part of a boat that hits obstacles in rapids head-on and drags on the ground when launching and landing, it's often reinforced with a piece of material called a *bang plate*. Some materials like ABS/Royalex are so durable that they don't need stems or bang plates for reinforcement. However, quality manufacturers include them on canoes made from those materials for extra protection from abrasions and impacts.

Gunwales are the strips of material added to the top edge of the hull to cover its sharp edges, to make a canoe easier to carry, and to attach other items like thwarts to the hull without piercing it. Fairly large outwales help keep water out of a boat, and small inwales let water drain from it easier when emptying it after a spill.

Decks are triangular sheets of material that cover the flotation chambers on aluminum and laminated canoes. They should have a rolled grip on the side closest to the canoe's interior for easier carrying. Consider painting aluminum decks a neutral, nonreflective black color to prevent the sun's reflection off them from blinding you when paddling.

The places where *grab loops* and *painters* attach to a canoe should be as close to the waterline as possible to reduce the chance of flipping the boat when used. Painters attached to the top of the deckplate are entirely too high for all but casual use, since the current can easily roll a canoe out from under a painter attached this way.

Bow caps and *stern caps* are materials that fit over the junction at the bow and stern where the gunwales, decks, stem, and hull meet. They frequently have a hole in them for attaching the painters or grab-loops, and some have a built-in handle for carrying the canoe.

Ribs are strips of material running perpendicular to the keel that give the hull support and rigidity. The longer a canoe is, the more ribs it should have. Fifteen-foot aluminum canoes, for example, need at least three or four ribs while 17-footers need at least four or five. Some quality whitewater canoes have additional ribs for more support in rough water.

Thwarts are bars that run across the top, open side of a canoe from gunwale to gunwale. They provide lateral support and stiffness for the hull, are used to tie gear into the canoe, aid in portaging it, and serve as a butt-rest when seats are not available or are occupied. The center thwart should always be the last item placed on a canoe and should be installed individually at each canoe's balance point (not necessarily its exact center) for the greatest ease and comfort when portaging. Thwarts and related peripheral gear like seats and gunwales, are made from wood, plastic, aluminum, or fiberglass materials. These *trim* attachments can be made of different materials than the hull and are often quite decorative on expensive boats.

Seats are used for sitting (obviously!), for securing gear in a canoe, and for stiffening the hull like a thwart. Though you can paddle most canoes more efficiently when kneeling, seats provide different paddling positions that make long trips more comfortable. Better seats are mounted low in the boat to lower your center of gravity and give greater stability, but they shouldn't be so low that you can't rapidly slide your legs in and out from under them when kneeling. In fact, the entire area under each seat should be free from support posts, ropes, and gear, since it's imperative that you be able to remove your legs from under the seats quickly when capsizing. Woven cane seats are comfortable, traditional, and not affected by temperature extremes. Nylon web, aluminum, or fiberglass seats are stronger and more durable than cane seats but not as aesthetically pleasing.

Specialized *saddle* or *pedestal seats* designed for solo canoes offer good comfort and excellent paddling control. *Seat cushions* help eliminate the uncomfortable feeling of extremely hot aluminum seats on sunny days and extremely cold ones in cold weather and help cushion your butt on long trips. *Contoured bucket seats* give you more control over your canoe when paddling but could be uncomfortable if they don't fit properly. Sliding, *adjustable seats* are ideal for achieving proper canoe trim (see page 116). *Drain holes* prevent puddles of water from collecting on solid seats during storms.

Some canoes, especially aluminum and fiberglass models, need foam or sealed air bag *flotation devices* to prevent them from sinking. These are usually placed out of the way in the bow and stern and are protected by *deck plates* and *bulkheads*. Built-in flotation devices are often designed to make the boat *self-righting* in the water, which means the canoe will tend to roll right side up after capsizing. This is called *positive flotation* and is useful on flatwater because it helps keep your gear inside the canoe and allows you to climb back inside it for safety after a capsize. However, this feature is not very useful in whitewater since an upright canoe filled with water is far more dangerous to swimmers and more likely to hit a rock and break apart than one that's floating through rapids upside down.

Sponsons or *safety foils* are wide air or foam chambers built in along the hull just above the waterline to increase a canoe's buoyancy and initial stability. They may also somewhat increase a canoe's cargo capacity and help keep splashed water out of the boat.

Spray rails are pieces of material attached to the outer hull to help prevent splashed water from entering the canoe. They're more useful when motor canoeing than when paddling.

MATERIALS

This section describes the materials used to construct almost every canoe hull currently available in North America. Both high and low quality canoes are made with all the materials described below, so knowing the kind of material a canoe is made from is not an indication of its quality. However, features that vary directly with the materials used are defined below and listed in Example 1-5.

The *price* of a canoe varies with the type and quality of construction and the materials used to make it.

Strength is a canoe's ability to withstand powerful impacts and stresses. This is quite important when whitewater paddling but of lesser importance for flatwater use.

Durability is a canoe's ability to withstand minor abuse over long periods of time.

Flexibility is the ability to absorb impacts. It's especially important for preventing damage to a hull in rough water, since canoes made with flexibile materials like plastic tend to slide over obstacles or bounce off them while those made from a rigid substance like wood tend to shatter on them. Too much flex, however, reduces a canoe's performance. An excessively flexible hull acts like a wet noodle floundering in the water instead of like a stiff knife cleanly slicing through it.

Some materials are *designed for use* in extremely rough conditions, while others are better suited for use in placid, unthreatening situations. Note that the "optimum use" category in Example 1-5 lists the very best use for a given canoe

MATERIALS

FEATURES	wood	aluminum	polyethylene	Royalex	fiberglass	Kevlar
price	high	low-moderate	low-moderate	moderate-high	low-high	high
strength	low	moderate	moderate	high	moderate	high
durability	moderate	high	moderate	high	moderate	high
flexibility	satisfactory	satisfactory	excessive	excessive	satisfactory	satisfactory
optimum use	flatwater	general recreation	general recreation	whitewater	varies with design	portaging, racing, rough conditions
upkeep required	plenty	almost none	almost none	almost none	minimal	minimal
ease of manufacture	moderate	fairly difficult	fairly difficult	fairly difficult	easy	easy
ease of major repair	difficult	moderate	moderate-difficult	moderately difficult	moderate	moderate
weight (lbs.)	60–80	70–85	70–90	70–85	50–80	35–60
additional flotation	not needed	needed	needed	often not needed	needed	needed
aesthetic appeal	beautiful	ugly	neutral-ugly	neutral	neutral	neutral
noise generated	almost none	excessive	low-moderate	low-moderate	low-moderate	low-moderate

Example 1-5: Features of various canoe materials.

hull material. This does not imply that materials are unsatisfactory for uses not listed.

The *amount of upkeep required* is the amount of effort you must put into your canoe to keep it in seaworthy, visually appealing, useful condition.

The *ease of manufacturing* is how easy it is to make a canoe with desired performance characteristics from a given material. It is not simply how easy it is to make a canoe from the specified material.

The *ease of repair* is how difficult it is to repair a damaged canoe yourself.

The lighter in *weight* a canoe is, the easier it is to carry on land and paddle in the water.

Some canoes need a great deal of *additional flotation* to keep them afloat, while others made from buoyant materials like wood float naturally.

Aesthetic appeal is a subjective criterion describing how beautiful and traditional a canoe appears to be.

Some canoe materials are *noisy* when used. which can be quite annoying. Noise results when your paddle bumps the side of a canoe, when water splashes against the boat, and when you move around or change positions in it.

Wood

Wood is the traditional material used for making canoes. Quality wood boats are works of art that demand respect in canoeing circles. Many people believe they're much more aesthetically pleasing than canoes made with other materials. Since they're almost always handmade, they can be individually crafted to personal needs and specifications. Wood canoes are quiet when paddled. This makes them ideal for activities such as hunting, fishing, and bird watching. Since wood canoes naturally float, no additional flotation must be added to them to prevent sinking, and this means they have more carrying capacity per length for your gear. While wood canoes aren't the most popular canoes sold nowadays, they sell at a steady rate year after year and have a dedicated following that swears by them.

Unfortunately, because they're handmade, wood canoes are expensive and fairly uncommon. Depending on their construction, they can be reasonably light in weight or fairly heavy, especially since they absorb up to 10–20% of their dry weight in water over a period of use. Because wood canoes are handmade, expensive, and not as durable as canoes made with synthetic materials, few people do any serious rough water paddling in them. While ideal on a lake or mild river, a wood canoe could quickly disintegrate in rough whitewater when paddled by inexperienced or careless boaters.

Almost every wood canoe has an interior structure consisting of closely spaced *ribs* running perpendicular to the keel from gunwale to gunwale and with wide, tight-fitting, usually cedar *planks* nailed or glued to them to form the hull. This basic hull is then finished in one of several ways. *Wood strip canoes* are boats with a waterproof coat of varnish or clear fiberglass covering thin strips (not planks) of wood glued together and attached to the ribs. Covering the internal rib and external planking structure with thick canvas or dacron cloth and then painting that for waterproofness is another method used to finish a wood canoe hull. A third, fairly popular method involves placing a layer of fiberglass either inside or outside or on both sides of the wood planking that forms the structural hull. Dacron and fiberglass outer materials are stronger and more abrasion-resistant than canvas but less traditional. Finally, a rare handful of wood canoes are still made with a birchbark hull. These canoes are quite fragile, difficult to repair, and exceedingly expensive. Some wooden canoes have a layer of planking inside them above their basic rib and planking structure that acts as an interior floor.

Unfortunately, wood canoes require a great deal of care during use and regular, often intense seasonal maintenance. Since they puncture and crack easily when compared with synthetic boats, you must be careful when using them in shallow water and rapids. Wash the insides of a wooden canoe occasionally to remove debris that eats away at its finish and retouch minor scratches to preserve its integrity. Annual sanding and repainting or revarnishing of the outer hull (and possibly the interior hull as well) is recommended. Though wood canoes require frequent care, when that's done properly, they'll remain in excellent condition through generations of use.

Aluminum

Aluminum is a very popular canoe material for several reasons. Aluminum canoes are strong, reasonably light, durable, economical, and maintenance-free. They'll last for years with no upkeep or care, and won't rot, warp, delaminate, or deteriorate in harsh weather or over long periods of time. Also, it's awfully hard to damage an aluminum canoe beyond repair. When you hit an obstacle like a rock in an aluminum boat, the aluminum stretches and dents but probably won't puncture and will rarely break. When dented, you can usually pound the dent out of it with a hammer, a rock, or your foot. You don't have to worry about scratches ruining the finish on an aluminum boat, because in reality, they have none. Quality aluminum canoes have a high resale value because it's hard to conceal their damages and disguise their repairs.

On the other side of the ledger, aluminum canoes are considered ugly to look at and noisy to paddle. It's extremely difficult to silently paddle an aluminum canoe, and this could pose problems for you when hunting, fishing, or photographing wildlife. You simply can't eliminate their noise, even when trying to be quiet. Aluminum is uncomfortably hot in the sun, icy to the touch in cold weather, and annoyingly reflects sunlight into your eyes. Since aluminum sinks, canoes made from it require flotation compartments which reduce their carrying capacity. Aluminum canoes occasionally develop hard-to-repair leaks along their bottom seam. Finally, aluminum tends to stick on rocks you hit in rapids instead of sliding over them. On occasion, this could cause you to lose control of your canoe in rough water.

Unfortunately aluminum canoes tend to hog more than any other canoe and this adversely affects their performance when paddled. *Hog* means that the bottom of the hull is bowed upward towards the inside of the canoe (Example 1-6). Check for this by resting an aluminum canoe right side up or upside down on a flat surface and looking at it sideways at keel level.

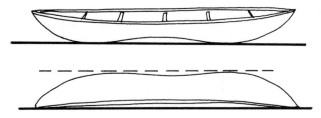

Example 1-6: Identifying a hogged canoe.

A major disadvantage of aluminum is that because of the high cost of machinery needed to manufacture canoes made from it, aluminum canoes cannot be built with sharp performance lines. This is why a handful of companies almost always mass produce them in a few almost identical designs and why they're usually generalized boats aimed at the broad recreational market and not specialty, high performance canoes designed for optimum handling under a few unique conditions. In general, aluminum canoes handle satisfactorily under a host of conditions but aren't the best possible type of canoe to use under any one condition.

Aluminum canoes are constructed in three major steps. First large sheets of aluminum are stretch-fitted to a mold. Then machinery stamps out each half of a canoe and the halves are joined together with a keel and ribs using rivets or spot welds. A thin layer of neoprene is usually placed between both sections before they are joined to guarantee waterproofness at the seam. Finally, the ribs, thwarts, gunwales, seats, decks, and other miscellaneous items are added.

The best quality aluminum canoes are made with a 6000 series grade aluminum (like 6061 or 6063) that's been heat treated to a T4 or a T6 temper for hardness and durability. An aluminum hull at least .05 inches thick is satisfactory for rough handling and whitewater use, though flatwater aluminum canoes that are either inferior discount brands or quality lightweight models have hulls as little as .03 inches thick. Aluminum parts like keels, ribs, and gunwales should be reinforced with extra material at critical stress areas. These occur at all shape discontinuities (like when a rounded edge suddenly becomes straight) and at major wear areas like the bottom of the keel.

Though considered maintenance-free, there are several things you can do to enhance an aluminum canoe. Specially fitted plastic *gunwale covers* placed over the gunwales will reduce the noise resulting when your paddle hits them. Painting the bow deck a flat black color will reduce the glare caused by the sun reflecting off it into your eyes. While painting the entire canoe is not recommended (really, why bother?), it will reduce the sunlight reflecting in your eyes from inside the boat and eliminate the occasional gray ''stain'' on your body, clothing, and gear caused by a rubbing contact with the aluminum. If possible, wash your aluminum canoe with fresh water after using it in salt water or after it has been exposed to winter road salts. Occasionally apply automotive paste wax to it to help preserve its outer shine.

Plastic

Plastic canoes are maintenance-free, tough, durable, and quiet. Some manufacturers even claim that plastic (especially Royalex) is the most indestructible type of material used in canoe construction. Plastic used to make canoes has a "memory." This means that it flexes to absorb the shock from an impact and then pops back in shape automatically afterwards. Due to this great flex, plastic canoes tend to slide over rocks that would snag other kinds of canoes. In very severe collisions, though, plastic canoes bend instead of crunching like aluminum or shattering like wood or fiberglass ones do, and have trapped a few unlucky canoeists inside them as a result. Also, although the main plastic hull will most probably remain intact after a severe wreck, you'll have to replace many nonplastic parts like the gunwales, thwarts, and seats after a rough collision. Plastic canoe hulls usually have no seams that could leak and no keel. They range in price from inexpensive, low quality discount store ones to high quality, fairly high priced ones.

Plastic canoes have two major disadvantages. Since expensive molding equipment is needed to manufacture them, they're made in a few "standard," general purpose models rather than many individualized, specialized ones. Thus, since it's hard to mold plastic into precise shapes with sharp lines, plastic boats with high performance features like an extremely narrow bow are usually not available. Secondly, plastic canoes tend to *oil can*, which means their hull flexes excessively when paddled fast or in rough water, and this reduces their paddling efficiency considerably. Also, their great flex causes an insecure, annoying "jelly" feeling under you. You can actually see and feel a bulge in a plastic hull when it scrapes over a rock. Quality plastic canoes often contain special stiffeners and stiffening construction techniques to reduce or control this unwanted flex.

Polyethylene plastic canoes (Coleman brand, for example) are low cost generalized canoes designed for the recreational market and not for specific kinds of canoeing like running rough whitewater. Unfortunately, this material is quite heavy, and canoes made from it tend to become somewhat brittle if exposed to sunlight for long periods of time unless treated with ultraviolet inhibitors.

ABS (Acrylonitrile Butadiene Styrene) is a durable, expensive thermoplastic material that's heated and then vacuum-molded into shape. There are two kinds of ABS canoe construction methods (Example 1-7). *ABS* refers to thin sheets of ABS plastic material. Canoes with this simple construction tend to puncture on impact with sharp objects unless reinforced with stiffening ribs along their hull. They also need additional flotation compartments to prevent sinking. Their ABS sheets are usually lined with an outer and inner layer of vinyl which provides the canoe's color and its durable, abrasion-resistant finish. The vinyl also blocks out the sun's ultraviolet rays to prevent the ABS from deteriorating over a period of time.

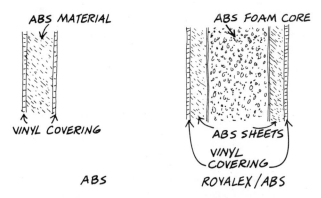

Example 1-7: Cross sections of an ABS and a Royalex/ABS hull.

Royalex/ABS refers to a material consisting of an ABS foam core sandwiched between two solid ABS layers. The ABS foam interior provides insulation from noise and cold water, extra buoyancy, cushioning to absorb impact, and rigidity to overcome the plastic's inherent, excessive flex. The foam is an ABS plastic that's thermally laminated to an ABS shell under heat so that air pockets form in it. It's usually about ¼-½" thick. The thicker the foam, the more rigid the boat will be. Royalex/ABS canoes with a foam core need no additional flotation compartments or rib stiffeners, and they're ideal for use on wilderness expeditions or in rough water where durability and reliability are desired.

It's important to note that all ABS and Royalex/ABS canoes are not identical in quality, since manufacturers can obtain these materials in several thicknesses and with various vinyl coatings, foam laminations, and selective reinforcements. Because of this, ABS and Royalex/ABS are occasionally referred to by different trade names. Old Town Canoe Company, for example, calls their Royalex/ABS material Oltonar, apparently to put some distance between themselves and other Royalex/ABS canoe manufacturers.

Plastic canoes need no special maintenance, but you can keep their surfaces shiny by occasionally applying automotive paste wax to them.

Laminates

Canoes made from fiberglass or Kevlar materials require little or no maintenance, are quiet, don't readily conduct heat or cold, are moderately but not excessively flexible, and are durable in rough water. A major advantage of these materials is that expensive equipment is not needed to make boats from them. This means that you can get a laminate canoe built to your specifications and individualized according to your needs for little additional cost, and that you'll have a wide variety of model selections to choose from. For example, if you're interested in a whitewater canoe that turns very quickly yet has a large carrying capacity for touring, you can probably find a fiberglass or Kevlar canoe manufacturer who either has a boat with those specs for sale or who will build one for you. Because laminates can be molded into canoes with very sharp lines, quality laminate canoes are performance canoes. They're typically designed to handle a precise way under specific conditions. Leaks aren't a problem with fiberglass or Kevlar canoes since they have a single body construction with no seams below the waterline. Also, they usually slide over rocks you hit in rapids instead of sticking to them like aluminum boats do.

Quality laminate canoes are generally lighter than similar aluminum ones, although their outer surface scratches easier than aluminum and shows wear readily. This could be a problem if you're concerned about looks, but any scratches present only affect a boat's visual appeal. The canoe's inner materials and durability remain undamaged, even if the scratches are never retouched. Fiberglass and Kevlar will break or puncture rather than dent in a rough collision with an obstacle, so while boats made of this material are quite durable, they're not indestructible. Fortunately, laminate canoes seldom are damaged severely and can be readily repaired at home. *Delamination*, a separation of the materials composing the hull, is an especially troublesome problem for improperly constructed fiberglass and Kevlar canoes.

In laminate construction, boat builders make a *plug*, which is the identical size and shape of the canoe they want to build. Then they make a mold of the plug and make finished boats from that mold. They do this by placing a thick resin called a gel-coat in the mold, placing layers of synthetic cloth on top of that, adding resin to secure the cloth, and removing the finished boat from the mold after the resin hardens. The *mold* is the pattern or shape used to construct the boat. All boats made from the same mold will be identical, much as all cookies cut from the same cookie shape will be the same.

The *gel-coat* is the smooth outer finish of a laminate canoe. Its main purpose is to hide minor construction blemishes and color the boat. It should be as thin as possible since it adds no significant strength to the finished product. A canoe without a gel-coat has what's called a *skin coat*. With a skin coat, the interior cloth pattern frequently shows through so the color of the boat is the color of the materials used to make it. Canoes with skin coats are up to 10 pounds lighter than those with gel-coats, but their performance and durability remain unaffected.

There are several problems associated with the gel-coat. Blisters in it indicate that impurities like air or dirt got between the gel-coat and the fiberglass or Kevlar layers during construction, and small cracks in it indicate that the hull has been or is stressed at those points. Fortunately these gel-coat blemishes generally don't indicate deeper structural damage.

In laminate construction the material and not the resin provides the strength. A *cloth* contains long, woven fibers, while a *mat* contains short fibers that are pressed together to make a felt-like material. A cloth consisting of fine threads is superior to one made from coarse threads but both are better than matted material, which absorbs excessive resin and is inherently weaker than woven cloth. Both mat and cloth are measured in weight per square yard. For example, 10-ounce cloth weighs 10 ounces for each square yard of material.

Different weights of cloth can be hand laid in various places for selectively reinforcing critical areas of the hull. *Roving* is a heavily reinforced material used for making fairly stiff, heavy, durable, modestly priced hulls. It's seldom used to make top quality boats.

Laminate canoes are made from various kinds of fiberglass, Kevlar, combinations of those materials, or combinations of those materials mixed with other synthetics like carbon fibers, nylon, and foam to achieve the desired amount of flex and strength with the least possible weight. Since *composite boats*, as laminate canoes made from combinations of materials are called, are usually high performance models, their high cost is a relatively minor factor in their construction. *Nylon cloth* is durable, tear resistant, and fairly inexpensive though excessively flexible; whereas, carbon fibers are both stiff and expensive. While *foam* increases a hull's stiffness, boats with foam cores have slightly less puncture resistance and are harder to repair than those with a solid hull layup. *S-glass* is a reinforced, especially designed fiberglass that's 40% stronger than the standard *E-glass* fiberglass material.

Because *Kevlar* is over five times stronger than steel by weight and up to 40% lighter than fiberglass cloth by size, canoes made from it are between 15 and 20 pounds lighter and much stronger than identical fiberglass models. However, Kevlar canoes cost several hundred dollars more than identical fiberglass boats. Kevlar canoes are primarily designed for racing or frequent portaging where light weight is a critical factor.

How the cloth is placed in the mold is called the *layup*. *Hand layups* are far superior to *machine layups* where a mixture of chopped fiberglass and resin is blown into the mold with a high-pressure spray gun. Boats with hand layups are lighter in weight, more durable, more flexible, of better overall quality, and (predictably) higher in cost than machined layups. You can identify a hand layup by the regular weaved cloth pattern on the inside of the canoe and by its lighter weight when compared with an identical canoe with a machine layup.

Resin is the gooey substance applied to the cloth to hold it in place. Various resins provide different amounts of strength, stiffness, and flexibility. Since the resin's only purpose is to hold the cloth in place, extra resin unnecessarily increases a canoe's weight. *Vacuum bagging* is an expensive process used to remove this excess resin. It involves sealing the mold containing the fresh, resin-impregnated cloth in a plastic bag and sucking the excess resin out of it. A dense, lightweight, tough layup results if vacuum bagging is repeated several times during the construction process. A vacuum-bagged canoe can be identified by wrinkles on the inside of the boat, especially in the bow and stern areas.

Laminate canoes need very little regular care. Store them indoors or in the shade when possible, since fiberglass canoes fade somewhat and Kevlar ones darken slightly with prolonged exposure to sunlight. You can restore the original color to laminate canoes by rubbing them occasionally with automotive rubbing compound. Automotive paste wax applied occasionally will help retain their original color.

PERFORMANCE CRITERIA

Performance criteria are specific qualities you could want your canoe to have. For example, you'll probably want a canoe to travel in a straight line so it goes where you want it to go and you'll probably want it to turn for maneuverability. While these two criteria—the ability to travel straight and the ability to turn—are both logically necessary, they directly contradict each other. A canoe that travels effortlessly in a straight line will be exceedingly difficult to turn, and a canoe that turns with ease will resist traveling on a straight course. With this in mind, remember that performance criteria are directly interrelated with each other. Whether they are complementary or contradictory depends on what qualities they're paired with. Common canoe performance criteria are explained in the next several paragraphs.

Tracking is the ability to travel in a straight line. This is important for paddling in winds, on flat water, in marathon races, and over long distances. *Directional stability* is synonymous with tracking.

Maneuverability is a canoe's ability to turn. Canoes used in rapids require a great deal of maneuverability, while those used primarily for lake paddling and long distance touring need little of it. As mentioned above, maneuverability and tracking are two performance criteria that contradict each other. It's very hard to design canoes that both track well and are highly maneuverable.

Speed is a vital criterion for racing canoes but is of lesser importance for recreational paddling. Closely related to speed, however, is how *efficiently* a canoe travels through the water with a given amount of effort. *Streamlined* hulls displace and replace water much more efficiently than those—like square-sterned models—which aren't streamlined. Related items that influence paddling efficiency include a low profile for minimum *wind resistance*, a comfortable paddling position in the canoe, and a narrow beam to allow the paddle blade to be placed close to the canoe's keel line and parallel to it.

Versatility is an important performance criterion for the large recreational canoe market. Versatile canoes must be "good enough" under all possible conditions to appeal to canoeists interested in a combination of whitewater, flatwater, and expedition canoeing.

Capacity is a boat's ability to carry cargo. The manufacturer's *recommended weight capacity* is a nonstandardized figure that should be used only for comparing the carrying capacities of boats made by that one manufacturer. Never use it to compare canoes from different companies. A somewhat more standard measurement is the *6" freeboard criterion*. You can calculate this by simply placing your canoe in calm water and loading it with known weights until you have a 6" freeboard. Try to center and balance the weights as much as possible when doing this so the canoe remains level. *Real carrying capacity*, as opposed to carrying capacity measured only with weights, is the amount of gear you can actually carry in a canoe. When canoe camping, for example, you'll be carrying sleeping bags that weigh very little but fill up a large volume of space in the boat. Thus, real carrying capacity depends on the volume inside the canoe as well as the weight of what you're carrying. Carrying capacity is critical on long distance canoe trips, but should pose no problems with average-sized canoes on trips less than a week in length.

Stability is a canoe's resistance to capsizing. *Initial stability* is the feeling of security you get when in a canoe resting level in the water. High initial stability is useful when you need a reliable platform for fishing or family outings on calm water. *Final stability* is a canoe's resistance to capsizing when near the capsize "point of no return." It's especially useful in rapids where leaning a canoe on its side is a necessary paddling tactic. Beginners generally feel more at home in canoes with great initial stability, while more experienced and whitewater paddlers prefer canoes with greater final stability.

A canoe's *performance when loaded* is especially important when paddling through whitewater or in heavy seas. Canoes usually handle much differently when loaded than when empty.

A canoe's *draft* is how deep it rides in the water. A small draft is useful in shallow water and in rapids, while a greater draft increases a boat's tracking in high winds.

Canoes used in large waves and rapids are designed with sides that *prevent water from entering* them. *Seaworthy* is a term describing the ability to remain afloat in rough water and waves.

FACTORS AFFECTING PERFORMANCE

The factors described below directly affect the performance criteria just explained and are also complementary and contradictory in nature. Understanding which factor causes which performance response and how various combinations of them influence the way a canoe handles in the water is the essence of the science of designing and building canoes.

Length

As you increase the length of a canoe, you get greater speed, weight, sensitivity to winds, tracking ability, better handling performance with heavy loads, and cost. In addition, long canoes have slightly less draft than short ones because their weight is supported by more water surface area, they travel more efficiently through the water because their elongated shape more effortlessly displaces and replaces the water, and they are easier to paddle a given distance than short ones since they tend to glide through the water while short ones plow through it. On the other hand, short canoes are easier to turn, easier to carry, lighter in weight, less expensive, and less affected by winds. Also, short canoes tend to float over large waves instead of charging through them like long canoes do, and they're ideal for poking around in narrow streams and coastal backwaters where long canoes are at a distinct disadvantage.

There's a real difference between a canoe's length from bow to stern and its effective length at the waterline. A boat's *effective length* is the length of its hull that's actually resting in the water. Most of the performance criteria listed in the previous paragraph actually related to a canoe's effective length and not to its bow-to-stern overall length. A canoe's horizontal hull shape, the amount of load it's carrying, its trim and its rocker (see below) could cause its effective hull length to be drastically different from its bow-to-stern length and could radically alter its handling characteristics.

Width

While wide canoes can carry more gear and have less draft, narrow ones are easier and more efficient to paddle and travel at a faster cruising speed. *Fullness* is how wide a canoe is and for how long up and down its length. Canoes with plenty of fullness have a large carrying capacity but move slower and with less efficiency because they displace and replace water less effectively than canoes that reach their maximum width for only a short section of their length. Note that stability depends far more on the shape of the hull than on its width.

Lines

A *line* is simply an outline of a canoe from a certain perspective (Example 1-8). For example, a *keel line* is the slope of a canoe's bottom as seen from the side. A curved keel line indicates plenty of rocker and a highly maneuverable canoe, while a flat keel line indicates little or no rocker and a boat designed for directional stability. Keel line also refers to the imaginary line running lengthwise down the center of the boat. You'll use this definition of it when studying the paddling strokes in Chapter 6. A *classic line* is the overall shape of a "traditional" canoe, while a *modern line* is the shape of a typical, newly designed, and somewhat odd-looking canoe. Some traditionalists favor canoes with classic lines for historical and aesthetic reasons. They feel a canoe should look like a canoe and not like anything else. Other canoe lines are discussed elsewhere at appropriate places in this book.

Horizontal Hull Shape

A line cutting completely through a canoe at its waterline is referred to as its *horizontal hull shape*. A canoe with a thin *entering line* or *leading edge* (Example 1-8) efficiently slices through the water and moves it out of the way; whereas, a canoe with a wide entry line uses the inefficient "brute force" method of getting water out of its way. Likewise, a thin *exit line* allows for a more efficient, gradual replacement of water behind a canoe. The thinner the entry and exit lines are, the more a canoe favors straight-ahead speed at the expense of maneuvering. Unfortunately, canoes with a narrow entering line tend to knife into waves rather than float over them like boats with wide entering lines do, and this could swamp them in rough water.

Canoes with square sterns designed for use with a motor have special problems. A typical, "normal" canoe handles much better than square-ended ones, since they have abrupt exit lines that drastically replace water in their wake. This results in a great deal of turbulence and produces a *water drag* in which the replacing water actually exerts a backward suction force on the for-

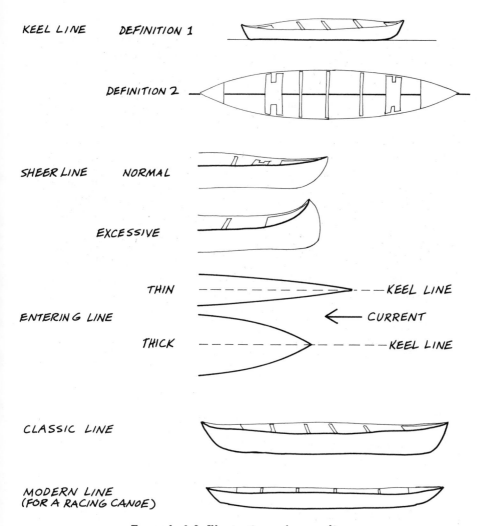

KEEL LINE   DEFINITION 1

DEFINITION 2

SHEER LINE   NORMAL

EXCESSIVE

THIN ————————KEEL LINE

ENTERING LINE   ←—— CURRENT

THICK ————————KEEL LINE

CLASSIC LINE

MODERN LINE
(FOR A RACING CANOE)

Example 1-8: Illustrations of canoe lines.

ward traveling canoe. Because of this suction, square-end canoes are sluggish and tiring to paddle on flat water. Also, they're not suited for rough whitewater because they can't maneuver as well in general, can't perform maneuvers like the back ferry at all, and restrict the stern paddler to a sitting position when flotation is stored under the rear seat. Because of these problems, better square-end canoes have a cut-off shape above the waterline for attaching a motor and a "normal" canoe shape below it for efficient replacement of water. Overall, though, because the disadvantages of a square-end canoe are large, many experienced paddlers recommend buying a canoe for canoeing and a motorboat for motored use. They feel that a square-ended canoe incorporates the disadvantages of a canoe and the disadvantages of a motorboat into a less-than-ideal craft.

There are several possible horizontal hull shapes (Example 1-9). A hull that's identical fore and aft of amidships has a *symmetrical shape*. The bow entry and stern exit lines are exactly the same, and the widest part of the canoe is amidships. Canoes with symmetrical shapes are slightly slower but more maneuverable than those with an asymmetrical shape.

The widest part of a canoe with an *asymmetrical hull* is located behind amidships. In this case, the part of the boat that displaces water is longer than the section of hull designed to replace it. While more difficult to turn, these canoes are faster and track easier than boats with symmetrical hulls, since their bow is narrow for a longer distance to more easily slice through the water. For the greatest possible speed and tracking, a hull should be quite narrow in the bow and somewhat pear-shaped in the stern, the widest part of the canoe should be wide for as short a distance as possible, and the bow should widen very slowly toward the stern.

To complicate matters, the hull shape at the waterline can vary considerably depending on the load in the canoe, its trim, the prevailing water conditions, and how you paddle it. Also, large waves could alter the part of the boat under water, a canoe's hull shape could be off center if you tend to lean the boat with each stroke, or if leaning and bracing techniques are used in whitewater.

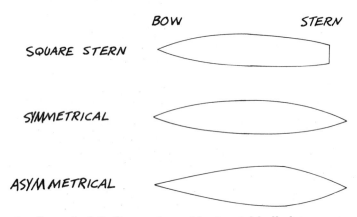

Example 1-9: Comparison of horizontal hull shapes.

Vertical Hull Shape

The *vertical hull shape* is the vertical shape of a hull at a specific point along it. There are several major kinds (Examples 1-10 and 1-11):

Canoes with *flat bottoms* have great initial stability when level, which is ideal for fishing, poling, hunting, and family outings. Experienced boaters can even stand up in a flat bottom canoe with little chance of flipping it over. Unfortunately, as soon as flat-bottomed canoes lean over past a certain point they'll tip suddenly, uncontrollably, and with little warning—and once they start capsizing, it's almost impossible to right them. In other words, flat bottom canoes are stable when upright but very unstable if leaned much to either side. Because it's very hard to properly *lean* a flat bottom canoe, they have limited usefulness in whitewater.

Because canoes with flat bottoms have a large area of water supporting them, they have a shallow draft. This means they require less water to float in, snag fewer obstacles under the water, are less affected by variations in water currents, and often turn easier and faster than canoes with deeper bottoms. However, flat bottom canoes don't track as well as deep canoes whose hulls act like keels providing directional stability in winds and rough water. Finally, because of their large volume, flat bottom canoes can usually carry heavier and larger loads than other canoes.

V-shaped hulls are at the opposite end of the spectrum. They have poor initial but excellent final stability. Canoeing in a V-shaped hull in flat water feels somewhat like trying to balance yourself on an inverted knifeblade. However, though tippy when level, you can lean far to the side in a V-hulled canoe with no fear of capsizing. In fact, up to a point V-shaped hulls gain stability as they lean

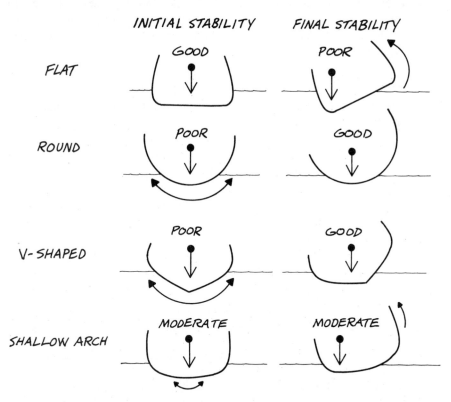

Example 1-10: Comparison of the initial and final stability of various canoe hulls.

over on their side. V hulls track very well through the water for efficient lake and wind paddling, but this makes them harder to turn and maneuver in rapids, since their hull acts like a keel providing directional stability.

Round hulls are somewhat of a compromise between flat and V bottoms. They tend to be faster, track better, and are more maneuverable than flat-bottomed canoes and have somewhat greater initial stability and slightly more carrying capacity than canoes with V shaped hulls. Round bottom canoes are especially useful in whitewater because of their great final stability and maneuverability.

A *shallow arch hull* is a compromise between a flat and round bottom design. For example, it provides more final stability than a flat bottom hull but less than that typical of a round design. Of course, exact qualities depend on its degree of flatness or roundness. Shallow arch hulls that are more flat than round favor the qualities of a flat bottom canoe, while those with a pronounced curve on the bottom of their hull handle more like round-bottomed ones.

In reality, though differences between hull shapes exist, there are few sharp distinctions between them. In fact, manufacturers often incorporate several shapes at various places along the hull in a single canoe to achieve their desired performance criteria. For example, a canoe could have a narrow V hull at its bow to slice through oncoming waves and a flat bottom amidships for a larger carrying capacity.

PERFORMANCE CRITERIA	round	flat	BOTTOM SHAPE V	shallow arch
draft	moderate	shallowest	deepest	moderate
initial stability	minimal	greatest	worst	moderate
final stability	fairly great	worst	greatest	moderate
speed	fastest	slowest	fastest	moderate
maneuverability	moderate	moderate	worst	moderate
tracking	moderate	worst	greatest	moderate
versatility	low-moderate	low-moderate	worst	greatest
carrying capacity	moderate	greatest	moderately low	moderate-great

Example 1-11: Comparison of the performance qualities of different hull shapes.

Depth

Depth is the vertical height of a canoe from its keel line to a designated point at the top of its gunwales. Canoes with a small depth are less affected by winds but can readily ship water over their sides in large waves. In other words, canoes with a large depth are ideally suited for whitewater since water can't easily pour inside them but aren't as useful when paddling on flatwater in winds. In general, the depth at the bow should be no more than 10–12 inches greater than the depth amidships, since the advantage of high ends keeping water out is negated by the greater wind resistance there. Of lesser importance, increasing depth increases a canoe's carrying capacity but makes it harder for your paddle to effectively reach the water when paddling. Except for its associated wind resistance, depth doesn't affect tracking, maneuverability, or speed to a significant degree.

Freeboard is simply the smallest depth above the waterline measured when a canoe is floating level in calm water. A minimum of a 6-inch freeboard is recommended for safety on all but the most specialized canoes (like racing ones, for example). Many paddlers prefer a large freeboard in spite of its greater wind resistance, since a small freeboard allows more water to enter and encourages swamping.

Sheer (Example 1-8) is the upward curve of the gunwales from amidships to each end of the canoe. Generally, a steady rise in sheer provides the greatest protection from water entering the boat and the least wind resistance. An exaggerated sheer curve immediately before the bow serves no useful purpose in keeping splashed water out, since the faster you travel the farther behind the bow it tends to enter a canoe.

Rocker

Rocker is the curvature of the keel line from amidships to the bow and stern. The more rocker a canoe has the easier it will maneuver but the harder it will track. Canoes designed for slalom racing where quick, responsive turns are needed have at least 6 inches of rocker; those used primarily in whitewater typically have 4–6″ of rocker; canoes made for general use under a variety of conditions have 2–3″ of rocker; and fast downriver racing canoes have virtually none. Increasing a boat's rocker reduces its bow and stern draft but tends to raise those ends up out of the water where the wind can easily affect them. Rocker also tends to reduce a canoe's stability since a boat with large rocker has less effective length than an identical canoe of equal bow-to-stern length with little rocker. Rocker is easily measured by looking at the curvature of a canoe's keel line when it's resting on level ground by pushing down on the bow or stern of a canoe resting upright on a level surface and noticing how far up the opposite end moves, or by holding one end of an upright canoe at waist height and seeing how easily it spins around upside down.

Keel

Keels are needed on all aluminum canoes to hold the two halves of the boat together and on some wood models for support or protection. They are optional on all other kinds of canoes. When present, a keel gives added support, rigidity, and abrasion resistance to the bottom of a hull and helps a canoe track through the water instead of sideslipping across it in winds. However, a keel interferes with maneuverability, since it tries to keep a canoe going in a straight line, snags on obstacles in whitewater, increases a canoe's draft, makes it harder to lean and brace a canoe in rapids, and makes it harder to sideslip around obstacles in rapids. In general, a keel is useful on lakes and calm rivers but not in whitewater or where quick maneuvering is done. It's interesting to note that hulls on well-designed canoes provide the advantages of keels without their disadvantages. For this reason, most high-performance boats have no keel, even when designed primarily for use on flatwater.

In a sense aluminum canoes are at a disadvantage because they must have keels. Aluminum canoe manufacturers have overcome this problem to some extent by designing the keel for different purposes. A *T-keel* for a flatwater aluminum canoe is typically a straight, up to 1 inch long, strip of metal that provides great tracking but restricted maneuverability (Example 1-12). Keels for whitewater aluminum canoes are called *shoe keels* and resemble rounded flanges of material often less than 1/2 inch high. A shoe keel snags less on underwater obstacles and offers more maneuverability and less draft than a T-keel. When designed properly, both kinds of keels offer the same amount of strength, support, and hull rigidity.

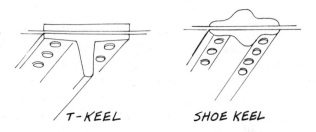

T-KEEL   SHOE KEEL

Example 1-12: Kinds of keels typical on aluminum canoes.

Tumblehome and Flare

Tumblehome (Example 1-13) is the degree that a hull curves in towards a canoe's center from the waterline to its gunwales. It adds some strength to the hull, makes it easier for your paddle to comfortably enter the water along the side of the boat, lets the paddle blade be used closer to the canoe's keel line for more efficient paddling, and helps keep splashed water out of the boat. *Flare* is the

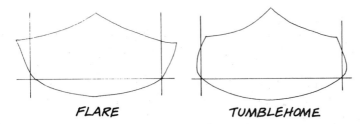

FLARE   TUMBLEHOME

Example 1-13: Flare and tumblehome on canoe cross-sections.

outward curvature of the hull above the waterline. It's useful in the bow of a canoe since it helps the boat ride over waves instead of sinking into them and amidships where it increases its carrying capacity. It's not desired along the hull at the paddling positions. Flare and tumblehome are often both included on a canoe to achieve the best combination of water repellency, paddling ease, stroke efficiency, and bow buoyancy.

To maximize this performance criterion	Make a canoe with these design features
1) Tracking	long length narrow width V or round bottom asymmetrical hull sharp entry and exit lines pronounced keel minimum rocker hull should widen slowly from bow
2) Maneuverability	short length pronounced rocker flat, shallow, or round bottom no keel symmetrical hull stubby entry and exit lines
3) Speed	narrow width asymmetrical hull V or round bottom minimum fullness long length no rocker narrow entry and exit lines hull should widen slowly from bow

Example 1-14: Summary of design features and performance criteria.

4) Carrying capacity......................large interior volume
                                          long length
                                          wide, symmetrical hull
                                          maximum fullness
                                          flat bottom
                                          flared amidships

5) General stability ....long length
                                          wide hull
                                          pronounced keel
                                          maximum fullness
                                          (initial and final stability
                                              varies with hull shape)

6) Versatility.............................medium length
                                          medium width
                                          symmetrical hull
                                          shallow arch bottom
                                          shoe keel (on aluminum canoes)
                                          2- to 4-inch rocker
                                          medium fullness

7) Low wind resistance ....minimum length
                                          minimum freeboard
                                          minimum rocker
                                          maximum weight
                                          pronounced keel
                                          minimum depth
                                          maximum draft

Example 1-14 (cont'd.)

SOLO CANOES

Solo canoeing gives you the freedom to do what you want, lets you canoe whenever you desire without waiting for a partner, lets you command your own ship, opens the spiritual door of solitude for you, and gives you a feeling of harmony with your boat and the water that's difficult to obtain in a tandem canoe. You may prefer paddling solo to avoid the countless compromises you'll have to make regarding things like paddling strokes, lunch stops, and bow or stern positions when tandem canoeing. Spending a few hours in a tandem canoe with a person you don't get along with will surely convince you of the virtues of solo canoeing.

With few exceptions, the performance criteria and design features discussed in this chapter apply equally well to both solo and tandem canoes. The major difference between them is that solo canoes are shorter and narrower than tandem models. Since a solo canoe is paddled from amidships, a wide boat interferes with the performance of each stroke and makes it difficult to place the paddle in the water without excessively leaning it. Likewise, for maximum efficiency, designers usually try to minimize a solo boat's length and weight without noticeably reducing its desired handling characteristics.

Solo canoes can be classified into several categories:

1) *Midget* and *pack canoes* are the smallest, lightest kind available. They range in length from 10 to 12 feet and weigh about 20 to 30 pounds. These are ideal for casual flatwater float trips in small streams and tidal backwaters and for backpacking into remote waterways. Their primary disadvantage is their limited cargo space.

2) *Whitewater canoes* have a large rocker for quick maneuverability and steep sides that help keep out splashed water in rapids.

3) *Marathon racing canoes* have no rocker, high tumblehome, a 16- to 17-foot length, and exceptional tracking ability. They're usually built to precise racing specifications.

4) *Touring canoes* are about 15 to 17 feet long and are designed to carry plenty of gear on long outings. Generally they track well and paddle efficiently, but aren't designed for negotiating difficult rapids.

5) *Sport canoes* are general purpose recreational boats suitable for short, several day outings, mild whitewater, and flatwater. They're about 13 to 14 feet long.

BUYING A CANOE

General Categories

To help you pinpoint your needs, the common features of the four categories of tandem canoes described on page 5 are summarized in Example 1-15. First, decide which general kind of canoe you're interested in buying, and then try to get one with as many of the features listed in the example as possible. When buying a canoe, deciding which kind to get is the most important decision you'll make. Other decisions, like what material it should be made of and how much rocker you'll need, will be relatively easy afterwards.

Price

Canoes can be categorized as low, moderate, or high in price. Those *low in cost* are generally lower quality, higher sales volume, all-purpose recreational models designed for moderate, casual use. Generally, this category includes less expensive plastic, lightweight aluminum, and chopped fiberglass models. *Medium-priced*, generally versatile recreational canoes include aluminum, plastic, most fiberglass, and some Royalex/ABS models. They're reasonably well-designed and can be expected to last far longer than inexpensive ones in rough use situations like in whitewater or at summer camps. *High-priced* canoes usually have a high performance design, an individualized fiberglass layup, or quality Royalex/ABS, Kevlar, or wood construction.

| FEATURES | KINDS OF TANDEM CANOES | | | |
	flatwater/ touring	whitewater/ slalom	recreational	downriver racing
rocker	1–2 inches	4–6 inches	2–4 inches	none
length	17–18 feet	15–17 feet	17 feet	17–19 feet
beam	33–37 inches	32–36 inches	33–36 inches	30–33 inches
hull shape	flat, shallow arch	round	shallow arch	round V
maximum depth	12–14 inches	13–15 inches	12–14 inches	9–12 inches
stability	great initial	great final	both moderate	not relevant
canoe weight	55–80 lbs.	55–80 lbs.	55–80 lbs.	30–45 lbs.
capacity	large	small–medium	medium–large	small–medium
keel	none–large	none	none–medium	none–medium

Example 1-15: Comparing qualities of various kinds of tandem canoes. Although the qualities are preferred amounts, they may vary greatly among manufacturers and canoe models.

As with everything else, you usually get what you pay for when buying a canoe. If you need a dependable boat for long term use in rugged conditions or a high-performance one for a specific purpose like racing, you should probably get a high-priced model. On the other hand, if all you'll do with a canoe is paddle around a small backyard pond, you can easily get by with the most inexpensive kind available. Be honest with yourself. You simply may not need a high quality canoe.

Odds and Ends

1) Question manufacturers' claims that a canoe is "easy to paddle." Experienced canoeists find all canoes easy to paddle; whereas, beginners find them all difficult to paddle. Also, by now you should realize that a canoe that's exceptionally easy to paddle on flatwater will probably handle poorly in rapids.

2) Ignore claims that a certain canoe can do everything from paddling on lakes to negotiating whitewater well. Versatile recreation canoes designed for use under a host of conditions can handle those conditions satisfactorily or adequately at best but not "well." No canoe can perform "well" in all conditions.

3) Avoid canoes with contradictions in design. For example, a large rocker on a canoe helps it maneuver quickly in rapids, while a bow with a long, narrow entry line is better suited for straight-ahead paddling. They probably should not be on the same boat.

4) Remember that except for expensive, individually built canoes, there's probably no canoe ideally suited for your needs. Buying a canoe involves making some compromises, especially when you want to paddle in a variety of situations.

5) Bright-colored canoes are easy to spot when in trouble in whitewater but are eyesores in environmentally sensitive areas. Canoes that blend into their surroundings are especially suited for hunting, fishing, and photographing wildlife. The inside of every canoe hull should be a neutral color that doesn't reflect sunlight into your eyes.

6) Large canoes can be carried on small cars. Don't let the size of your vehicle influence the length of the canoe you buy.

7) Avoid specially designed craft unless you will only canoe in one kind of situation. Avoid extremes in design unless you're sure you'll use those features. Usually a general-purpose recreational model is best for people who will own only one canoe and will use it in a variety of conditions.

8) Carrying capacity is a somewhat overstated criterion. It's often better to reduce the volume and weight of your gear on a few extended trips than to paddle an excessively large canoe around on frequent short outings.

9) Be wary of companies with only general information in their catalogs. All information manufacturers distribute should be clear, specific, and up-to-date.

10) While the weights of standardized canoes like mass-produced plastic and aluminum ones closely match their advertised weights, individually made, specially designed boats can weigh up to 10% more than advertised. Weigh a boat on your bathroom scale to verify its weight.

11) Large companies are typically in business to sell canoes, while smaller companies are often in business because their owners enjoy building quality canoes that sell themselves.

12) Owners of aluminum and lower-cost plastic canoes are generally happy boaters but not the most dedicated or educated ones. People who own expensive plastic, laminate, or wood canoes have often paddled several kinds of canoes before settling on the one they have now. Ask them, and not general recreational paddlers, for advice about things like performance criteria and handling characteristics.

13) If at all possible, paddle a canoe in the water for a period of time before buying it. Tip it over to test its stability, paddle one stroke and then observe its glide, try portaging it, and test its maneuverability and tracking abilities.

14) Always buy a laminate canoe from people or stores who are familiar with fiberglass and Kevlar construction. Ask the person selling the canoe to tell you the kind of layup and its *order* (the pattern the cloth was laid in) as well as the number of cloth layers used to make the boat. When buying a laminate canoe,

lean on its hull to check its flex and compare it with other models. Some flex is desirable to prevent shattering on impact, but too much will cause oil canning and is an indication of an unresponsive, sluggish boat. Sight along the hull with your eyes and avoid any canoes that have ripples or irregularities in their finish. White-colored areas inside the hull indicate regions of *resin-starved cloth*, and pools of resin on the bottom inside of the hull indicate *resin flooding*. Both of these conditions are signs of inferior workmanship.

15) The best way to judge the quality of a canoe is to know the reputation of the manufacturer. The second best way is to associate cost with quality. Expensive canoes are usually of better quality than inexpensive ones.

Buying a Used Canoe

Chances are you'll get a great deal when buying a used canoe from a friend or fellow member of a canoe club, since you can test it before actually buying it and since you know its owner firsthand. Often experienced paddlers or racers unload quality canoes at down-to-earth prices because they don't handle to their precise specifications. Consider going to races or canoe club meetings to buy a canoe this way. Buying a used canoe from a retailer, rental outfitter, or newspaper ad is somewhat more risky, since you don't know how the owner cared for it and any abuses it's had. Also, the owner may be hesitant to let you paddle it on the water first before buying it.

Be especially cautious when buying a used homemade canoe unless you know all the previous owners and its builder and can paddle it in the water. Many are lemons. Be wary of homemade laminate canoes that are delaminating.

Know the going retail price for canoes and for the model you're interested in. This will give you a starting point when you negotiate its price. In general, plan on paying about 70–80% of the list price for a used Kevlar, Royalex, or high-quality aluminum canoe and about 50–60% of the list price for a fiberglass and lower-quality aluminum boat, assuming they are in good condition.

Judge the quality of a used canoe by its construction, materials, and amount of wear, not by the superficial and meaningless surface scratches on it. If at all possible, check for leaks in the water. Often a minor canoe leak is a real nuisance and is difficult to repair, especially on aluminum models. Check for missing or broken rivets, cracked or bent gunwales, cracked ribs, indications of major repairs, damaged flotation compartments, and rotten wood or canvas hidden under a new paint job. Avoid a canoe with a bent keel, since this indicates a major confrontation with a rock and is difficult to repair. Beware of a person selling a laminate canoe if he doesn't know the canoe's layup. No one will sell a Kevlar canoe at a low price unless there's something wrong with it.

BUILDING A CANOE

Building a canoe at home is fairly inexpensive, allows you to design it for your paddling needs, and can give you a sense of personal accomplishment, but this requires much hard work, demands extensive knowledge of materials and construction techniques, and limits you primarily to laminate construction. Also, you'll have to live with your creation afterwards. While you'll always be proud of a well-built canoe, you'll never hear the end of it if you build one that sinks or springs a leak the first time you use it. Building a canoe is recommended only if you can work with other people who have had direct experience building boats and have necessary molds and tools at hand. Because you'll need constant supervision with a project of this nature and because designs and construction methods are virtually unlimited, instructions for building a canoe are not included in this book.

CANOE STORAGE

In general, store a canoe indoors as much as possible for the best weather protection. If you can, store your canoe horizontally upside down on sawhorses, suspended from your garage ceiling, or hanging sideways on a rack secured to your basement wall. Leaving a canoe exposed to the elements for long periods of time and especially throughout the winter can significantly damage it. Never let a canoe get frozen in a lake, and be careful that it's not stored outside in areas of high snowfalls, which could crush its hull. Wet snow sliding off a roof is especially threatening. Vandals and falling trees also claim unprotected canoes each year.

With the above precautions in mind, *aluminum* canoes can be stored outdoors in harsh climates and direct sunlight for long periods of time with no adverse effects. You should always store a *wood* canoe upside down off the ground when not in use. If you don't have a canoe rack, simply storing a wood canoe propped up on logs or rocks is better than leaving it lay unprotected on the ground or floating in the water. Also, it's best to protect a wood canoe from precipitation and excessive, continuous sunlight whenever possible. Store *laminate* canoes indoors or in the shade when possible to preserve their original color. Likewise, plastic canoes are best stored indoors or at least in the shade, since they decay unless treated with ultraviolet inhibitors at the factory. If you must store a wood, laminate, or plastic canoe outdoors, follow the precautions just mentioned and cover it with a fabric canoe cover for maximum protection from harsh sunlight and moisture.

2

BOATING GEAR

PADDLES

Example 2-1 illustrates the parts of a canoe paddle and the proper way to hold a paddle. When holding a canoe paddle, be sure you place one hand around the top of the grip and the other hand in the throat region about one or two hand widths above the blade. Beginners tend to hold a paddle below the grip with their upper hand and excessively high above the blade with their lower one.

Factors Affecting Design

Several important factors affect how a paddle handles in the water and how comfortable it is to use. These are listed below.

1) Paddles light in *weight* are easier and less tiring to use than heavier ones. This is very important, since you'll be moving your paddle in and out of the water several thousand times each day.

2) A paddle's weight should be *balanced* for better handling control. Well-balanced paddles have slightly lighter blades than shafts when held in one hand at the normal throat paddling position.

3) Slight *flexibility* is preferred by many canoeists because it gives their paddle a nice feel when in the water and a subtle "kick" at the end of each stroke. Test the flexibility of a paddle by holding its grip in your left hand, resting the blade on the floor so the shaft slopes at about a 45° angle, and pushing down on the lower middle part of the shaft with your right hand. Then compare with other models.

4) Efficient paddles have a *low moment of inertia*. This means that they have little weight at their ends. To simplify this important engineering concept, 1 pound at the end of a 3-foot-long section of paddle (measured from its center of gravity or pivot point, see also page 116) feels like 3 pounds would feel 1 foot from that pivot point. Thus, the weight at the extreme ends of a paddle has a far greater effect on how you'll feel that weight when swinging the paddle around all day.

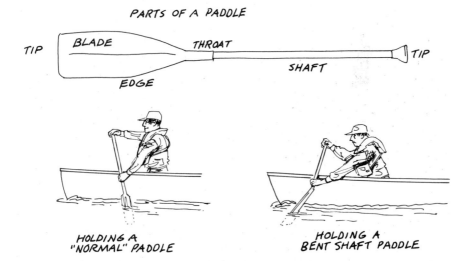

Example 2-1: The parts of a canoe paddle and the correct way to hold a paddle.

5) The greater a paddle blade's *surface area*, the more energy you'll need to put into each stroke, but the more response you'll get from it. In general, a strong, experienced paddler will travel faster with a large blade than with a smaller one, but paddling with a large-bladed paddle is no guarantee of a fast canoe unless you put a lot of effort into each stroke.

A blade's surface area varies with its length and width. A wide, short blade is useful when traveling in shallow water or through rapids; whereas, many people prefer a longer, narrower blade for flatwater use. Typically, paddle blades are from 7 to 9 inches wide and from 20 to 27 inches long. *Beavertail*, *rectangular*, and *square* are the three prominent blade shapes (Example 2-2). Note that rounded edges wear somewhat less then sharp corners and tend to splash less water each time you plant the paddle in the water to begin a stroke. *Spoon blades* cup the water better than flat blades for a slightly more efficient stroke.

6) Paddles with *bent shafts* are designed for efficient, powerful canoeing on flatwater or in a race. Avoid them if you're just getting started in canoeing or need the better steering control straight shaft paddles offer. The angles in bent shaft paddles range from 3 to 15 degrees off the vertical position. The greater the angle, the more efficient and powerful your strokes will be, but the less control you'll have when steering. Blade angles up to about 7 to 9 degrees are satisfactory for recreational, flatwater use, while those with angles greater than about 10 degrees are designed primarily for racing.

7) Upper paddle *grips* are either round or T in shape. Although many whitewater canoeists prefer a T grip because it gives them better steering control and a more secure hold on their paddles in rough water, both kinds are popular and comfortable for general recreational use.

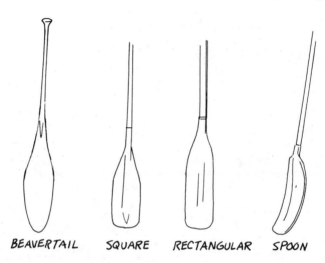

BEAVERTAIL   SQUARE   RECTANGULAR   SPOON

Example 2-2: Kinds of canoe paddle blades.

8) Paddle *shafts* in the lower grip area are either round or oval in design. Oval ones are more comfortable for extended paddling and more responsive in use, since they fit your hands better.

The factors listed below do not affect how a paddle handles in use, but are still important design criteria:

1) All paddles should *float* so you don't lose them in the water.

2) A paddle should be *strong* to support the forces exerted on it in rough water. The rougher the water you canoe, the longer your trips are, and the farther from civilization you journey, the stronger your paddle should be. Note that with the host of synthetic materials on the market, thickness is not needed for strength anymore. Thin synthetic paddle blades are usually exceptionally strong.

3) *Durability* is a paddle's ability to withstand wear for long periods of time. Many paddles fray or chip annoyingly at their tips, others tend to break along their shaft, and wood ones in particular are noted for splitting up the blade.

4) *No-maintenance* paddles are ideal when you don't want to bother caring for them, for use in demanding situations like summer camps, or with a family of wild kids. Virtually all paddles except wood ones can be classified in this category.

5) Some people prefer traditional, *aesthetic* wood paddles. They feel synthetic ones are ugly and out of place in a wilderness setting.

6) Brightly *colored* paddles are easy to locate when lost in a rapids. However, colored paddles could be a disadvantage when hunting or fishing or an eyesore in popular areas.

Materials

Paddles are made from wood or synthetic materials such as plastic, fiberglass, and Kevlar. *Synthetic paddles* are virtually maintenance-free, lightweight, durable, strong, and reliable in demanding situations, though often quite expensive. They're ideal for use in rugged whitewater and wilderness areas where you can't chance breaking a paddle. Often synthetic paddles have an aluminum or fiberglass shaft and an ABS, plastic, fiberglass, Kevlar, aluminum, or polypropylene blade. Foam-filled shafts are slightly warmer and stronger than hollow ones. Sometimes aluminum shafts are coated with a thin polyethylene sleeve for comfort and warmth and to prevent the aluminum from "staining" your hands as it oxidizes. When buying a synthetic paddle with a shaft and blade made from different materials, be sure they fit together securely. Avoid inexpensive plastic paddles which break with little encouragement.

Some synthetic paddles are available oversized and with detached handles. With them, you size the paddle to your body (see below), saw off any excess shaft material, and attach the grip to the shaft according to the directions accompanying them. Avoid using this method to size a paddle with a normal, permanently attached grip, since you'll never be able to connect the grip to the shaft as well as the manufacturer did.

Quality *wood paddles* are aesthetically beautiful, comfortable in hot or cold weather, inherently pleasing to hold, and generally inexpensive, though top quality ones often rival synthetic ones in price. Wood paddles are the standard for flexibility that synthetic paddles can't come close to imitating. They are usually made from maple, ash, spruce, or pine. Paddles made from a hardwood like maple are generally heavier but more durable than those made from a softwood, but quality paddles are made from all kinds of wood, so it's unfair to judge a paddle only by the kind of wood it's made from. Laminated paddles constructed from layers of various woods are usually stronger, more durable, and lighter than paddles made with a single type of wood. Generally, the cheaper in price a wood paddle is, the heavier, weaker, thicker, more prone to splitting, unresponsive, and less durable it is. Avoid any wood paddles with a crooked grain or knots in them.

Unfortunately, wood paddles split or break fairly easily and their tips wear rapidly in use. For greater durability, place a layer of fiberglass cloth over the blade of your wood paddle to prevent splitting and fiberglass its tip to prevent fraying. Even a layer of hardware store epoxy glue added to the tip of a wooden paddle will greatly prolong its life.

Wood paddles are usually completely varnished to protect them from the elements. However, a few models are sold without varnished hand grips, since some canoeists prefer paddles with no varnish on the grips because they claim it causes blisters. If you buy a completely varnished paddle, try it first before desecrating the finish on it. Then, if you think the varnish on the grips is giving you blisters or sore hands, lightly sand the grip areas to smooth out any imperfections there. Finally, if you're still not satisfied with it that way, sand the varnish completely off the grips.

Buying a Paddle

If you're just getting started in canoeing, almost any properly sized paddle will suffice, since you'll neither notice nor need high-performance features common on expensive models. However, while inexpensive, mass-produced paddles are suitable for kids, when you don't want to worry about someone stealing your priceless paddle, or if you're a beginning canoeist, buy the best possible paddle for your needs when you plan to race, canoe extensively on long trips, or paddle in challenging situations. While beginners generally prefer fairly inexpensive wood paddles, experienced canoeists often favor more expensive, higher quality wood or synthetic ones.

Sizing a paddle properly is not very difficult to do, although it can be confusing. It seems like every canoeist has their own personal rule explaining how to do this. Some of the more common ones are listed below:

1) One long-standing rule instructs you to buy a bow paddle reaching from the floor to your chin and a stern paddle reaching from the floor to your eyes. This is somewhat useless since it measures your leg length as much as it measures your more important trunk size, and it ignores important factors like your canoe's depth, width, and seat height. Also, while a stern paddle is somewhat more effective if slightly longer than one used in the bow, it's impractical for you to use one paddle in the bow and a different one in the stern.

2) A method based on your arm length states that a paddle's shaft should be about 6 to 8 inches longer than your arm from the armpit to the tips of your extended fingers. Many of the problems associated with 1) above also apply here.

3) Another method claims that a paddle shaft should be as long as the distance from the tops of your shoulders to the ground when sitting on the floor, plus the height of the seat above the bottom of the canoe. This method tries to compensate for different canoe seat heights but ignores personal factors like arm length.

4) A far more accurate rule than all the preceding ones is that a paddle's blade should be fully immersed in the water and its grip at upper shoulder level when held vertical in the middle of a forward paddling stroke in your usual paddling position inside your personal canoe. Few people can actually try out a paddle like this before buying one, though.

In general, then, there's no set rule for sizing a paddle. A paddle's length depends on factors like the position of a canoe's seat, the canoe's depth in the water, the blade height, and your personal paddling style and body size. When standing, an upright paddle that reaches your upper neck is most probably too small, while one taller than your forehead is most probably too large. You'll have to hold different paddles within that range or test some of the methods described above to find one that's comfortable for you. If you're a beginning canoeist almost any paddle 1 or 2 inches on either side of your "ideal" size is satisfactory. Experienced canoeists, however, often prefer paddles less than 1 inch from their "ideal" size, and they know immediately if a paddle is too short, too long, or just right.

When you have found several paddles that seem like they're the correct size, buy the one that "feels" best when holding it in the correct paddling position. This is a very intangible, horse-sense kind of thing but it seems to work. A paddle that feels right in a store will probably serve you well on the water.

As a final note, a handful of solo canoeists prefer a double-bladed kayak paddle instead of a single-blade canoe paddle because of its greater efficiency. However, most proficient soloists recommend mastering single blade use as described in this book before experimenting with kayak paddling methods and advise using a double blade paddle to supplement—not replace—one with a standard single blade. You can get additional information about kayak paddles from local kayaking friends or from books that focus on that sport.

Paddle Care

Canoe paddles will last a long time if you care for them properly. Avoid using paddles as poles to push off the bottom when launching or landing a canoe, and avoid fending off rocks in rapids with them. Don't use them as cutting boards when camping, to pound in tent stakes, or as seats on the ground around a campfire. Carry your paddles in a *paddle bag*, which is a specialized, usually nylon bag designed to protect them when traveling to and from waterways. Store paddles hanging up on a paddle rack when not in use, and use specially designed, commercially available paddle *retip kits* to repair their worn blade tips.

Wood paddles require extra care. To prevent warping, keep a wood paddle out of intense, direct sunlight whenever possible and especially when wet. Store wood paddles in your tent or hanging from a tree branch when camping at night so porcupines can't chew them up. If your wood paddle begins to split, either replace it or try to repair it, but remember that repaired paddles seldom perform like new ones. To repair a split wood paddle, remove all loose splinters at the split section. Then apply waterproof glue where needed and tape the blade securely until dry. To repair a large crack in a paddle blade, remove all loose splinters, fill the seam with plastic wood, tape it until dry, and apply a layer of fiberglass cloth over the blade for added durability.

LIFE JACKETS

Life jackets, also called *life preservers*, *life vests*, and *personal flotation devices (PFDs)* are needed for safety on all canoeing trips. Their primary goal is to keep your head afloat so you can breathe when in the water, but they also protect you from sharp objects like rocks in rapids and insulate your body to help prevent hypothermia (see page 249). Life jackets are an extremely important piece of boating equipment. Buy and use the best possible one for your needs, *always* wear one when in a canoe, and carry one spare per boat. Note that government agencies often require the use of life jackets on water in their jurisdiction and federal regulations state that you must have at least one properly sized, functional, Coast Guard-approved life preserver for each person on board a water craft.

A PFD's *buoyancy* is the weight of the water it displaces. This factor gives you an indication of how well it will support you in the water. Although bulky life jackets with as much as 40 pounds of buoyancy are used when closed boat canoeing or rafting in very rough water, something like 15–20 pounds of buoyancy or a buoyancy factor equal to about 10% of your body weight is sufficient for most open boat canoeing trips. Of course extra buoyancy is useful in cold water, for nonswimmers, and when wearing many layers of clothing. Every new life jacket should have its buoyancy and type (see below) printed on it at a prominent location.

Safety Ratings

PFD's are Coast Guard-rated according to the following criteria (Example 2-3):

A *Type I* PFD provides a large amount of buoyancy (at least 22 pounds) and is *positive righting*. This means it's designed to turn an unconscious person from a face-down position to a face-up position in the water, and will maintain him in a vertical, slightly backward, face-up position in it afterwards. Obviously, this is a very desirable quality for a life jacket to have. Type I PFDs are often required on commercial canoeing and rafting trips, but tend to be excessively bulky and overdesigned for general paddling use.

Type II PFDs are designed for recreational boating. They have at least 15.5 pounds of buoyancy and are also positive righting, though less so than Type I life preservers. These PFDs are not suited for whitewater use because they offer no back protection and can slide off in rough water unless carefully secured around your chest.

Type III PFDs have at least 15.5 pounds of bouyancy, support and maintain a floating person in a vertical, slightly face-up position in the water, but aren't positive righting. They're designed primarily for greater comfort and mobility when worn, and because of this are popular with water sports enthusiasts. Type III PFDs are usually a vest style that completely encloses your upper body for the greatest insulation from cold water and maximum protection from river obstacles.

Type IV PFD's have a minimum of 16 pounds of buoyancy and are designed to be held in the hands or thrown to a swimmer. Seat cushion and life buoy styles are examples of this type. Use these only as auxiliary PFD's and not as your main life preserver protection, since they're too unreliable for most canoeing uses.

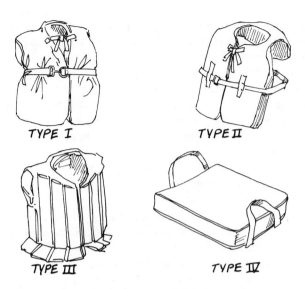

Example 2-3: Types of life preservers.

Type V is an open category of life jacket approved for specific uses under certain conditions. River runners on the Colorado River, for example, have PFDs of this type rated exclusively for the large waves and dangerous rapids typical there. This kind is generally not used when open boat canoeing.

Other Features

Life jackets are usually *filled* with closed cell foam or kapok, which is a plant material imported from tropical regions. PFD's containing kapok are somewhat fragile, since when the plastic bag holding the kapok breaks, it soaks up water and ruins the jacket. However, with proper care—like not walking on them and not using them as seat cushions—kapok-filled life preservers will last for years. The kapok pouches are not ruptured if they remain firm but flexible when squeezed. Kapok fill is common in Type I and Type II life preservers.

Closed-cell foam filling is common on Type III life jackets. This material is durable and reliable, though somewhat expensive. PFDs with this type of filler work even if used extensively as seat cushions, since they contain no inner waterproof plastic bag that can puncture. The foam itself contains thousands of tiny air pockets that are inherently waterproof. PFDs containing separate "ribs" of foam are more comfortable than those containing large "plates" of it, and padded shoulders are ideal for padding when portaging.

Avoid inflatable PFD's which are too fragile, avoid solid foam life preservers popular with water skiers but too restrictive for canoeing, and avoid all life preservers that attach only to your waist.

The *shape* of a PFD greatly influences how much insulation and protection it provides. The more traditional horseshoe collar style is relatively inexpensive but chafes your neck and exposes your back to underwater obstacles and the cold environment. Quality jacket or vest PFDs are usually rather expensive but provide significantly more protection from rocks and insulation in harsh weather. Typically these are filled with closed cell foam for more durability. PFD's with a waist strap and a lower "skirt" that can be folded up above the waist strap are designed so that kayakers can sit inside their craft with them on. They're adequate for open boat canoeing as well. Some PFDs have an additional flap of buoyant material behind the neck to protect your head when floating through rapids.

A PFD with a bright *color* is especially helpful in an emergency, while dark green, blue, or camouflage colors are designed for hunting, fishing, and photographing wildlife.

A cotton *outer material* is not as durable as nylon, since the cotton rots when stored wet and tears and decomposes with use. In addition, wet cotton chafes your skin while wet nylon has a softer, smoother feel. A fishnet *inner material* dries faster and is cooler and less clammy in hot weather than solid materials.

Ride-up, where a life jacket tries to float off your body over your head when in the water, is a major problem with many PFD's. A proper *closure* system consisting of elastic cords, buttons, snaps, and zippered openings with appropriate adjusting straps helps secure a PFD to your body and prevent this. However, avoid any PFD with a complicated system of dangling straps, which are a hassle to put on or remove and dangerous in a capsize. Quick-release buckles are handy to remove a PFD rapidly. Highly adjustable straps are useful when sharing a life jacket with different people or when wearing clothes for insulation under it. Avoid all PFDs that don't fit securely and comfortably around your chest area when properly worn.

Buying a PFD

Buying a life jacket is a relatively simple task. First of all, decide which type you need. Then, select a preserver that's rated to support your body weight and one that's designed to fit your chest size. These measurements should be clearly marked somewhere on it. Finally, select a PFD with the durability, freedom of movement, price, filler material, and closure method you prefer. Selecting the kind of fill a PFD has is often an irrelevant decision, since Type I and Type II preservers are usually filled with kapok while Type III preservers usually contain closed-cell foam filling.

Buy a comfortable PFD so you'll be more inclined to wear it when paddling. Comfortable life jackets are sized properly for your body's dimensions and have a secure, easily adjusted closure mechanism, a minimum of bulk, and deep arm holes for great freedom of movement when paddling. Always try a PFD on in a store to test its closing system and comfort. When wearing one, swing your arms around as if paddling to test its freedom of movement, and have someone try to pull it off over your head to test its ride-up tendency. Above all, buy a life jacket for the comfort and protection it offers, not for the style or fashion it portrays.

ROPES AND RESCUE EQUIPMENT

Rope

There are several kinds of ropes available for canoeing use. *Polypropylene* is a colorful plastic rope useful for rescuing people because it floats. Unfortunately, polypropylene lacks the high strength typical of nylon rope and is somewhat hard to handle because it's slippery and stiff, kinks easily, and doesn't coil neatly or readily. Also, its light weight makes it hard to throw long distances unless secured to a heavy object like a rescue bag. *Nylon* rope is noted for its high strength, comfortable feel, indestructibility, and shock absorbing properties. When stressed, a nylon rope stretches a great deal to absorb the load on it. While this helps relieve the shock on a victim holding a nylon rope in moving water, it could be a disadvantage when you need to apply a strong force to remove a pinned canoe with it. Another disadvantage of nylon for canoeing use is that sizes thick enough to handle comfortably are fairly expensive. *Perlon* is similar to nylon but lacks its elastic, "rubber band effect" when heavily loaded. In normal use, environmental factors like moisture, sunlight, and cold weather don't noticeably affect nylon, polypropylene, or perlon ropes, and they don't rot, splinter, or decay over a period of time. Avoid *manila*, *cotton*, and similar *natural fiber* ropes which have low breaking strengths, are adversely affected by moisture, and wear rapidly in use.

A rope's *test strength* is the amount of weight it can hold without breaking under ideal conditions. Its *safe working load* is one-fourth or one-fifth its test strength and is the load it can be expected to support with normal use. For example, a rope rated at 600 pounds test will safely support a weight of 150 pounds when canoeing if used properly. Remember, though, that jerking a rope doubles the strain on it, and a knot in it decreases its safe working load by at least 50%. Except for thin cord useful for tying gear in canoes, all canoeing ropes should be at least 3/8 inches thick so you can grip them easier.

Painters are 10- to 15-foot sections of rope you attach to the bow and stern of your canoe for use when lashing it to your car, wading it through rough rapids or shallow areas, and securing it to the shoreline when beached. Nylon painters are safest for securing a canoe to your vehicle because of their great strength, although polypropylene painters are ideal for use on the water because they float. In reality, though, the differences between them aren't worth the hassle of changing painters every time you begin and end a canoe trip. Avoid floats or knots on the ends of your painters, since they could snag on underwater obstacles, and avoid excessively long painters which could become tangled around your body if you spill. Some canoeists recommend coiling your painters and securing them to your canoe to get them out of your way when paddling, while others think they're more useful if left laying loose in the canoe where they're more accessible in a capsize. For safety, be sure you stow or secure your painters in an out-of-the-way location so they won't interfere with your paddling position or a quick exit from the boat in an emergency.

You should always carry several 30- to 50-foot sections of rope for lining canoes through rough rapids or shallow areas and for freeing pinned canoes and rescuing overboard people in rapids. Several sections of line distributed among the canoes in your party are much handier than one large coil of rope which can easily tangle into a huge ball of knots. As with painters, rescue and lining rope should contain no separate floats, attachments, or knots which could snag on obstacles and interfere with their use.

Rescue Bags

Rescue bags or *throw bags* are weighted nylon stuff sacks containing polypropylene rope (Example 2-4) ideal for rescuing people because of their ease of use and accuracy when thrown. On most models, the polypropylene rope can be detached from the bag and used separately if desired, and some models have a convenient *sling strap* that noticeably increases their throwing range.

To use a rescue bag, hold the loose end of the rope with one hand and throw the bag underhand towards your target with your free arm. If you missed your target in an emergency, you can quickly retrieve the bag, fill it with water, and throw it again without coiling the rope or restuffing it in the bag first. For storage, simply stuff the rope in the bag. You don't have to coil it or repack it in any special way at all.

While *life buoys* may be useful for water rescues at summer camps, swimming beaches, and on a few flatwater outings, avoid them on long canoe trips where they get in the way and on all whitewater outings where they snag on obstacles in the water. Instead, rely on ropes, rescue bags, your swimming ability, your PFD, and good, old-fashioned common sense for safety.

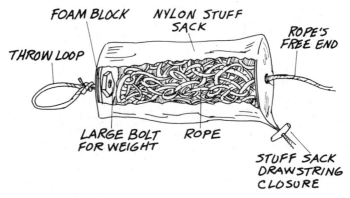

Example 2-4: A rescue bag.

CARRYING CONTAINERS

Containers (Example 2-5) suitable for carrying your gear on a canoe trip should be:

1) Above all else, *waterproof*. This means absolutely, completely, and totally waterproof. Even pinhole leaks in plastic bags or stitch holes on packs will leak an unacceptable amount of water in a capsize or prolonged storm.

2) *Durable*. Carrying containers should be able to withstand common abrasions for long periods of time. Round corners on all types of containers resist wear better than square ones. 200 denier weave nylon and 20 mil thick vinyl are the minimum safe values for containers made from those materials.

3) *Strong*. The stronger your containers are, the better they'll resist severe impacts that can occur when dropped or in a capsize. Rigid containers provide greater impact resistance than soft ones unless fragile items in them are padded well.

4) *Easy to carry*. All containers should have shoulder straps or handles for easier carrying to and from your canoe at launch areas, campsites, and portage locations. In general, the fewer containers you have, the fewer trips you'll have to make carrying your gear. This is especially important when portaging frequently or for long distances.

5) *Easy to use*. You shouldn't have to fuss with your equipment containers whenever you want to get something out of them. Likewise, you shouldn't have to worry about how secure and waterproof the openings on those containers are.

6) *Brightly colored*. Equipment containers that contrast sharply with their background are much harder to lose at camping and launching areas and when floating through rapids after a capsize.

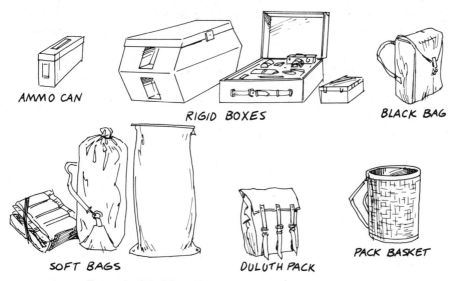

AMMO CAN

RIGID BOXES

BLACK BAG

SOFT BAGS

DULUTH PACK

PACK BASKET

Example 2-5: Miscellaneous canoe storage containers.

Ammo Cans

Ammo cans are fairly small metal containers useful for carrying fragile things like sunglasses, often needed items like sun tan lotion, and supplies like a first aid kit that must always be readily accessible. Durability is their hallmark. Their rigid shape resists impacts and abrasions better than almost any other type of container available. Most ammo cans are quite waterproof, but double check for this by filling them with rocks and immersing them in a bathtub of water overnight before using them outdoors. Unfortunately, these containers are heavy and bulky for the relatively small amount of gear they can carry, and this makes them a real pain on trips requiring much portaging. In fact, their usefulness tends to decline as the number of days you are on a trip increases. Ammo boxes painted white reflect sunlight better and thus stay cooler than darker ones. This is important if you're carrying heat sensitive things like film in them. Also, white ones are easier to locate at camp and in a capsize than drab ones that blend into their background.

Rigid Boxes

Rigid boxes are useful for storing odd-shaped items like cooking gear that could puncture waterproof bags and fragile foods like bread that could get crushed. Commercial ones made from materials such as fiberglass, metal, ABS, and polypropylene are durable, waterproof, and often guaranteed for life against defects in workmanship or breakage. Some even have padded interiors for storing delicate gear, detachable legs so you can use them as tables, and interior compartments for categorizing their contents. Unfortunately rigid boxes are bulky, difficult to pack, and awkward to portage. Also, they retain their bulk when empty instead of compressing into a tiny bundle for storage. While this empty bulk may be useful as added flotation in rapids, it's generally an unnecessary hassle.

Used plastic *bulk food storage containers* with snap-on lids available at no cost from restaurants are suitable for storing your gear. Check to be sure they're waterproof at home first before relying on them outdoors. If not, use plastic bags inside them to keep water away from your gear.

Black Bags

Black bags are stiff rubber containers useful for storing canoeing gear. Often they're modeled after the heavy rubber bags used in the armed forces and occasionally available at army surplus stores. Usually they come with shoulder straps which aid in portaging them and for securing them to a canoe. Black bags generally are about 2 feet tall, 1 foot deep, and a foot and a half wide. Their closure system is waterproof, durable, and reliable, though somewhat more complicated than those found on other containers.

Soft Bags

Soft bags are nonrigid containers that easily fit inside most canoes and collapse when not in use. Quality ones are made from a variety of materials including polypropylene, polyethylene, neoprene, vinyl, plastic, coated nylon and coated dacron. Those made from a plastic-type of material are often bonded to a tough fabric like dacron or nylon for greater support, durability, and puncture resistance and have heat-welded—not stitched—seams. Soft bags are usually less expensive than black bags and rigid boxes but lack the durability typical of those containers. This disadvantage can be reduced by carrying them inside tough, not necessarily waterproof, nylon or canvas sacks and by padding sharp objects like silverware and rigid items like a stove with soft materials like clothing before packing them. For the greatest reliability, always carry a repair kit for them anywhere outdoors. Soft bags are sealed with a plastic strip that slides over their opening or by folding down a neck of fabric and securing that with straps, velcro fasteners, or drawstrings.

Small, soft bags with *inflatable air chambers* cushioning their contents are ideal for carrying delicate items like eyeglasses and cameras. Bags of *mesh netting* are useful for carrying wet gear or for immersing foods and beverages in the water to keep cool. Even a high-school *gym bag* lined with several plastic bags is reliable on short trips.

Backpacks

Backpacks are ideal storage containers because they're easy to portage. Inexpensive, lower quality packs work just as well as quality ones for all but extended wilderness trips. Avoid using backpacks with fancy features like an elaborate suspension system, since constant immersion in water and frequent exposure to the elements could damage those features. Also, avoid "tissue paper" backpacks made from thin materials and designed primarily for light-weight hiking. Internal frame packs fit inside a canoe better than those with external frames, though a frame on the outside of a pack acts like a floor board that elevates it above any water in the bottom of the boat. Unfortunately, however, your sleeping bag is usually exposed on external frame packs while it's stored inside internal frame ones for greater wetness, abrasion, and impact protection. You'll need to line all packs, including those made from waterproof materials, with plastic bags to ensure waterproofness before use, since water can easily enter through their numerous seams. Single compartment packs are much easier to use and to waterproof than those with several main compartments.

Duluth packs or *rucksacks* are simple, large, frameless, usually canvas packs with shoulder straps, a single top opening, and no fancy components like waist belts or pockets. They're quite popular in many canoeing areas because of their low cost and great durability, although you must line them with plastic bags since they aren't completely waterproof.

Consider placing an appropriately sized plastic garbage pail or similar rigid container inside a backpack to prevent gear from tearing your inner waterproof layers and to prop it open for easier access. Do this by lining your pack with several layers of plastic bags, placing a container slightly smaller than the pack inside them, and placing your gear in it. Then seal the opening by putting the lid (if available) on the container, sealing the waterproof plastic bags over it, and closing the pack's main opening.

Pack baskets are rigid wooden baskets with shoulder straps attached to them. They're useful for carrying soft or fragile items and many small, easily lost things. They aren't waterproof, so you'll have to line them with several layers of plastic bags; they aren't compressible when empty, so you'll always have to deal with their bulk; they are somewhat fragile, so you can't treat them with the disrespect that rigid boxes can handle; and they are somewhat awkward to carry on portages because their contents can shift around as you walk. Generally, modern gear has replaced this more traditional container.

Day packs are small packs useful for storing compact, often-used items like your towel, sunglasses, map, and compass. They are handy to have along when you'll be going on short hiking trips away from your canoe. A *fanny pack* is a specialized day pack that wraps around your waist when hiking and easily straps to a canoe thwart when boating. Both of these kinds of packs are somewhat difficult to waterproof effectively because of their small size.

Plastic Bags

You may have to use *plastic bags* in combination with some of the containers just described to waterproof your gear. Though this method is initially inexpensive, it's probably quite costly in the long run when their fragile nature is compared to the almost lifetime durability of containers like black bags and rigid boxes. In addition, gear stored in plastic bags is far more difficult to access quickly when needed than equipment stored in commercially made waterproof containers. Plastic bags should only be used to waterproof gear inside a durable container such as a backpack, gym bag, or a duffel bag. Those used unprotected in your canoe will get torn to shreds long before the trip is over and often long before the drive to the launch site ends. Always use the thickest, strongest kind of plastic bag available and double or triple them for extra strength. For the longest possible life, seal holes in them with duct tape as soon as they appear, and never store unpadded rigid or sharp objects inside them since they'll tear through the plastic with ease.

Tarps and Ground Sheets

Several outdated canoeing books describe how to "waterproof" your gear by wrapping it in a bundle inside a tarp or ground sheet. What they neglect to show is their author sullenly drying his soaked equipment by a campfire after a capsize or sudden storm. No matter how carefully your gear is secured inside a tarp or ground sheet, it will be ten times better protected inside one of the modern storage containers just described.

ROOF RACKS

There are four methods you can use to carry canoes on your car (Example 2-6):

1) *Roof racks designed for cars with roof rain gutters* are considered the safest tie-down system since they clamp directly and securely to your vehicle. With this system the load on the racks is supported by the major frame braces along the edge of the roof and not by the weaker sheet metal on the roof itself. Roof rack cross bars are usually made from wood, aluminum, or rustproof, coated steel. For greater versatility, be sure they're long enough to support two canoes, even if you only have one boat and a small car. Adjustable racks are more versatile than permanently sized ones, and locking racks discourage thieves. Vertical eyelets at the ends of rack cross bars aid in securing canoes to the rack, although they make it slightly harder to initially get a canoe on them.

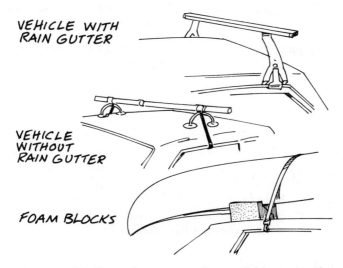

Example 2-6: Typical commercially available roof racks.

2) *Roof racks designed for cars with no rain gutters* are slightly less reliable than those just mentioned. With them, vertical posts rest directly on your vehicle's roof, and tie-down straps with small hooks on their ends fasten under the metal lip along the edges of it above the side windows. Often these vertical posts use rubber pads or suction cups to distribute the weight evenly on the roof. Note that suction cups are not designed to secure the rack to the roof at all. In fact, there's very little suction under them and not nearly enough to support a

canoe. For maximum effectiveness, the support posts on this kind of rack should be placed as far away from the center of the roof as possible.

3) *Foam blocks* install quickly to almost any car and are less expensive than racks. To use them, just slip the blocks on your canoe's gunwales when it's resting upright on the ground, put the canoe on your vehicle roof, and secure it with cross and end lines attached to special hooks that accompany the blocks and fasten under the lip along the edges of your vehicle's roof. When the car that dropped you off at the start of your trip is not the same car that will pick you up afterwards, simply carry them in your canoe on your trip. Another, more insignificant advantage of blocks is that you don't have to drive around with roof racks on your vehicle all the time. The blocks are easily removed and stored out of sight when not in use. Unfortunately, a canoe transported with blocks is potentially less safe than one secured with a properly applied set of roof racks, and you'll have difficulty carrying more than one canoe on a vehicle at a time with them.

4) Placing your canoe on *blankets or rubber pads* on your roof before tying it down is the least reliable method but should be satisfactory for short distances at low driving speeds on smooth roads. Unfortunately, it's quite difficult to properly tie cross lines around a canoe resting on a blanket without running them through the windows and tying the car doors shut in the process.

Luggage racks (except possibly those attached to the vehicle by the manufacturer), bicycle racks, ski racks, and other kinds of roof racks are generally not strong enough for carrying canoes.

MISCELLANEOUS GEAR

A *bailer* is used to empty water from a canoe. Ones with flexible, flat sides and a large opening scoop water out more efficiently and faster than stiff, rounded, or narrow ones. For example, a plastic gallon bleach bottle with its top screwed on and its bottom cut off is ideal. It's a good idea to have a bailer at each end of your canoe when paddling in rough water so you and your partner can use them instantly if needed. Always tie your bailers to a thwart with a 2- or 3-foot length of thin nylon cord to prevent loss. *Sponges* are useful only for removing the last few drops of water from a boat. They're agonizingly slow and inefficient for removing quantities of water.

You'll need *knee pads* for comfort when paddling from a kneeling position. Closed-cell foam pads are comfortable, absorb a great deal of shock, and soak up virtually no water. Pieces of neoprene or closed cell foam glued to the floor of your canoe in the correct kneeling positions are handy, convenient, and impossible to lose. However, they're useless when you want to alter your position and uncomfortable if dirt collecting on them isn't removed. *Gardener's* or *roofer's knee pads* are ideal for canoeing, though walking with them on is somewhat difficult. When new, seal the seams between the foam pad and the rubber cups with waterproof rubber cement to prevent them from falling apart there. Commercially available "pull-on" *neoprene kneepads* are also ideal for canoeing when sized properly. Ones that don't fit well tend to uncomfortably bunch up behind your knees or annoyingly slide off. Avoid elastic or cotton *athletic knee pads* which absorb water when wet, are uncomfortable when worn for long periods of time, and aren't as durable as other kinds available. Avoid kneeling on open-cell foam sponges or soft clothing because they rapidly become waterlogged, and avoid using loose gear like seat cushions that could become lost in a spill.

Eyeglass retaining straps are essential for eyeglass wearers in rapids and cheap insurance against loss anywhere near the water. Commercial ones are usually adjustable elastic bands while homemade ones are generally pieces of string attached to both ends of the frame and encircling the back of your head.

A *repair kit* is useful when canoeing in rough water or for long periods of time. Items that should be included in every repair kit are listed in Chapter 11.

Flotation devices prevent a swamped or capsized canoe from filling up with water to reduce the chance that it will get damaged or pinned against an obstacle in moving water. They are recommended for use on class II or rougher rivers. Vinyl *flotation bags* should be at least 20 mils thick and nylon ones should have a minimum of a 200 denier weave for satisfactory puncture resistance and durability. Grommets in their corners aid in securing them in your canoe. *Inner tubes* are inexpensive and readily available but a hassle to inflate. Either place them in position beneath your canoe's center thwart and inflate them at a service station enroute to the river or carry a hand pump and inflate them as needed on your trip. Inflate inner tubes and air bags hard enough so their shape holds them in the canoe but soft enough so they are less likely to puncture. What matters is that you fill as much of your canoe's volume as possible with the air they contain, not that you put as much air in them as possible. Both bags and inner tubes are ideal because they fold up into a manageable bundle for storage and portaging when not in use. *Foam blocks* are bulky and difficult to portage but can't puncture. If using blocks, remove your center thwart (if possible), cut the blocks to fit in the center of your canoe beneath and around the center thwart, install them, and replace the thwart. It should firmly secure the blocks in place. If you replace the center thwart with wing nuts or other easily removed fasteners, you can install and remove the thwart and the blocks with ease.

For all but occasional short portages, use a wood, plastic, metal, or "canoe paddle" *yoke* when carrying a canoe for greater comfort. Removable yokes that either replace the center thwart or attach directly to or over it usually have a system of pads for greater comfort, but an unpadded yoke permanently built into a canoe as a modified center thwart is convenient because it's always there when you need it. You don't have to bother carrying and rigging a separate piece of gear whenever you must portage. Of course, removable yokes are necessary for solo canoes since you paddle them from amidships.

There are several styles of portaging yokes available (Example 2-7). Example 2-7A illustrates two foam pads that simply attach to the center thwart. They are light, small, and portable but somewhat less reliable than a full yoke system. Example 2-7B illustrates a built-in yoke which is really just a molded center thwart. This style usually isn't padded so you'll have to use a foam pad, old life jacket, or piece of clothing for padding when carrying a canoe with it. An aluminum yoke designed to fit over a center thwart is pictured in Example 2-7C. Rigging two canoe paddles to form a yoke is illustrated in Example 2-7D. This method is convenient and simple to use but offers less comfort than commercially available yokes. When rigging this system, be sure to position the paddles far enough apart so they ride on your shoulders and so their handles are in front of you when walking. If you're a resourceful person, you can build a yoke ideally suited for your canoe with materials from any hardware store.

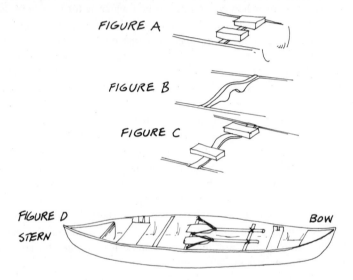

Example 2-7: Kinds of portage yokes.

Carabiners are fist-sized, metal rings used extensively in technical mountain climbing. When canoeing, they're handy for attaching items like bailers to thwarts, for securing end lines to a canoe, and for rigging harnesses or pulleys in water rescues. If you have a technical climbing background, other uses will immediately become apparent, much as a handyman has a thousand and one uses for a pair of pliers. Don't be concerned if you have never used carabiners, since almost everything they're used for—except ropework and rescues—can be done equally well with something else.

Floor racks are wooden platforms that raise your gear above the bottom of a canoe to keep it dry from splashed water that puddles there. Commercial ones are designed for more permanent use, while driftwood or blowdown logs will suffice for temporary use and on trips involving portages.

A *spray cover* is a sheet of nylon, plastic, or neoprene material that covers the canoe's opening and prevents water from entering when paddling through rough waves, rapids, or rainstorms. Quality ones form a complete seal around the canoe's gunwales and paddlers' waists to effectively shed external water. In effect, because a spray cover makes your canoe a closed boat, you should wear a helmet, use flotation devices, be an excellent swimmer, and be experienced in exiting a capsizing canoe when enclosed inside one. Practice exiting from a capsizing canoe when inside a spray cover in calm water with friends nearby for assistance before venturing into rapids with one. Always keep an extra paddle tied securely to the canoe on the outside of the spray cover for easy access if needed in rapids. Unfortunately, spray covers are a hassle to rig on trips involving frequent portaging, severely limit your freedom of movement inside the canoe, and restrict access to your gear.

While tarps or ground sheets spread out over the center of your canoe are easily rigged, they're ineffective spray covers since water pools on them and then flows down their sides and into the boat.

Thigh straps (Example 2-8) are pieces of webbing attached to a canoe and running around your thighs. In effect, they secure you to the boat so it responds faster and more efficiently to your strokes, braces, and leaning maneuvers when paddling in rough whitewater. Their primary disadvantage is the difficulty of getting out of them in a capsize. To somewhat overcome this, top paddlers recommend using knee pads permanently glued to the canoe rather than the kind that strap on your legs. Thigh strap kits are available from numerous suppliers listed in the Appendix.

In conjunction with thigh straps, *toe braces* give your entire body a secure hold on a canoe for maximum responsiveness when paddling, bracing, and leaning in rough water.

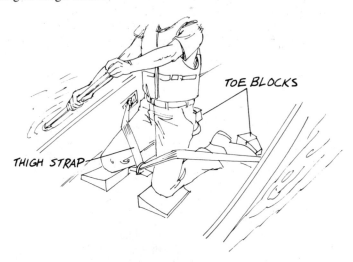

Example 2-8: Using thigh straps and toe braces.

You should use a *helmet* for safety when canoeing in very rough white water. Quality, specially made canoeing and kayaking helmets are brightly colored for visibility, have vents that rapidly drain water from them when you flip, don't impair your vision or hearing, are adjustable so you can wear a hat under them in cold weather, are large enough so you can wear eyeglasses with them, are as light as possible, and have a secure chinstrap to prevent loss. While not ideal, using climbing, cycling, skateboarding, or motorcycle helmets for protection in dangerous rapids is better than wearing nothing at all. Generally, closed boat canoeists and kayakers need helmets much more than whitewater open boat canoeists do because they can drift upside down underwater for a long period of time after a capsize; whereas, open boat canoeists can usually swim clear of a capsizing canoe with their head out of the water.

A *motor mount* is designed to secure a small horsepower motor to a canoe. Side mounts are made for regular canoes while stern mounts are built for square-ended ones. Motors mounted in the stern require no course corrections when used since they propel a canoe directly in line with its keel, but you have to sit in an awkward, sideways position and reach completely around to your back to control a motor mounted in this fashion. On the other hand, while side-mounted motors require a slight course correction to compensate for their placement off-center of the keel line, they're much more comfortable to use over extended periods of time since you can control them from a comfortable, face-first sitting position.

Motors designed for use on a canoe should be 5 horsepower or less and as light as possible, since the greater the weight of a motor, the more it adversely affects a canoe's trim, handling characteristics, and balance. While motors are useful for carrying heavy loads, in emergency rescues, when supplying base camps, and when quickly traveling to a prime fishing location, they usually complicate a recreational canoe trip and are no substitute for honest, traditional paddling. Also, motors are often too heavy, fragile, or awkward to portage, require a host of peripheral support equipment, like gas cans, tools, and spare parts, and are noisy, smelly, and somewhat unethical for much outdoor use.

A *tumpline* is a wide band that slips over your forehead and attaches to a heavy item like a canoe to help carry it. In principle, it transfers some of the load from your shoulders to your neck muscles. Tumplines used to be quite popular among professional voyageurs but have become quaint novelties to the hordes of out-of-shape suburban warriors flocking to the waterways every weekend. Avoid using one unless you're an experienced canoeist with a very strong neck.

Pontoons are long cylinders of foam that attach to the gunwales of a canoe for additional final stability when a capsize is imminent. While not needed for general canoeing, they could be useful for parents paddling with small children or for fishermen who want a mobile, stable craft with little chance of tipping over.

Skid plates are sheets of a tough material like Kevlar that attach to the lower bow of your canoe for additional protection from abrasions and impacts in rough water. They're available in kit form from major outfitters listed in the Appendix.

Passenger seats made of net, nylon, or similar material attach to a canoe's gunwales so your passengers don't have to sit on a wet, cold floor.

Homemade *seat cushions* can be improvised from a piece of closed cell foam secured to a canoe seat with velcro attachments or rope. Commercial ones can be Type IV PFD's or 1/2-inch thick closed cell foam with a coated nylon cover for added durability. Avoid open-cell foam cushions which easily become waterlogged.

A folding *anchor* is useful for emergency stability when canoeing on windy lakes or when you need to remain in one location to photograph, hunt, or fish. A large bucket secured to a rope works almost as well as a commercial anchor in an emergency.

You can install a *nonskid floor* inside your canoe for greater traction. These are available in kit form from boating suppliers.

A *rowing kit* attaches to a canoe's gunwales so you can row it like a rowboat. Its true function is debatable, though. After all, a canoe is made to be paddled not rowed. If you want to row something, get a rowboat.

Likewise, a few manufacturers market portable *sailing rigs* that attach to a canoe. These are somewhat gimmicky, ineffective items only occasionally useful since they're too heavy to cart around constantly and since a canoe is designed to be paddled, not sailed. If you want a boat efficiently propelled by the wind, use a sailboat designed specifically for that purpose.

3

CLOTHING

On canoeing trips clothing should protect you from the sun, poisonous plants, abrasions, insects, and poisonous snakes. In deserts and along coastlines, it should protect you from other poisonous creatures as well. Clothing should also insulate you from excessively warm or cold temperatures, keep you dry, and be loose-fitting for freedom of movement when paddling. Finally, clothing should be versatile for effective use under a wide range of conditions.

MATERIALS

Materials used to make *undergarments* should be noted for comfort and have a high vapor transmissibility to prevent a buildup of annoying, chilling water vapor next to your skin.

An *insulating* or *filler material* is designed to trap a great deal of air to keep you warm. The thickness of the insulating material is called the *loft*. Generally, the greater a garment's loft, the warmer it will be, though specially made *thin insulators* provide warmth without thickness because their fibers have a large surface area and efficiently trap insulating air.

An *outer* or *shell material* is made to hold the insulating filler in place and to keep wind, dirt, and water from it. Ideally, outer materials should be waterproof to shed external water yet breathable to allow your body's water vapor to escape through them. These two qualities are, of course, contradictory in nature but possible with a handful of specially designed, modern materials. All other fabrics used as an outer layer either sacrifice waterproofness for breathability or breathability for waterproofness. (Terms that deal with protection from and passage of water are explained on page 64.)

Because of its superb comfort, *cotton* is best used to make pants, shirts, and undergarments worn close to the skin. Unfortunately, cotton becomes useless when wet, and this makes it ineffective as an outer material and dangerous as an insulator. For safety, avoid cotton clothing in anything but comfortably warm weather.

Unlike cotton, *wool* is a satisfactory material to use in cold or wet conditions because a wet wool garment keeps you a lot warmer than a similar wet cotton one. Since cotton has a strong *wicking action*, you'll remain damp and chilled in clothes made from it until they completely dry, while wet wool ones dry from the skin out from your body heat alone. In addition, wool garments are warmer than similar cotton ones because their naturally curly fibers resist compression and have a larger surface area which traps more insulating air. Despite these advantages, wool is declining in popularity among canoeists because modern synthetics are far better in adverse conditions.

Polyester is used to make shirts and pants suitable for use on mild weather trips and for making pile insulating garments for cold weather use. Polyester's major advantage is it absorbs almost no water. You can soak a polyester garment in a river and then completely dry it by wringing it out and placing it in the sun for a few minutes. Consider carrying polyester clothing in unsettled weather conditions when you want the comfort of cotton without its terrible insulating qualities when wet.

Because *polypropylene* has great water vapor passing properties and doesn't absorb moisture into its fibers, it's an excellent material for use in adverse conditions. Polypropylene is commonly used to make clothes like long underwear worn as a vapor transmission layer next to the skin and pile sweaters, jackets, and pants worn for insulation.

While *down* is considered the best available cold weather insulator, it's far less than ideal when used on canoeing trips. Its Achilles heel is its tendency to soak up water. A wet down garment offers no insulation and requires several days of direct, intense sunlight to dry. To make matters worse, down products become extremely fragile when wet. Even a slightly wet down garment loses almost all of its insulating ability and is dangerous to handle without great care. Because of these problems, *down garments should never be worn when actually canoeing or when in foul, wet weather*. You should also avoid using down garments on canoe camping trips because the damp environment along waterways greatly reduces their insulating properties.

Several *new synthetic* insulating materials (primarily Polarguard, Hollofil, Fiberfill, and Quallofil) have appeared on the market to compete with down. Clothing and sleeping bags made from them are ideal for use in wet conditions because they retain about 80% of their insulation value when wet, absorb very little water, and can be almost completely dried by simply wringing them out by hand. Unlike down garments, you can quickly dry new synthetic materials by a fire without damaging them, and you can conveniently wash and dry them in machines at home. Unfortunately, these modern synthetics seem to lose a great deal of their insulating value after only 2 or 3 years of casual use.

Because *thin insulators* like Thinsulate and Sontique absorb less than 1% of their weight in water, they're ideal for use in the cold and wet conditions typically found along waterways. They are commonly used as insulating materials in jackets, parkas, and gloves.

Pile is a shaggy insulating material made from nylon, polyester, or polypropylene fabrics. Because it absorbs only about 1% of its weight in water, you'll feel almost as warm and dry in a soaked pile garment that's been wrung out by hand as in a completely dry one, and this makes it ideal for use on canoe trips. Pile is used to make insulating clothing like jackets, sweaters, pants, and gloves.

Neoprene is a closed-cell foam material ideally suited for use as an insulator in cold and wet conditions. It's used to make garments like dry suits and wet suits that completely shed external water and wind.

Nylon is an ideal outer material because it's breathable, strong, dries fast when wet, can easily be coated for waterproofness, and sheds wind effectively. Woven nylon in the form of pile is the only time it's used as an insulating material.

KINDS OF CLOTHING

Although *short pants* provide very little protection, they're ideal for use in warm weather because of their great freedom of movement and comfort. They're also useful when wading your canoe and when there's a great chance you'll get wet in a capsize or from splashed water.

Generally, you should carry at least one pair of *long pants* for warmth and protection on every canoe trip, but consider taking two pairs if you'll be canoeing for lengthy periods of time or in cooler or wetter weather. Long pants with wide bottoms you can slip on over river footgear and roll up when walking in shallow areas are especially convenient.

On most canoe trips, you'll need at least one or two *t-shirts* and one *long-sleeved shirt*. If you prefer long-sleeved shirts instead of sweaters or jackets for warmth, it's better to carry several light ones than one thick, heavy one for better heat regulation.

Wear a *bathing suit* instead of *underwear* when canoeing, because you'll be constantly in or near the water. Carry a spare to change into at the end of the day, and two or three pair at most on overnight trips of any length. Thin nylon swim suits are ideal because they dry fast when wet, although you should wear them under an outer pair of shorts because they lack durability.

A wide-brimmed *hat* provides shade and sunburn protection on sunny days and keeps the rain off your face and eyeglasses in foul weather. Wear a ski hat for insulation when canoeing in cool weather and carry one for use around your camp on cold nights.

A *turtleneck sweater, bandana*, or *scarf* keeps you noticeably warmer in cold weather by sealing your neck area from drafts and reducing heat loss there. Zippered turtlenecks are useful for heat regulation.

In colder weather your main insulation layers can consist of combinations of *sweaters*, *sweatshirts*, extra *shirts*, *pants*, *coats*, and garments discussed below. Always carry plenty of insulating clothing in cool or cold weather when the threat of hypothermia is greatest.

On cool weather canoeing trips carry only one insulating garment like *long underwear* for your legs if you'll use it only in the morning or evening around your campsite or at launch areas before and after a trip. If you're in weather so cold that you must paddle in these garments as well, wear a set and carry a spare for day trips and wear one set but carry at least two spares for emergencies on longer trips.

A *paddling jacket* is a loose-fitting coat designed for use while canoeing. Paddling jackets usually have neoprene wrist, neck, and waist closures that seal out external water and zippered or velcro openings in those closures for easier access through them.

Paddling pants are designed to protect your legs from wind, moisture, and abrasions while canoeing. Like paddling jackets, quality ones have neoprene cuffs that prevent water from entering their openings and are commonly made from breathable nylon, coated nylon, neoprene, or PTFE materials (see pages 64 and 65).

A *windbreaker* is a very thin, lightweight shell coat that keeps the wind away from your inner insulating layers. It can roll up into a bundle about the size of a closed fist for packing.

A *wind parka* is a durable windbreaker coat designed to keep the wind and a light snow, brief drizzle, or condensing fog away from your insulating layers as well as provide a limited amount of insulation itself. *Shell parkas* are simply a durable, outer, windproof layer, while *lined parkas* have various amounts and types of insulation attached beneath their outer shell.

Dry suits are full length, baggy neoprene, nylon, or PTFE garments that enclose your body for insulation and wetness protection in inclement weather. They have tight-fitting neoprene seals around their neck, ankle, and wrist openings to shed external moisture. While most are primarily designed to keep you dry in your canoe, a few will keep you dry when immersed in the water as well. Pile and polypropylene garments worn under a dry suit provide excellent insulation in cold weather.

Wetsuits are specialized neoprene garments that insulate your body by trapping a layer of warmed water next to it. While divers frequently use wet suits made from 1/4-inch thick neoprene fabric for protection during long periods of exposure to cold water, 1/8-inch thick neoprene wetsuits are adequate for almost all cold weather canoeing trips where infrequent, quick immersion occurs rather than planned, extended swimming excursions. In other words, canoeing wetsuits primarily offer insulation from the cold when paddling and shock protection from sudden but temporary immersion in cold water.

As a general rule, you should wear a wetsuit whenever the sum of the air temperature and the water temperature (both in degrees Fahrenheit) is less than

100. For example, it's best to wear a wetsuit when the water temperature is 55°F and the air temperature is less than 45°F. Another guideline states that you should wear a wetsuit if the water is so cold that you can't swim unprotected in it for at least five minutes. Of course, since a wetsuit provides a great deal of protection from the elements, it's better to wear it and not need it than to need it and not have it on.

Wetsuits are available in a host of styles (Example 3-1). Wetsuit *vests* are nice to have in marginal conditions when you want to protect your body's core without risking overheating or restricting your freedom of movement when paddling. *Shortie wetsuits* that extend from your elbows to your knees offer more protection than *farmer john* wetsuits, resembling farmer's overalls. *Full length* wetsuits should only be used in severe conditions, since you'll rapidly overheat in them in moderate weather.

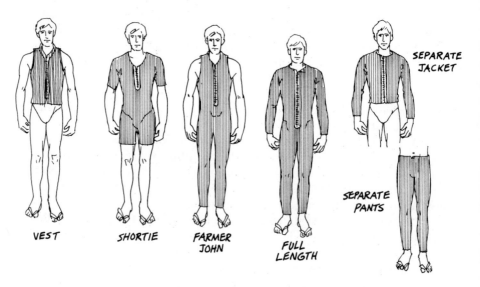

VEST   SHORTIE   FARMER   FULL   SEPARATE
                               JOHN   LENGTH   JACKET

                                                             SEPARATE
                                                             PANTS

Example 3-1: Wet suit styles.

Wetsuits should fit tight enough to prevent the flow of water inside them but loose enough so they don't restrict your body's circulation. Custom-made ones are more expensive but provide a better fit than standard-sized models. Two-piece suits are easier to put on and remove and more versatile than single-piece ones, since you can wear their parts separately in mild weather or together in colder conditions. Zippers aid in regulating your temperature and in putting them on and taking them off. For maximum temperature control, you should have zippers at wrist, ankle, and neck openings as well as at the main entry opening. Those made with a nylon inner lining are more expensive but stronger, more durable, more comfortable, and easier to put on and remove than standard, all-neoprene models.

You'll need to wear *gloves* or *mittens* for insulation in cold weather. Mittens are warmer than gloves because your fingers can huddle together for warmth inside them, but gloves are better where finger dexterity is needed to do something like tie knots in the cold. Wear hand protection noted for its insulation value and not its water repelling properties when not actually paddling your canoe or exposed to precipitation in cold weather. Gloves or mittens designed for this purpose are usually made from wool, pile, a thin insulator, or a new synthetic type of fill.

In wet conditions wear gloves or mittens that shed as much external water as possible, since anything worn on your hands will get exposed to large amounts of water from paddling or precipitation. Neoprene gloves or mittens are ideal in severe conditions, since they retain their insulating properties when wet, while uninsulated rubber handyman gloves are suitable for use in mildly cool, wet weather.

Commercially available *paddling gloves* are primarily designed to prevent blisters when paddling for long periods of time. They typically have a mesh back for ventilation and leather palms for durability.

INSECT PROTECTION

Powerful insect repellents and thick clothing are your best lines of defense against hordes of insects that could plague you on a canoe trip. When repelling insects, completely cover your entire body with clothing and seal all joints between clothing layers by tucking each layer into the preceding one so no bare skin is exposed. The last thing you want to do is tempt these voracious creatures with a patch of easily accessible flesh. Then apply your insect repellent to critical parts of your body that are hard to seal. Always carry and wear long-sleeved shirts, long pants, gloves, socks, a scarf, and an insect head net in heavily infested areas—and be sure your clothing is thick enough so they can't drill through it to your skin. Many materials, including cotton shirts and demin jeans, will only keep a fraction of them at bay.

Insect head nets are often invaluable on a canoe trip. They have insect netting completely encircling them, several stiff rings that keep the material away from your face, an insect-proof top, and a drawstring closure system to seal them shut around your neck.

RAINGEAR

Garments made for use in the rain should be waterproof to shed external water, offer freedom of movement when paddling, be well-ventilated to prevent internal condensation, and not impair your vision. Raingear should be loose-fitting to provide plenty of ventilation and allow room for extra insulating cloth-ing layers under it in cold weather.

You should assume that any clothes worn under raingear will become wet from external leaks or internal condensation in a storm. Therefore, when canoe-ing in foul but warm weather, wear a short-sleeved shirt and short pants under your rain gear to keep your remaining garments protected in your dry bags for later use. In colder weather, wear synthetics like polypropylene and pile for warmth under your raingear because they keep most of their insulating value when wet. Remember that it's often better to wait out a storm in a shelter than to paddle in it and risk soaking your insulating clothing. Never leave a shelter in a storm unless you have a complete dry change of clothes to wear later in the day.

Materials

Waterproof materials are complete barriers against water. Thus, you'll get soaked and then chilled from your condensing body vapor when canoeing for a few hours in a waterproof garment, even though it completely protects you from the elements.

Waterproof raingear is made from several kinds of materials. *Plastic* is only suited for day use in mild conditions because it's so fragile. Relying on a plastic rain garment over long periods of time or in harsh conditions is foolish and dangerous. *Rubberized cloth* and *vinyl-coated materials* are tough, moder-ately priced fabrics, but they're heavy and uncomfortably stiff and their coatings often crack or peel off after a small amount of use. *Coated nylon* materials offer reliable waterproof protection with more comfort and less weight, though at a significantly greater cost.

Water repellent materials shed external moisture for a short time before leaking. Avoid them when canoeing in cold conditions or in regions with fre-quent or prolonged storms, since they offer no reliable wetness protection.

Breathable fabrics let moisture readily pass through them. While wearing a breathable outer layer helps prevent a buildup of moisture in your insulation layers, it does little to restrict external water from entering.

Waterproof but breathable *polytetra-fluorethylene (PTFE)* materials like Goretex are ideal for use in the rain because they completely shed external water yet allow your internal body moisture to escape. In addition they can double as a windbreaker or insulating parka in fair weather without causing a buildup of water vapor within your insulation layers.

Styles

There are several styles and combinations of raingear suitable for canoeing. On an extremely cold, stormy day, a *wetsuit* is probably the safest protection available. In more mild, foul weather conditions, a *dry suit*, *paddling jacket*, *rain parka*, or *rainsuit* used in conjunction with appropriate underlying insulation layers could provide the proper amount of external wetness protection, breathability, ventilation, and insulation you'll need for safety. Avoid *ponchos* which billow annoyingly in the wind, snag on obstructions, and invite water to enter their large arm openings when paddling. Also, avoid traditional *raincoats* which excessively restrict your arm movements when paddling.

FOOTGEAR

Canoeing footgear should provide protection from sharp objects, insulation from cold water, and traction on wet surfaces. Drain holes that let water empty out of them quickly, lightweight materials that dry fast, and a flexible sole for freedom of movement are additional useful qualities. Always use shoes you tie on rather than those that just slip on your feet to prevent loss in the water.

On overnight trips, take at least two sets of footgear so you can wear one during the day on the river and have a dry set to wear around your camp in the evening. Always use the same set in the water even if that means putting a wet pair on in the morning so your other pair stays dry for evening use at camp. On long trips or in wet weather, consider taking as many as three pairs of footgear for the best possible foot protection.

Shoes

Sneakers are popular canoeing shoes because of their low cost, comfortable fit, and superb drainage. High top styles resist falling off better than low cut ones and offer some ankle protection as well. While old, worn sneakers are satisfactory for casual weekend canoe trips, new ones offer the best reliability on longer outings.

Avoid using traditional leather *hiking boots* while canoeing because they're unnecessarily heavy, easily become waterlogged, are difficult to swim in, and dry very slowly. Canvas top, leather bottom *Vietnam (jungle) boots* and lightweight, *nylon* or *nylon/leather hiking boots* are ideal when canoeing because they offer superb traction and durability and have the advantages of sneakers without the problems of leather boots. Avoid wearing open-topped *rubber hip waders* when canoeing because they can easily fill up with water and are hard to swim in after a capsize. Avoid wearing *sandals* when paddling in your canoe, because they fall off easily and offer insufficient support and protection in the water. Specially made, commercially available *river shoes* with neoprene uppers and molded rubber, no-slip soles are useful in cold or rough water but aren't needed for casual recreational boating.

As a word of caution, always wear some kind of foot protection outdoors. Pieces of glass, pop tabs from beverage cans, sharp rocks, and thorns exist everywhere out there, and they threaten to cut your feet with your first barefoot step. In fact, the farther you are from civilization the more you must be careful about preventing injuries like cut feet because of the difficulty involved with getting to medical help if hurt.

Socks

Socks cushion your feet from impacts, protect them from debris that collects inside your shoes, and insulate them in cold weather. Avoid them on warm days unless you need them for comfort, since they quickly become waterlogged. In mildly cool weather, a pair of pile or wool socks worn inside your sneakers will provide some insulation even when wet. In colder weather wear *neoprene socks* inside oversized sneakers or wetsuit socks with nonslip soles for additional protection, and wear polypropylene or pile socks under them for even greater warmth in very cold weather.

SELECTING CANOEING CLOTHING

In conclusion and as a word of warning, *always carry more clothing than you think you'll need on every outing*. It's better to carry an excessive amount of clothing and be warm and dry than to cut your clothing supplies to the bone and risk soaking them and getting hypothermia. Avoid playing the survival game with the gods of fate unless you deal the cards.

TECHNIQUES

4

INITIAL PREPARATIONS

The next section is a basic introduction to canoeing on a river. Generalized preparations for canoeing on both flatwater and moving water then follow.

CANOEING ON MOVING WATER

River Ratings

The major concepts you should learn from this section are that rivers are rated according to their difficulty and that some rivers require far more skill to negotiate than others. If you're not familiar with specific terms, like holes, reversals, and gradient, appearing in this section, just read it to get an idea what river canoeing is about and then return to it again after reading Chapter 8.

Rivers, sections of rivers, and rapids are typically rated in the following way:

A *class I* river is easy to canoe. It's great for beginners since it's wide, unobstructed, and slow. It has a small gradient, riffles instead of rapids, a predictable current, and obvious channels. Common sense, rather than river reading skill, is needed to negotiate a class I river.

A *class II* river is of moderate difficulty. It's suitable for canoeists with prior experience on class I water and a mastery of basic whitewater skills. Class II rivers have fairly wide, usually unobstructed channels, moderate rapids with waves a maximum of 2 feet high, a faster and less predictable current, and distinct eddies. With some river reading ability, it's not difficult to avoid obstacles in these rivers. Class II rivers are usually the limit of navigability for heavily loaded canoes.

Because a *class III* river is fairly difficult, it's considered the roughest water an open canoe can negotiate. A class III river usually contains plenty of 3- or 4-foot waves, confusing channels, overlapping eddies, fast currents, potentially dangerous holes, and obstacles that should be avoided for safety. Often you should scout class III rapids from shore before canoeing through them and will need to make quick route decisions when maneuvering in them. Class III rivers are suitable only for highly experienced paddlers.

A *class IV* river should be run only by expert, helmeted paddlers in closed canoes, kayaks, or open canoes with spray covers over them. This kind of river typically contains long sections of violent rapids, large and frequent waves, fast and tricky currents, a steep gradient, large reversals, and sharp drops. Scouting from shore is mandatory for all class IV water.

Class V rivers challenge even advanced expert closed boaters. They contain large drops, a very steep gradient, obstructed channels, dangerous currents, unreliable eddies, and huge holes. Navigation is difficult on them and death is possible with any mistake.

Class VI rivers are classified as impossible to run safely. The "limit of navigability" is a frequently used term describing these rivers.

Often rivers don't fit into the neat categories just described. To compensate for this, they can be tagged with a "+" or a "−" sign to indicate greater or less than the stated numerical difficulty. For example, a class II+ river is harder than a class II but not as hard as a class III river. Likewise, class III− is harder than class II but not as hard as class III water. The "+" and "−" signs also give you an invitation to try slightly more difficult water. If you can handle class II water without anxiety, then try a class II+ or a class III− river before embarking on a trip through class III water.

That's how it works in theory, anyway. Because judging a river's difficulty is so subjective, one man's class II+ river is another's class II and a third's class III. Generally, rivers are slightly underrated in regions of the country containing much whitewater and somewhat overrated in difficulty in areas that have mostly meandering, peaceful streams.

While these ratings help estimate the difficulty of a section of river or a rapids, they are no guarantee that it will be precisely of that difficulty. There are several factors, almost always *not* taken into account when assigning the numerical rating values described above, that influence the *true difficulty* of a river:

1) *The length of a rapids*. The longer a set of rapids, the more dangerous it is to paddle through. A long class III rapids could really be of class IV difficulty and not recommended at all for open canoes, especially if it contains few reliable eddies, limited accessibility for rescuers, and few safe landing spots in it.

2) *Water temperature*. Because of the dangers of hypothermia, increase a river's rating by one notch if it's colder than about 50°F. Thus, treat a class II river as if it were a class III if its water is cold.

3) *Accessibility*. Increase a river's difficulty rating by one degree if it's in a remote location with little or no quick access to civilization. For example, ex-

perienced paddlers treat wilderness class II rivers as if they were class III by scouting their rapids from shore before running them, even though they almost always would never scout class II water in an accessible region.

4) *The location of a particularly difficult section.* Increase a river's difficulty rating by one degree if its hardest section is near its top. If you spill at the beginning of a rapids, you'll have to somehow get yourself and your equipment to safety with the current continually threatening to wash you into the bulk of the rapids awaiting downstream. On the other hand, if the hardest part of a rapids is near its end and if you get in trouble there, you're only a short swim from the safe, calm water below the rapids.

5) *The water level.* Rapids usually become much worse at higher water levels. Though rocks and obstructions tend to wash out as the water level increases, holes generally get much worse, standing waves grow to roller-coaster-sized monsters, and reliable landing spots become flooded. Also, river currents become fast and tricky at high water levels. In low water, rapids usually become rock gardens that are less threatening, though more difficult to navigate through. In general, then, increase the difficulty of a river by at least one category to compensate for the greater dangers associated with high water levels, but do not decrease its rating at lower water levels.

6) *A river's character.* A mild river rated as class II could contain one class III rapids that would effectively limit a trip there to canoeists capable of handling class III water, unless class II canoeists portage around the difficult section.

7) *The time of year.* Rivers are usually much higher in spring than in fall. Beware of ice flows in early spring.

8) *Dam releases.* Water released from upstream reservoirs can change a mild class I river into a roaring, feisty, class III bronco in a very short time. Always check the release schedule before canoeing on these rivers.

Another way to look at this concept of increasing a river's difficulty rating is by saying something like "the *river* we'll be canoeing on is class II in difficulty, but this is a class III *trip* because of the cold water" (or because of the isolated location or whatever). Although class II canoeists could probably negotiate the rapids on it without difficulty, allowing only class III or greater paddlers to go on the trip assures you that they have a greater than minimum competence level which will reduce the chances of anyone capsizing into the cold water (or getting hurt in the remote area, etc.)

Rivers are also rated according to their volume of flow in *cfs* (cubic feet per second). This term is useful for comparing various sizes of rivers and various water levels on the same river. When considering paddling a river new to you, get an indication of its difficulty by asking local canoeists familiar with it what its flow is presently, what its normal flow is for that time of year, and how that river behaves at its present and normal water levels. The percent difference between the present and normal cfs flows is far more important than the actual volume difference between them. For example, a small stream with a normal 1,000 cfs flow will be extremely dangerous at 3,000 cfs, while a large river with a normal flow of 50,000 cfs will have virtually no change in character at 55,000 cfs, even though it gained more than twice as much water as the smaller stream.

Some rapids are rated on a 1–10 scale. With this system, 1 is the easiest, while 10 is the most difficult. A rapid rated a 10, for example, will flip 50% of the boats traveling through it. This scale has limited use for open boat canoeists, since most rapids rated with it are located in the southwestern states and are best traveled by raft, kayak, or closed canoe.

Canoeists, as well as rivers, are rated. *Class O* paddlers are people who have never canoed before. These people should limit themselves to flatwater until they master the basic strokes. Depending on the person and the method of instruction, this may take several hours or several days. *Class I* canoeists are familiar with the basic canoeing strokes and should be capable of paddling on class I streams. *Class II* canoeists are novices who have mastered the basics of reading moving water and simple rapids. They should be able to handle class II water without difficulty. *Class III* canoeists are experienced paddlers capable of canoeing class III water. They can perform complicated maneuvers like leaning, bracing, and eddy turns instinctively and with ease.

Sources of Information

Always obtain as much advice as possible about a river you're planning to canoe on, and never paddle in moving water without first being absolutely sure it's suitable for your skill level. Sources of information you can use to find out about a waterway are listed below:

1) *Experienced canoeists* are probably your best source of information. You can obtain information about canoeing rivers from boaters you meet outdoors, from paddling friends, or from people in a neighborhood canoe club. Boating clubs are goldmines of regional information, since chances are every river within a few hundred miles of your town has been paddled by someone in the club. To find information about a river or area far from your home, request a list of affiliates from the American Canoe Association (its address is in the Appendix) and write to the one closest to your area of interest. Someone in that club can probably provide the information you need to plan a trip there.

2) *Guidebooks and tourist brochures* often list put-in and takeout pints, nearby roads, river mileages between landmarks like bridge crossings, gaging locations, nearby canoeing services like rental outfitters, the river difficulty rating at a given cfs level, and river dangers. Regional guidebooks are often much more accurate, complete, and up-to-date than national ones, since they contain mostly firsthand information, whereas much of the information in na-

tional guides is necessarily second- or thirdhand. Guidebooks and tourist brochures are usually published for popular waterways, so you'll probably have company if you canoe on rivers discussed in them.

3) *Canoe dealers and outdoor store clerks* who are experienced paddlers can probably direct you to local canoeing streams suited for your ability.

4) *Topographic maps* are quite useful for planning a canoe trip if you know how to use them. Consult standard camping references for information in this regard.

5) Contact the USGS *gaging station* closest to the section of river you want to canoe to find its current flow rate in cfs. As explained earlier, this information is useful when you can compare it to the average flow for that time of year. Usually, you'll learn little other helpful information about a river's difficulty from this source, unless the people who work at the stations are experienced canoeists or unless the river contains well-known dangers. Write to the

United States Geological Survey
Department of the Interior
Reston, VA 22092

and request the free booklet "WRD Information Guide" which lists state and regional addresses you can contact to find the location of gaging stations on particular rivers.

6) Obtain information about a specific river from the *government agency* or *utility* responsible for regulating it. These organizations include the Army Corps of Engineers, power companies, parks and recreation commissions, and state fishing departments. In the past, they've probably been approached by canoeists and should be familiar with the canoeing opportunities and dangers there.

7) Research *historical accounts* of canoe trips in your public library to learn some background information about a waterway and its potential for canoeing. These accounts abound in areas like Canada and the northern states where travel- ing by canoe was the most reliable method of transportation until a few years ago. In general, accounts in the form of scientific observations and ongoing notes are more useful than those written as personal diaries or post-trip reflections.

8) *Local people* living near a waterway are often poor sources of informa- tion, unless you know them and their canoeing ability personally. Most people who don't canoe have no idea what a river is like for canoeing, even though it could be flowing right through their backyard. They may see people canoeing on it, but won't know anything about how difficult it is to paddle or where suitable access points are. While most local people will try to help you when approached, a rare few that despise outsiders will pass on false information to you to discour- age you from returning again.

You can try calling service stations or businesses along a waterway to get a general idea of the canoeing conditions there. Ask them what the present weather is like (a storm could indicate rising water levels), what the color of the water is (muddy water indicates high water), and if the river is lower or higher than normal. By asking carefully worded questions and diligently separating the wheat from the chaff, you may be able to get an idea about the canoeing potential in the area at the present time.

Always double check your information, and be wary of non- and beginning paddlers loaded with advice on canoeing a river. Rely on first- more than second- or thirdhand information and discard any that seems unreasonable or contradictory. If you're an experienced boater, take information from beginning paddlers with a grain of salt, since their "difficult" river could be blasé to you. Likewise, be careful when receiving advice from experienced canoeists if you're new to canoeing. Their "easy" river could be a real challenge for you. Of course, the less information you have about a river, the more cautious you must be when planning a trip to it and when actually traveling on it for safety.

Wild and Scenic Rivers

The Wild and Scenic Rivers Act of 1968 and recent amendments to it have designated parts of over 60 rivers as National Wild, Scenic, or Recreational Rivers. For inclusion in the system, a river must be free-flowing, have high water quality, and be noted for its scenic, geological, recreational, wildlife, cultural, or historic values. According to the law, *wild rivers* are primitive and inaccessible, *scenic rivers* slightly show the effects of development, and *recreational rivers* have some shoreline development and a reduced wilderness character. You can obtain more information about this law or about specific wild, scenic, and recreational rivers by contacting the National Park Service (see the Appendix).

Several states and provinces have designated their own wild and scenic rivers. Contact the appropriate state or province recreation, tourism, or fish and game department for more information about any of these waterways of interest to you.

The Refuse Act of 1899

This law prohibits anyone from dumping foreign material into a navigable waterway, which by definition includes any lake or river you can travel up or down by canoe or floating log. This law is an extremely powerful legal tool that canoeists can use to stop and prevent water pollution. As an added benefit, it awards half the fine to anyone providing information leading to a conviction! This means that if you report a pollution violation to the proper health or environmental authorities or sue the polluter yourself, you are entitled to half their penalty. Since polluters can be fined up to $2,500 per day, this can be a substantial amount of money. Contact the Army Corps of Engineers (see the Appendix) for more information.

GENERAL CONSIDERATIONS

Access

While you can legally canoe waterways deep enough to float a canoe, you may not be able to access them at convenient places or times. Access is limited in these ways:

1) *Landowners* along waterways occasionally post their land to keep outsiders away. They've learned through unfortunate experiences that people bring garbage, disrespectful manners, and a degradation of the natural resource. Always get permission from the landlord before crossing private land to get to or from a waterway, and prevent additional posting by treating all landowners with respect. Help dispel the notion that all canoeists are beer drinking slobs.

2) *Agencies* occasionally regulate canoeing areas with a *permit system* to monitor the human impact there, to prevent further environmental destruction, to preserve a quality outdoor experience for everyone using the area, and to promote safe boating in dangerous areas. Usually permits for access to a regulated waterway or for permission to float a controlled section of river are free or very inexpensive and can be obtained through the mail or by phone. You should arrange to get any needed permits as long as possible before beginning your trip to be sure they're available. While few of us enjoy the wave of bureaucracy controlling our lives, these permits achieve a valuable purpose. Avoid hassling the people issuing them or enforcing these regulations.

Agencies issuing permits may require that you carry items like life preservers, rescue gear, sewage containers, insurance, and at least one extra paddle per boat. On popular or dangerous rivers, they may have rangers actually checking for them before letting you proceed on the water. Some states require boating licenses for flatwater as well as whitewater paddling. Inquire about all these things from the agencies involved or from experienced canoeing friends in your local area before actually embarking on a trip to avoid disappointments at the launch site.

3) *Undeveloped, shoreline areas* are another obstacle you could face when trying to get to a waterway. Use a highway map to find locations where roads cross or parallel water bodies. Access points usually occur at bridges, small towns, or places where roads are closest to the water. If you want to canoe a section of river or lake not bordered by roads marked on a highway map, use topographic or county road maps to find secondary roads that can take you there. As a last resort, inquire at farms or villages about possible, isolated dirt roads in the area. Be cautious and reserved when dealing with country people. They live where they do because they enjoy the peace and solitude. The last thing they want is a caravan of boaters traveling through every weekend.

4) *Obstructed shorelines.* Natural features like cliffs, dense thickets, patches of poison ivy, fields of stickers, and swamps can pose formidable access barriers for even the most diehard canoeists.

5) *Poor road conditions* can ruin your most carefully made plans. A rainstorm can turn a dirt road into a swamp surprisingly fast, high winds can easily topple a tree across a road, deep ruts can tear the bottom out of a low riding car, and vegetation can quickly obliterate a road in less than a generation of infrequent use. Always be sure you can drive back out of a county road if the weather turns bad and be sure you can turn around anywhere along it. Backing out of a dead-end road can be a long, tedious affair.

6) *Insufficient parking space* at a potential put-in or takeout location could mean you have to alter your shuttle plans to start or end at that spot. When parking along a roadway, pull your car as far off the pavement onto the shoulder as possible. When parking in more remote areas, don't block the main access road, don't block the access to the water itself, and don't restrict the room needed to turn a vehicle around in the area. When parking your vehicle in a congested area before heading off in your canoe, be especially careful that an inconsiderate person can't park you in when you're gone.

Where to Canoe

Access locations and paddling difficulty primarily determine where you can canoe. If you're new to canoeing, you should paddle at popular lakes, developed recreation areas, or on calm sections of rivers until you learn more about the sport. If you're an experienced paddler, you're limited much more by access or your available time and money than by the difficulty of the waterway. Some people enjoy canoeing wild, scenic, or recreational rivers because they're of generally good quality, others are happy paddling waterways that leisurely meander through the countryside, and still others enjoy charging down rapids on difficult mountain streams. Many wild areas like the Adirondacks offer unlimited canoeing opportunities, and, of course, canoeing in a true wilderness is possible, especially in Alaska or Canada. Although a city is not the most natural setting for a canoe trip, the feeling of exploration and adventure there is just as real as in the wilderness. In short, then, with a few common sense precautions and the proper combination of money, time, and experience, you can canoe almost anywhere. As an extreme example I live in the middle of the endless Arizona desert, yet superb canoeing streams and countless high country lakes abound within a few hours drive in any direction.

Distance and Traveling Speed

How fast and far you'll travel varies with the current, the wind speed and direction, the amount of portaging you'll do, the amount of available daylight, your physical condition, your canoe's design, the degree of cold or wet weather, the amount of gear on board, and the amount of time actually spent paddling. You'll travel faster and farther when the size of your group is small, when you paddle at a steady pace, when you rest infrequently and for short periods of time, and when everyone in your group is skilled in canoeing techniques and has equal levels of physical endurance. As a rough estimate, you'll travel about 2 to 4 miles an hour on flat water, about 2 to 4 miles an hour plus the river's speed on moving water, and far less than 1 mile an hour when portaging. While experienced canoeists can cover more than 20 miles a day for many consecutive days, expect to paddle much less than that if you're just beginning or if you're paddling in less than ideal conditions.

Be flexible with your long-distance canoe camping plans. Allow an occasional *rest day* in case you become stormbound, get sick, or decide to linger at an attractive campsite. Experienced canoeists should allow at least one rest day for every six to eight consecutive canoeing days, while average canoeists should allow one for every four to six canoeing days, and people with young children need at least one rest day for every two or three days spent paddling. Note that you don't have to rest on a rest day. They are just free blocks of time you insert into your schedule to help eliminate the pressures of time on your outing. Rest days can be used for canoeing as well as for resting.

Weather Conditions

Be aware of the predicted and potential weather conditions where you'll canoe so you'll know what kind of gear to pack and will be able to survive comfortably in those conditions. Always carry extra wet and cold weather protection for those "just in case" hypothermia situations that arise more frequently than expected or desired.

Average monthly temperature and precipitation tables indicate the typical or average weather conditions in a location for a given time of year. While useful for getting a general idea what the weather will be like where you'll canoe, they don't indicate potential extremes or the specific conditions that could confront you outdoors. Tables listing these average values for the United States are available from:

> U.S. Department of Commerce
> National Climatic Data Center
> Federal Building
> Asheville, NC 28801

Local *weather reports* and *five-day forecasts* indicate specific conditions you'll probably encounter on the first few days of a trip. These are available in local newspapers, from TV or radio stations, or by calling the U.S. Weather Bureau in the region where you'll canoe.

Consider carrying a *radio* to keep abreast of changes in the weather when traveling for a long period of time or in the colder spring and fall season, to help avoid a confrontation with hypothermia. For example, when canoeing in cold weather you could use the radio to get a weather forecast to determine if a light rain will blow over or if it's the advance guard of a dangerous snow or sleet storm.

Vehicle Transportation

Throughout this section detailing how to get to and from a waterway, the pronoun "you" is used to mean a group of people. With a few common-sense exceptions, getting to and coming home from a solo canoe trip is identical to the methods described.

Typically, on short flatwater trips, you drive your cars to the waterway, paddle around all day, and then return to them and drive home. On longer flatwater trips and on almost all river trips your starting and ending locations are not the same, so you must arrange to either be dropped off and picked up or *shuttle* your vehicles from the *put-in* to the *takeout* points. There are two ways to arrange the transportation if your put-in and takeout locations are not the same:

1) *Someone drops you off at your starting location and picks you up at your destination.* A major advantage of this method is that you don't waste time shuttling the vehicles. You can begin canoeing almost as soon as you unload your gear. This method works best when paddling fairly close to home because the expense and hassle involved with having other people drive you a long distance to and from a waterway are quite large. However, arranging the meeting at the takeout so that neither you nor the drivers have to wait very long is difficult to do. Waiting for a ride in cold, wet weather can be dangerous and discouraging.

2) *Shuttling your vehicles* can waste a significant amount of time, involve a confusing exchange of gear like roof racks, and require a minimum of two vehicles. Its advantages include potentially lower travel costs, fewer problems when compared with coercing friends or spouses into driving your vehicles for you, the opportunity for everyone in your group to store dry clothes and food in the vehicles left at the takeout for immediate use at the end of the trip, and using the vehicles left at the takeout as a shelter when off the water. These last two items are important considerations when paddling in inclement weather.

A shuttle generally works like this. First, everyone in your group meets at a designated place in your community on the day of the trip, travels to the launch site in as few vehicles as possible, and unloads them. Then the drivers transfer the cars to the takeout point, leave all but one vehicle there, and rejoin the rest of the group at the launch site in that one car. This way, at the end of the trip, people can load the gear in and the canoes on the vehicles at the takeout location while a single vehicle returns to the launch site to retrieve the lone vehicle left there. If time is of the essence, everyone should unload the vehicles at the launch site as quickly as possible so the drivers can begin the shuttle without delay. Then the other paddlers can carry the canoes to the water and secure gear into them while the drivers are performing the shuttle.

If you have excess room in your vehicles, you can perform a shortened version of the previously described shuttle to save gas and time. With this procedure, you drive to the takeout location, transfer the gear and passengers from the smallest vehicle into the other ones, leave that car at the takeout spot, and proceed to the put-in. At the end of the trip, the drivers return to the launch site to retrieve the cars in the one vehicle left at the takeout location. When performing this shuttle, be sure the vehicle you leave at the takeout spot can hold all the drivers for the shuttle at the end of the trip.

Always lock unattended shuttle vehicles, hide valuables left in them, and leave nothing like paddles or roof racks visible in them to indicate you're on an extended river trip instead of a short hike or other activity. If possible, avoid parking in obvious canoe launching areas in regions where vandalism has occurred in the past. A car left parked near a roadside pullout will attract far less attention than one parked at a boat river access area. For added security, leave your vehicles at homes, gas stations, restaurants, or motels near your entry and exit locations, with permission, of course, from their owners. All the previous shuttle directions assumed someone in your group was responsible for watching your gear while the vehicles were shuttled. Only a group of fools would leave their boating gear lying unattended while they shuttled vehicles.

Learning to Canoe

If you're a beginning canoeist, there are several ways to learn canoeing techniques and skills:

1) *Joining a canoe club* is an excellent way to meet people willing to teach you about the sport. You may feel out of place the first few times you go to a canoe club meeting, especially when it seems like so many people there socialize with each other so readily. Remember, though, that canoe clubs are groups of people that have shared experiences and through time have become close friends. If you go on a few trips with them and take an interest in club activities, you'll break into the group with ease. You might notice a subtle split between the recreational paddlers and the racers or between the open boat canoeists and the closed boaters in the club, but don't let that bother you. With time you'll find your niche in the group. Travel on the carefree, enjoyable outings frequented by the recreational boaters if that's what you prefer, but learn from the closed boat paddlers and the racers, for they are the cutting edge of the sport. They'll help you perfect your paddling techniques in a very short time and will give you opportunities to try closed boat canoeing and kayaking, which are exciting sports in their own right.

2) *Professional guide services* offer a host of canoeing, camping, hunting, fishing, and exploring programs in often highly scenic areas. Their addresses are listed in popular outdoor magazines, Chamber of Commerce brochures, and standard telephone directories. Quality outfitters will mail you a pamphlet describing their programs and a list of previous customers you can contact for testimonials about them.

Before signing up with a professional guide service, be sure you fully understand exactly what insurance, food, equipment, transportation, medical, and repair costs are involved, and know what gear you are expected to bring with you from home. Check to be sure you have the proper canoeing and outdoor skills for the planned route and that none of your physical handicaps or dietary problems will interfere with the intended plans. Be sure your goals for the trip match what the outfitter can provide. For example, don't be disappointed if you spend very little time running rapids on a predominantly fishing expedition.

Some professional outfitters encourage you to assume a relaxed spectator role on their outings, while others expect you to perform your fair share of chores like washing dishes and digging the latrine. While the first kind of trip is a great way to spend an unpressured vacation, the second type of trip just described will give you an opportunity to increase your outdoor skills under the guidance of trained outdoorsmen.

3) *Canoeing schools* differ from guide services in that their primary goal is to teach you how to canoe, not to serve you a full course meal of outdoor experiences. In other words, canoeing schools are ideal places to learn paddling techniques, water safety principles, and river reading skills firsthand. They range in length from weekend to week-long sessions. Some people incorporate them into their vacation so they can see a different part of the country while learning to canoe. Like guide services, canoeing schools advertise extensively in popular outdoor magazines.

Before enrolling in a paddling school, compare brochures from several different ones and learn as much as you can about them. Find out what equipment each school provides and what you need to bring with you to it. Some advanced paddlers prefer using their own boating gear, although convenience should be your primary concern if you're a beginning paddler since the equipment you use matters relatively little at that level of experience. Better schools have facilities that can be either rustic or luxurious but are always adequate, a low instructor/ student ratio (no more than 1:6), instructors experienced in their sport as well as in teaching it, instructors trained in advanced first aid and rescue techniques, a location close to various kinds of water conditions, a solid reputation, and a short drive to the water.

The more time you spend canoeing with the instructor, the more you'll learn, although long hours on the water could be torture if you're not in good physical condition. Find out if you can end any lesson when tired or if you must finish long paddling sessions each day to get back to a base area or shuttle vehicle. Better schools divide their students up into groups of people with similar abilities. Be wary of schools that group students with different interests and skill levels together, those that emphasize a certain aspect of canoeing if you have little interest in it, and schools that make unrealistic claims of the progress you'll achieve there. Avoid schools that don't publish a brochure and those that don't clearly list the details of their program in writing.

4) *Community organizations* like YMCAs, the Red Cross, Boy Scouts, community colleges, local recreation departments, and public school adult education programs frequently offer canoeing instructions. These programs are ideal if you're just getting started in the sport because they emphasize basic techniques like the paddling strokes that are forever useful on the water.

5) Finally, you can use *this book* to learn about canoeing. If you have no experienced paddling friends nearby to teach you, simply read it several times as needed and practice the skills explained in it. This volume also makes an excellent reference manual that complements instructions you may receive in a formal class. Since this book is compiled from a host of sources, it probably contains more information than many experienced paddlers acquire from years of canoeing.

And now a few words of caution are appropriate, especially since it's so tempting to believe everything you hear about canoeing when just getting started in the sport. Unfortunately, many canoeists are only too willing to teach you paddling techniques they learned improperly years ago, and contact with misinformed woodsmen will quickly tarnish your soul with outmoded camping practices. It seems like every lake and stream has its resident "canoeing expert," and libraries are filled with canoeing and camping manuals that teach you how to pollute the water and desecrate the land. It's far better to selectively sip canoeing, camping, and wilderness travel techniques from a handful of reliable sources than to quench your thirst for outdoor knowledge from every cup of information that passes your way.

Leading a Canoe Trip

If you're a member of a group of people like a canoe club or a Scout troop, you may have an opportunity to lead a canoe trip. While you should have some canoeing experience before doing this, you don't have to be an expert paddler or the most experienced person on the trip. Often people are willing to go on a trip but just lack the time, effort, or initiative needed to organize it.

While the information in this section focuses on leading a river canoe trip because of its greater complexity, the underlying concepts are identical for leading trips on flat water as well. Also, the following information includes many details that you as a leader should do when canoeing with several beginners. Canoe trips composed of experienced paddlers usually fall comfortably in place with little obvious "leadership." Finally, while this section emphasizes leading a canoe club trip, the principles discussed in it are relevant for any trip you take, whether it's with a group of friends or a specific organization.

Depending on how your club operates, there are several methods of informing people of upcoming trips. Two are explained below:

1) *Place sign-up sheets at designated locations.* Many canoe clubs like those at large universities meet once or twice a month but have a large enough membership to paddle every weekend. In this case, a person leading a canoe trip on an "off week" posts an information sheet describing his plans and listing information like the length of the trip, equipment needed, skill level required, and expected cost on a bulletin board in a centralized location like the student union building. This way people can simply read the information, sign up on nearby sheets if interested, and meet at the designated place at the specified time. No organizational meeting is required beforehand.

For smoother operation of this system, the leader should phone everyone who signed up on the sheet as a driver to verify that they can indeed drive their vehicles on the trip and should phone everyone else to be sure they're definitely going. On more difficult trips, the leader should check everyone's paddling skills to be sure they can handle the expected water conditions. Additional coordination, particularly involving planning the food for overnight trips, may be needed depending on the experience levels of everyone involved.

2) *Bring sign-up sheets to meetings.* Canoe clubs with no centralized information spot or those with infrequent outings usually distribute trip sign-up sheets at their meetings. In this case, a trip leader explains all relevant information about an intended trip and then passes a sheet around so everyone present can sign up for it if interested. Then, early in the week before the outing, the leader calls everyone on the list to confirm who will be going, makes arrangements for food, and verifies the transportation.

As a trip leader, you should arrive at the designated meeting place early on the day of the trip to conclude administrative details as people arrive, direct the loading of any club-owned canoes, and oversee the shuffling of personal canoes between vehicles as needed to optimize the transportation. You or a designated experienced boater should check beginners' gear to be sure they didn't forget items like knee pads and life jackets. Except on very difficult rivers, a verbal and not an actual physical check will suffice. Before leaving, be sure to distribute sketch or photocopied maps to any driver not familiar with the route, and plan a driving caravan (see below) and arrange any meeting places along the way for it if needed. Finally, check to be sure everyone who signed up for the trip is accounted for, and make last-minute phone calls to rouse late sleepers from bed if necessary. Of course, always leave word with an experienced boater who knows where you'll be, when you expect to return, and the names and phone numbers of everyone on the trip. This is especially important for solo canoeists and when traveling on difficult waterways or in remote areas.

Having the drivers meet at the launch site is satisfactory if the put-in location is nearby, but if you must drive a long distance to the waterway, it's best to drive in a caravan to be sure no vehicles break down along the way. Nothing's worse than the feeling of anxiety you get when waiting at a launch site for a vehicle that should have arrived a long time ago. When driving in a caravan, designate "lead" and "sweep" cars and always keep the vehicles in front of you and behind you in sight to prevent getting lost and to keep track of everyone in the group. Consider arranging headlight signals for food, bathroom, or gas breaks. If you'll be traveling a long time on one highway or through a confusing maze of city streets, arrange to meet every two hours or so at specific interchanges or mileage markers to lessen the trouble of keeping in sight all the time. A major disadvantage of caravaning is that it seems like it takes forever to get where you're going, since you travel at the speed of the slowest vehicle and must stop frequently for breaks or to keep together at road junctions. Vehicles hauling canoe trailers are inherently slow. Be sure to give them a head start or allow for greater-than-normal driving times when traveling with them.

As soon as possible after arriving at the put-in, you need to be sure that everyone understands they must wait there while the drivers shuttle the vehicles before beginning the journey in the canoes. This is taken for granted among experienced paddlers, but it may have to be stated explicitly on trips that include beginners. It's disheartening to watch a boatload of inexperienced paddlers carry their canoe to the water, launch it, and paddle downstream around a bend believing that everyone else will quickly follow. Your group can save a fair amount of time at the put-in by quickly unloading the vehicles, sending the drivers on their way, and then carrying the boats to the water and loading the gear in them while the shuttle is in progress. The rest of the time spent waiting for the drivers to return is ideal for practicing canoeing strokes and maneuvers. Good rules to follow when doing this are that everyone should stay equal to or slightly upstream from the launch site and that beginners should be paired with experienced paddlers for more efficient learning. You as the trip leader should remain with the group to supervise the launch area and teach the beginners, but don't hesitate to ask for an experienced paddler in the group to handle these responsibilities if you don't feel qualified or have to drive on the shuttle.

When the drivers return from the shuttle, you need to gather everyone in the group together and explain safety concepts like the purpose of lead and sweep canoes (see page 185), specific dangers on that section of river, and how to float downstream feet first through rapids (see page 231). Also, since you as the trip leader are responsible for organizing and directing any rescue operations, you should briefly review what rescue equipment is available and how to use it. Finally, you may need to review the basic paddling strokes and correct methods for launching and boarding a canoe with any drivers new to canoeing, since they missed the previous practice session. Again, have a person more experienced than you do these things if you don't feel qualified.

During your trip, safety should be your primary concern. When on the water strictly enforce the standard canoe safety rules explained throughout this book. These include not crowding in rapids, having everyone stay in sight of the canoe behind them, and respecting the position of lead and sweep canoes. You'll seldom have any "enforcement problems" if you explain the reasons for these rules to beginning canoeists and if experienced paddlers accompanying you set a good example by following them.

Before closing this section, there are some additional considerations that you as the leader should be aware of for a better trip. For safety, always try to have someone who has previously been on that section of river accompany you, and try to have at least one person along who's trained in advanced first aid skills. Clearly establishing the trip's goal before people sign up for it will help prevent personal problems from developing on it. Some common goals are a relaxing recreational trip, a long distance ramble, and an intensive whitewater challenge. Nothing can ruin a canoe trip faster than having people along who expected something other than what they are getting. Finally, don't hesitate to yield the leadership of your group to those more experienced than you whenever necessary. For example, don't adamantly maintain leadership of a group in a first aid emergency if others nearby are better trained than you to deal with the situation.

While a minimum of three canoes is required for safety on whitewater river trips, a group of six or seven boats is the largest that you can effectively deal with at one time. As the size of your group increases, its flexibility decreases, it travels slower and with more inertia, it loses its personal character, and it gains a party atmosphere. Of course, these changes aren't necessarily bad, as long as the size of your group remains below the six-to-eight-boat recommended maximum. You'll have to decide if you want an intimate canoe trip in tune with the natural world or a social trip where companionship and having a good time are of prime importance. As a trip increases in size, though, it will be harder for you to find suitable camping spots, congestion in rapids will occur, arranging for the transportation and food becomes more difficult, it gets harder to account for everyone on the water, and greater environmental damage is more likely to occur from your group. Because of these considerations, a group of something like three to five canoes and six to ten people is considered ideal.

Hopefully you didn't get the impression that I'm overly worried about safety or that there are too many details to take care of when leading a canoe trip. You'll find that the whole procedure discussed here seems to fall right in place, especially after you've gone on a few trips and especially if experienced paddlers accompany you.

Canoeing with Children

Never take *young children* canoeing or canoe camping unless you're experienced and comfortable in a canoe and while camping. Relaxed, unpressured flatwater or class I trips in mild weather are far safer and more enjoyable than fast-paced or intense journeys. Avoid all dangerous or trying situations like rough rapids, cold weather, rain, and the mosquito season until your children are capable of dealing with those conditions. Always be sure at least one competent adult swimmer accompanies each small child on your trip. Set a good example by always wearing your life preserver and requiring that your children do the same, and be sure they're wearing a properly sized child's model and not an extra adult one you had lying around the house. Swim aids and inflatable objects don't count as life preservers, although they're nice to have in your boat as toys. Carefree parents should note that a life preserver is no substitute for proper adult supervision. Teach every child how to put on their life jacket, tell them what it is designed to do, show them how it works, and let them wear it in the water to gain confidence in it. Teach your children to respect the water, not to fear it. If the weather and water are warm, encourage them to swim, even if it's just floating inside their life preserver. Slightly older children should become comfortable swimming in the water and swamping the canoe to get used to the fact that they might one day capsize when in it. Issue snack foods as special treats throughout the day, and bring cushions or pads that they can sit on for comfort. Letting small children use a toy paddle gives them a feeling of belonging in the family. When they're young, don't worry about teaching them the proper strokes. Just let them have fun.

It's often difficult to supervise *older children* or *teenagers* on a canoe trip because they're usually interested in having a great adventure while you're mostly (often overly) concerned about safety. Try to be firm and fair with necessary safety precautions like wearing life jackets, but flexible enough in general so everyone has a great time. It's important to give older kids as much freedom as possible when on the water and when planning a trip, since experience is the best teacher and responsibility is the cornerstone of experience. Avoid the temptation to plan the details of an outing for your older children, to help them pack for a trip, or to check the gear they've packed. Rummaging through their equipment giving suggestions on what or what not to take is a painful insult not easily forgotten. When canoeing with a group of older children or teenagers, you should have at least one adult for every five youngsters and at least two adults on each outing.

Costs

Since canoe trips are primarily group affairs, you should work out an agreement with your partners as to who pays what costs before actually going on one. Though rare, damages to equipment can occur and can turn close friends into fierce enemies in a very short time. Canoeing expenses break down into these categories:

1) *Transportation costs*. In general, the trip's drivers should cover the wear and tear on their vehicles, which includes the cost of basic auto supplies like oil and repair bills for things like flat tires and overheated radiators. All passengers should split the gasoline bill evenly among themselves. Drivers shouldn't be expected to pay for both maintenance costs and gasoline. Passengers can pay the driver before the trip, during the trip at each gas stop, or at the end of the outing. Gas payment before a trip is usually based on an estimate of the gasoline expenses, while payment at the end of a trip should be based on the actual costs. Though usually not formally discussed, passengers should offer to pay for the driver's coffee and meals enroute as a gesture of courtesy. Some canoe clubs also let their drivers use group equipment at reduced rental rates.

2) *Food costs*. If you're sharing food on your trip, its cost should be divided up evenly among all participants, unless some of the heavier eaters volunteer to pay more than their share. Everyone sharing food should pool their money as long as possible before a trip begins to guarantee that they're actually going. This also gives the people buying the food a fund to use for that purpose so they don't have to forward their own money for the cause.

3) *Damaged equipment* and *rescue costs*. Paddlers often avoid discussing these issues because of their sensitivity. However, it's important that everyone in your group understands what they're liable for before a trip begins because of the high cost of rescues, of replacing damaged gear, and of mending torn friendships. Requiring people to be responsible for group equipment they damage encourages them to take care of it but could make paddling partners bitter enemies, like when arguing over who made the critical mistake that destroyed the canoe. On the other hand, a canoe club that assumes the responsibility for repairing damaged club-owned gear encourages reckless use of that equipment. As a general rule, private owners are completely responsible for their own equipment. They should refuse to loan anything to untrustworthy people and to anyone not willing to assume complete responsibility for it. Unfortunately, while common courtesy dictates that anyone borrowing equipment should accept full responsibility for it if damaged, the greater the damage and the higher the cost of repairs, the faster this principle is swept under the rug and ignored.

Almost always, individual victims bear the cost of their own rescues. For example, if a person has a heart attack on a canoe trip, he shouldn't expect anyone else along to pay for his emergency evacuation and medical treatment.

Drinking Water

You may think that water will be the last thing to worry about while canoeing, since there's so much of it around. Unfortunately, much of it isn't safe to use anymore because of the host of impurities flowing into our waterways. Many smaller communities pipe only partially treated sewage into the nearest stream, fertilizers and pesticides drain off farmlands, cattle wastes cloud beautiful mountain creeks, and industrial and chemical pollutants like mercury contaminate water near larger cities. Combinations of all these pollutants make water near developed areas most dangerous to drink and to swim in. Even water far removed from inhabited areas is of questionable quality because too many people camp nowadays with unclean practices.

Unfortunately, most waterways contain excessively high levels of bacteria and infectious organisms as well as chemical pollutants. *Giardia*, a microscopic protozoan spread by animals and people, is of primary concern to outdoorsmen because it's so hard to kill. Symptoms of *giardiasis* include a miserable collection of ailments like diarrhea, nausea, loss of weight, loss of appetite, upset stomach, vomiting, and headaches. These symptoms can appear up to several weeks after ingesting contaminated water. Treatment for giardiasis is available but—like rabies shots—is nothing to look forward to or to be proud of receiving. To throw insult on top of injury, giardiasis is much easier to get again after you've had it once before.

Never consume water directly from an outdoor source unless you're absolutely sure it's safe. On short day or overnight trips, carrying and using water from home may be the safest thing to do. If doing this, use the water you brought with you for everything from cooking and drinking to brushing your teeth. Only use local, untreated water for washing your dishes and only when sterilizing them in boiling water for several minutes afterwards. On longer trips when carrying sufficient water is impractical or at other times when it's a hassle, you must purify all locally obtained water before using it for maximum safety.

Water sources contain both *chemical pollutants*, like insecticides, oil, and industrial wastes, and *biological pollutants* such as bacteria and other microorganisms. While quality water purification devices such as specially made filters can be designed to remove both kinds of pollutants from water, traditional purification methods like boiling and treating with chlorine tablets only kill biological microorganisms in it. They have no effect on chemical impurities. Thus, a filtration device that removes both chemical and biological impurities is safer than traditional purification methods and may be needed in developed areas.

There are several ways to purify your water:

1) *Boiling water* for at least five to eight minutes (longer at high altitudes) will kill all biological pollutants including *Giardia*. Unfortunately, boiling water rapidly consumes your camp fuel, requires much time and effort for a limited supply of pure water, and is not an exciting thing to do on a hot or adventuresome day.

2) *Water purification tablets* available in stores are convenient and inexpensive but occasionally kill microorganisms less effectively than boiling. Halazone (chlorine) and iodine tablets are both popular. Consider the dosages listed on their containers as the minimum recommended. Don't hesitate to increase them as needed (see below).

3) Use a small amount of *household bleach* to purify your water if it has sodium hypochlorite as its one and only active ingredient. Use an eyedropper to place two drops per quart of bleach with a 5–7% concentration of that chemical in your canteen. Apply up to 4–10 drops per quart for weaker bleach solutions, depending on its concentration. If your water has an overpowering chlorine taste after treatment, treat a different batch of water with a smaller dose, let the treated water stand uncovered for a while to dissipate the chlorine, or mask the chlorine taste with a powdered fruit drink as described below. Carry bleach in a small 1/2-ounce plastic container sealed inside a plastic bag to guard against leaks. Rinse the eyedropper out with water after use, since bleach will corrode its rubber stopper.

4) *Tincture of iodine* available at drugstores and *iodine crystals* available from chemical supply sources effectively kill most biological pollutants, though, like chlorine products, aren't as effective against *Giardia* as boiling. Use about 6 to 10 drops of a 2% solution of tincture of iodine (the concentration usually found in drugstores) per quart of water. To use iodine crystals, place about 5 grams of them in a 1-ounce glass vial of water, shake vigorously for a minute, and mix about 5–7 "small capfuls" (about 10–15 cc.) of the solution (not the solid crystals!) for each quart of untreated water. The solution containing the crystals can be used for a long period of time by simply topping off the vial containing the

undissolved crystals with water and shaking it as needed. Disadvantages of these liquid iodine preparations include the danger to people sensitive to iodine, the possibility of ingesting the solid crystals, the need to store them in tightly sealed *glass* containers, and the possibility of leaks in your packs.

Chlorine products rapidly lose their potency. Use a new bottle of halazone tablets or a new vial of bleach every few months for maximum effectiveness. If you can't taste a chlorine "swimming pool taste" in your water after purifying it with the recommended dose of a chlorine product, replenish your supply immediately. *Iodine materials* are much more stable than chlorine ones and will last a fairly long time when stored at home. A problem with using chlorine or iodine in any form is that their effectiveness depends on conditions like the water temperature, water pH, the amount of time between when they're applied and when you drink the water, and the strength of the dose. In general, the higher the water temperature, the closer it is to being neutral in pH, the longer the time between application and use, and the greater the dose, the safer your water will be.

After applying tablets, liquid bleach, or iodine, shake your canteen vigorously, wait about five minutes, and then shake it again with the lid loose enough so some water leaks out to cleanse its opening. This is not a trival point. It's important that you kill every organism in your drinking water, since only a few of them can make you terribly sick. Finally, wait at least 30 minutes longer before using. Double the times mentioned above when using tablets, bleach, or iodine to purify water colder than about 40°F or when purifying cloudy or noticeably contaminated water. Water with a strong dose and a horrible taste is much safer than halfway purified water that tastes fresh. You can mask the chemical taste of purified water with a fruit-flavored powdered drink and improve the taste of boiled water by pouring it back and forth from container to container several times, by adding a pinch of salt to it, and by letting it chill. For maximum effectiveness, always add beverage powders to purified water *after* the recommended contact times given above have passed.

5) Commercial *water filters* are becoming increasingly popular because of their reliability. When buying a filtering device, be sure it strains out both biological and chemical impurities for greater protection, and avoid any that make extravagant purification claims without experimental test data to back them up. Also, check the filter's weight, size, flow rate, pumping system, cost, and expected life, and buy one with features appropriate for your needs. A very important safety criterion is the size of the filter in a filtration device. Filters that allow particles larger than 4 or 5 microns to pass through them are ineffective against *Giardia*. Initially straining water through a coffee filter before running it through your filtering device will prolong the life of its rather expensive inner filter. Before storage, run a strong chlorine bleach/water solution through a filtering device to sterilize it.

Always collect your drinking water from a waterway's main channel and not from eddies, stagnant areas, or along the shore, and avoid water containing sediments stirred up from wading, swimming, or upstream obstacles. It's important to *clear muddy or dirty water* before purifying it, since sediments in water often contain harmful microorganisms and nullify the effect of chemical and filter purifiers. Do this by letting it stand still for a while so gravity can pull the particles in it to the bottom. Then slowly pour the clear water into another, clean container and treat this water with one of the methods outlined above. Another method is to simply pour the muddy water over a filter made by piling a thin layer of sand over a shirt held above a clean container.

Canoeing Etiquette

Always be considerate of other people on or along a waterway. Detour wide around swimmers and fishermen to avoid a confrontation with them. They have as much right to be there as you do. Get permission to cross or camp on private land. Landowners near potential access points like bridges are especially sensitive to life-jacketed trespassers. Be as clean and courteous as possible when entering local businesses like restaurants and motels. No one wants a bunch of filthy gorillas descending on their well-kept establishment. Properly dispose of your garbage and body wastes when canoeing, and leave all campsites cleaner than when you found them.

NO-IMPACT CANOEING

Sadly, those not blinded by the glittering promises of progress can see a time coming very soon when no wild areas will remain on this planet. Even now logging roads and highways bisect areas that used to be wilderness only a few short years ago, powerlines string across formerly expansive sunset vistas, and rivers that used to teem with fish now only transport garbage and the scavengers that feed on it. To some these are signs of industrial, commercial, and human progress, but to others more in tune with the natural world, they're dangerous signs of the times. Now, more than ever before in the history of our species, we need to be careful stewards of this planet that's our home. In the coming years, huge battles will be fought in the world's political arenas that will have a tremendous impact on the quality of life on this planet and on our outdoor experiences.

Yet, another war, much more subtle in nature and subdued in character is being fought along the planet's waterways. Where once you could canoe alone for days on most rivers, now hordes of boaters, fishermen, hunters, tubers, swimmers, and other outdoor enthusiasts flock there every chance they get . . . and leave their filth behind. We, the people who enjoy the outdoors, are simply loving it to death. There's not enough room out there anymore for us to do whatever we want to do. Our rivers and lakes are being used so heavily that even a few people can ruin the quality of these resources for the many others that will surely follow.

No-impact canoeing and camping means leaving no impact on the natural world. There are three components of this important philosophy:

1) *Preserve everyone's outdoor experience.* Always canoe with respect for those you meet along your way and for those who will follow in your wake. Don't blast your radio up and down the river, don't toss garbage in the water, and don't skinny-dip in popular areas.

2) *Preserve the immediate resource.* Never wash yourself, your dishes, or your clothes directly in any waterway. Always leave a campsite cleaner and more wild than when you found it. Avoid all glass containers on river trips, since one broken bottle could ruin a beautiful beach and injure people using the area in the future. Avoid building campfires whenever possible, and never build more than one fire at each campsite.

3) *Preserve remaining wild areas.* Politely educate other canoeists ignorant of proper outdoor practices. Join hands with misinformed boaters instead of shaking your fist at them, for they're really your allies in a world filled with people who would send a bulldozer in to "channelize" a stream just as easily as they send a dirty coat to the cleaners.

At times you may feel like your voice is but a tiny echo of sanity in a very confused world. You may be saddened by the cloud of filthy air hanging over your city, by the chemical water pouring from your kitchen faucet, by the traffic jams threatening your composure, and by the wave of development sweeping over the country. You may begin to feel that there's nothing you can do to stop the onslaught of environmental dangers confronting us. Take heart despite these problems, for there are millions of people out there who care about the quality of life as much as you do. Get out of your prefabricated suburban closet, discard your Burger King and disco queen TV images of the "good life," and support those who value clean air, pure water, open space, and a healthy way of life. Join several conservation organizations listed in the Appendix. Then put on your political boxing gloves, get inside the ring where environmental decisions are made, and fight for the kind of environment you'd like to live in and pass on to the next generation.

5

GETTING STARTED

CARRYING A CANOE

The two primary difficulties involved with carrying a canoe are lifting its weight and managing its bulk. While most people in good physical condition can support the weight of a canoe themselves and almost anyone can learn to balance it with practice, it's probably safest to have at least one other person help you carry your boat if you're not in condition or aren't familiar with the solo carries described in this section. The next several pages explain popular canoe carrying techniques, while *portaging* (carrying a canoe a long distance) is discussed in Chapter 9.

General Carrying Tips

General tips for carrying a canoe include:

1) Completely drain any water from the bottom of a boat before carrying it to lighten the load you'll have to move and to keep from getting soaked as you flip it upside down when beginning an overhead carry.

2) Use a closed-cell foam life preserver, soft clothing, or a canoe yoke to pad your neck and shoulders when carrying a canoe with an overhead carry.

3) Secure all dangling painters before beginning a carry.

4) Often carrying a canoe is easier when several people help with the chore. Occasionally, however, additional helpers get in the way and create problems if everyone involved doesn't communicate their intentions and coordinate their actions. Carrying a canoe along a rough trail with an out-of-step person can be especially annoying.

5) Some hardened outdoorsmen can solo carry a backpack and a canoe at the same time. Attempt this with caution if you're out of shape or new to canoeing, lest you hurt more than your pride.

6) Remove as much gear as possible from a canoe before beginning a solo or overhead carry to lighten your load and to achieve optimum bal-

ance. Even something as light as a life jacket attached at one end of a canoe could radically alter its equilibrium when on your shoulders.

7) Place lightweight, bulky items like bailers, paddles, and life jackets in a canoe before tandem carrying it in a right-side-up position to reduce the number of trips you'll have to make transporting your gear. Never, however, carry a canoe loaded with heavy items or with a full complement of equipment, since this excessively strains its hull.

One-Person Thigh Carry

Though somewhat awkward, this method is useful for carrying a canoe a short distance when it's not worth the effort to lift it over your head.

Procedure:

1) Stand facing your canoe and amidships of it. Hold the closest gunwale with both hands.

2) Lift the canoe up so it hangs with its opposite gunwale low to the ground. Rest the part of the canoe's bottom nearest you on your thighs (Example 5-1).

3) Slowly and deliberately walk or sidestep to your destination.

One-Person Overhead Carry

This carry is useful for moving a canoe distances greater than about 50 feet. Unfortunately, getting a canoe over your head easily and efficiently is difficult to do and requires much practice. If you have trouble mastering the flipping technique described in Method #1, work your way under the canoe using Method #2 or rest its bow on a tree branch or have a friend hold it up while you position yourself under it (Example 5-2F). Always practice this technique on a soft yard and with friends nearby who can "spot" the canoe if it begins to fall.

Method #1—Procedure:

1) Stand amidships with the canoe rolled on its side and its open end away from you. Face the canoe with your left side in the direction you intend to go.

2) Hold the near gunwale with both hands placed on either side of the center thwart. Then lift the canoe up and rest it against your thighs as if performing a thigh carry (Example 5-1).

3) Hold the far side of the center thwart or the far gunwale with your left hand, and either grip the near gunwale or the near side of the center thwart with your right hand. Be sure both wrists point in the direction you want to go.

4) Pull in with your left hand so the canoe rolls toward your body (Example 5-2A). (Note the position of the wrists in the photograph.)

Example 5-1: A one-person thigh carry.

Figure A

Example 5-2: One-person overhead carry. The solo flip technique (Method #1) (Figs. A and B), the solo end entrance technique (Method #2) (Figs. D and E), and with assistance (Method #3) (Fig. F).

5) In one quick, fluid motion, pull the high side of the canoe over your head and down on your left shoulder with your left arm, push the near side of the canoe up with your right hand and your right thigh, and straighten your knees (Example 5-2B). It's crucial that you *toss* and *roll* the canoe in a single, fast motion. This maneuver is very hard to do if you deliberately try to *lift* it.

6) Gently rest the canoe yoke on your shoulders. If you're not using a yoke, position the center thwart on your shoulders and across the back of your neck.

7) Place your hands far forward along each gunwale to balance the canoe. Tip the front of the boat up slightly for better visibility before walking (Example 5-2C).

Example 5-2 (Cont'd.) **Figure B**

Method #2—Procedure:

1) Stand at one end of the canoe and roll it upside down.

2) Lift that end up over your head (Example 5-2D).

3) Walk under the canoe with your hands supporting its gunwales (Example 5-2E). Simply slide your hands down along them as you go so the boat rises higher and higher in the air. During this step, almost all the canoe's weight should rest on the stern on the ground, not on your arms.

Example 5-2 (Cont'd.)   Figure C

Example 5-2 (Cont'd.)   Figure D

4) When you reach the center thwart, carefully switch hands and turn around so you're facing the uplifted end of the boat.

5) Position yourself under the yoke or center thwart, tip the canoe onto your shoulders, raise the front slightly for visibility, and begin walking.

Example 5-2 (Cont'd.)   Figure E

Example 5-2 (Cont'd.)   Figure F

Setting a Canoe Down

Two ways to get a canoe down off your shoulders are explained as follows and illustrated in Example 5-3. Never simply drop a canoe to the ground when done carrying it to prevent damaging it.

Method #1—Procedure:

1) Begin with the canoe resting on your shoulders in an overhead carry. Then tip it backwards so its stern rests on the ground.

2) Walk forward out from under it by sliding your hands along its gunwales (Example 5-3A).

3) When you reach the bow, roll it right side up and set it down.

Figure A

Example 5-3: Setting a canoe down from an overhead carry.

Method #2—Procedure:

1) Begin with the canoe resting on your shoulders. Then steady it with your left hand while it rolls off your shoulders towards the right and into a cradle formed by your right hand (Example 5-3B).

2) Let the canoe roll gently to your thighs and then to the ground. This "rolling" should be in one continuous but controlled motion from the time the canoe leaves your shoulders until it reaches the ground.

Example 5-3 (Cont'd.)   **Figure B**

Two-Person End Carry

This method is useful for carrying a canoe a fairly short distance over fairly rough terrain.

Procedure:

1) Point the canoe in the direction you want to go. Have one person stand on one side of it at the bow while the other person stands on its opposite side at the stern.

2) On a given signal, both lift the canoe to about knee height and begin walking (Example 5-4). The flange of the deck where it connects with the bulkhead, handles built into the deck plate, and the grabloops at the far ends of the canoe are all convenient lifting and carrying points.

Two-Person Overhead Carry

This method is suitable for two people to use when carrying a canoe over relatively level ground in fairly unobstructed terrain. Visibility can be improved somewhat by having the taller of the two people carry the bow of the canoe.

Procedure:

1) One person stands just in front of the bow seat and the other person stands just in front of the stern seat. Both must face the intended direction of travel and must be on the same side of the canoe.

Example 5-4: A two-person end carry.

Figure A

Example 5-5: Two-person overhead carry.

2) Both people grasp the far gunwale with their right hands and the near gunwale with their left ones (Example 5-5A).

3) On signal, they decisively roll and lift the canoe up to shoulder height and over their heads (Example 5-5B).

4) Finally, both people carefully lower the canoe until the front of the bow seat slightly rests on the first person's shoulders and back of his neck and the front of the stern seat slightly rests on the rear person's shoulders and back of his neck. When walking, both people's arms remain in their initial position on the gunwales and are used as shock absorbers to prevent sudden weight shifts from bashing the canoe into their shoulders.

Figure B

Example 5-5 (Cont'd.)

Carries with More than Two People

Carrying a canoe is often less tiring if more than two people help, especially over steep or rough terrain. Carrying a canoe *with three people* is relatively easy if the strongest person performs an end carry at the stern while the other two end carry it at the bow (Example 5-6A). Carrying a canoe *with four people* (Example 5-6B) is even easier if two people help carry each end of the boat.

PLACING A CANOE ON A CAR OR TRAILER

The best way to solo position a canoe on a vehicle roof rack is to carefully lower it there from a one-man overhead carry. Only strong, experienced paddlers

Figure A

Example 5-6: Carrying a canoe with three people (Figure A). With four people (Figure B).

Example 5-6 (Cont'd.)   Figure B

should attempt this though, because it's easy to lose control of the boat and damage the vehicle in the process. Most canoeists prefer having at least one other person help them load and unload boats from their vehicles as described below. Removing a canoe from a vehicle is done by carefully following the steps outlined below in reverse.

Procedure:

1) Place the canoe open side up about 5 to 7 feet from and parallel to the vehicle.

2) One person should stand at the bow and the other at the stern. Both should be at the extreme ends of the canoe and should face each other.

3) On signal, both people lift the canoe off the ground (Example 5-7A) and roll it upside down in a predetermined direction.

4) Finally, they lift the canoe as high as needed (Example 5-7B), sidestep over to the vehicle, and place it on the roof racks.

SECURING A CANOE TO A CAR

As discussed in Chapter 2, you can use roof racks, foam blocks, or a blanket/padding system to support your canoe on your vehicle. Although the information that follows describes how to secure a canoe to a roof rack support system, the underlying principles in this section apply equally to all kinds of roof attachment methods. Likewise, securing canoes on a canoe trailer is essentially identical to securing them to your car. The major difference is that with a trailer, there's no need for bow and stern end lines because trailer support bars are spaced so wide apart.

It's a good idea to place your roof racks as far apart as possible on your vehicle's roof to better distribute the load on them and to reduce the great effect wind has on a canoe secured at points close to each other. For maximum stability, racks should be at least 4 feet apart and should be placed on the level part of the roof. Also, be sure the imaginary line connecting the top of both racks is horizontal and the middle of the canoe is centered between them.

Small cars handle slightly better if a single canoe is centered in the middle of their racks (as seen from the front of the car) (Example 5-8). When carrying two canoes, place them on the racks as shown in the illustration. You can carry three canoes on almost all cars including compact models by centering the third one above the previous two. Carrying more than three canoes on a vehicle other than a canoe trailer is not recommended. When transporting three canoes, secure the two bottom ones separately first as described below. Then center the third one over the other two and secure it exactly the same way. Avoid carrying more than two non-aluminum canoes on a vehicle roof rack to preserve their finish.

It's best to carry a canoe upside down on your roof because the wind tends to lift a canoe off a vehicle if it's secured with its open end up. In addition,

Figure A

Example 5-7: Loading a canoe on a vehicle with several people.

Example 5-7 (Cont'd.)   **Figure B**

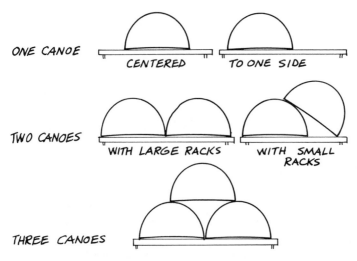

Example 5-8: Positioning canoes on vehicles.

securing a canoe to your roof with its open end down prevents rainwater from collecting inside it during a storm. This added water and its associated weight could make removing a canoe from a vehicle a difficult and wet experience.

Securing Cross and End Lines

You secure canoes to vehicles with cross lines and end lines. *Cross lines* hold the boats you're transporting to your car's roof rack, while *end lines* secure their ends to your vehicle's front and rear bumpers. Both cross lines and end lines must remain unaffected by road vibrations and high winds, be durable for reliable use, and be easy to use under often cold, wet, and dark conditions. There are several possibilities:

1) Although *nylon rope* is extremely reliable when used properly, it's harder and more time consuming to use than the methods explained below, and knots in rope could become almost impossible to remove when wet or tight. Standard knots used to secure canoes to roof racks are illustrated in Examples 5-9 and 5-10.

2) Nylon rope tipped with *shock-corded hooks* or specially made *rubber rope* is far easier to use than the rope-tying method just described. When using the customized shock-corded system illustrated in Example 5-11, you simply load the canoes on the racks, stretch the cross ropes permanently attached to the racks over them, and hook the hooks fastened to the end of each line into the eyebolts at the outer edges of each rack. you can secure bow and stern end lines to eyebolts fastened to your vehicle's bumpers in a similar fashion. Either buy commercial shock cord in a hardware store and attach it to the ends of your lines or cut 2-inch thick, donut-shaped cross-sections from an old inner tube and use them instead.

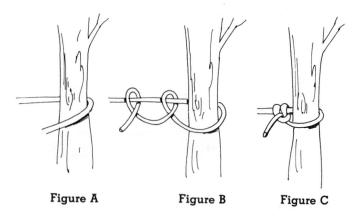

Figure A   **Figure B**   **Figure C**

1) Loop a rope around the object you're tying something to (Fig. A). When using this knot to secure a line under tension, tightly wrap the rope around the permanent object several times before proceeding.

2) Loop the free end over the rope twice (Fig. B). Add an additional loop for greater reliability.

3) Pull tight (Fig. C).

Example 5-9: Two half hitches. This knot is useful for fastening your cross and end lines to your vehicle's bumpers and to its roof racks.

3) Commercially available *nylon webbing* with adjustable, rustproof, quick release buckles is reliable and easy to use.

4) Commercial *bungy cords* designed for securing things to motorcycles are simple to use but of questionable reliability and durability. Often their excessive softness doesn't provide the security needed on rough roads, at high speeds, and in windy conditions.

5) A system of *metal slip rings and hooks* available from discount boating suppliers is easy to use but not as reliable as the first three methods described above.

After positioning canoes on your vehicle, tie two *cross ropes* over them from one end of each rack to the other. When carrying two canoes, tie them to the rack as if they were one. That is, take a rope from one end of a rack completely over both canoes and secure it to the far end of that rack, and then repeat the procedure for the second cross line and second roof rack. There's no need to tie both canoes down separately as long as they snugly touch amidships. The knots where cross ropes attach to the roof racks should be placed as close as possible to the outside gunwales of each canoe to reduce the possibility of them shifting around inside the rope, and the cross lines should travel the shortest possible distance over each boat to prevent a loss of tension when in use. Consider placing strips of old carpet or cloth between these cross ropes and fiberglass or wood

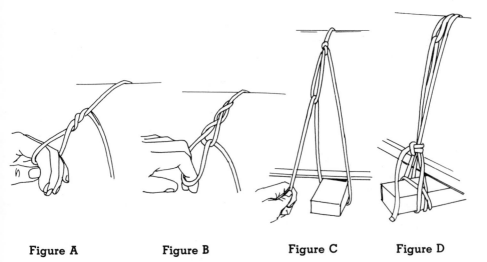

Figure A   **Figure B**   **Figure C**   **Figure D**

1) Fasten one end of the rope to your roof rack with a two-half-hitches knot.

Run the rope over your inverted canoe and then position yourself on the side of the roof rack where you want to tie the knot.

2) Hold the rope high at the canoe's bilge, form a 6-inch loop in it, and twist it around clockwise twice (Fig. A).

3) Reach through the loop you just made and hold the rope close to the coils.

4) Pull that part of the rope down through the first loop you made and tighten the resulting knot (Fig. B). A resulting loop about 2 or 3 inches long is adequate.

5) Run the rope's end down, under, and around the roof rack and up through the small loop you made in step 4 (Fig. C).

6) Pull down on the rope end to achieve a pulley effect. While maintaining tension on the line, run its end around the roof rack several times and secure it by tying several half hitches around the ropes at the base of the rack (Fig. D).

Example 5-10: Trucker's knot. This knot is ideal for actually securing your end and cross lines. Securing a cross line is illustrated above.

canoes to protect their finish, and don't tighten them as hard as you would for "indestructible" aluminum or plastic canoes.

If you're transporting a canoe on blankets, rubber mats, foam blocks, or similar objects, you may have to tie cross lines through your car's door or window openings to secure them adequately. This is an inferior method because

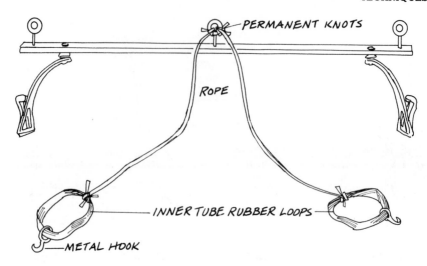

PERMANENT KNOTS

ROPE

INNER TUBE RUBBER LOOPS

METAL HOOK

Example 5-11: Constructing a shock-corded system for securing canoes to your roof rack.

the canoe can easily slide around on the roof underneath the ropes since they aren't secured close to its gunwales. Inconvenience, as well as insecurity, is the hallmark of this method. Just try climbing through the windows of a car with its doors tied shut sometime.

After the cross ropes are secure, tie *end ropes* rope from the bow and stern of each canoe to your bumpers for additional protection against canoe movement when driving. For the greatest security, tie two separate end lines to each end of each canoe you're carrying (Example 5-12). Then secure the other end of each of those ropes to your bumpers so that both the bow and stern of each canoe has one rope secured to the extreme left end and another, separate rope secured to the extreme right end of each bumper. Slightly less dependable systems involve using one long rope for each end of each canoe or one very long rope for all the canoe ends at each end of your car. Place strips of carpet or cloth rags under any end lines that rub on your car's surface to protect its finish.

There are two ways to secure end lines to your bumpers. You can attach heavy duty *eyebolts* to them and then run each end line around one of them before securing it with a knot or similar closure system. A second method involves running your end lines around the main posts supporting your bumpers and then securing them with a knot or other fastener. No matter which system you use, always secure the end lines as far to the extreme ends of your bumpers as possible for the most lateral support, and be sure they can't slide in towards the center of your vehicle and loosen in use.

Finally, after your cross and end lines are tied, secure their loose ends so they can't flap around and damage your car's finish when traveling.

TIE BUMPERS
WIDE APART

Example 5-12: Properly secured cross and end lines.

Safety

Safety should be of paramount importance to you when securing canoes to your vehicle, since high speed driving and traveling on rough, bumpy roads places great, sudden stresses on roof tie-down systems. Always check the condition of your roof attachment equipment at the end of every trip and again before beginning an outing, and repair it as needed. Always secure canoes to your car so that if one line breaks, the others will be strong enough and tied correctly enough to support the added stress, and always carry extra rope in your vehicle for emergencies. Tie brightly colored pieces of cloth to the extreme ends of canoes that overhang your vehicle for added visibility when driving.

After securing a canoe to your vehicle and before driving anywhere, test the reliability of your system by trying to push the gunwales up away from the roof racks at the places where they touch. Any gap there is too much. Then grip the canoe at various points and shake it violently. The whole apparatus—canoe, racks, and vehicle body—should move as one solid unit. Immediately before driving, look through your windshield and note the position of the canoe in relation to your rear view mirror, sun visor, or convenient windshield fingerprint smudge. If the canoe gradually or suddenly shifts position as you drive, stop and check the entire canoe and rack assembly for broken lines, damaged attachments, and loosened knots.

When hauling boats on a canoe trailer, be sure it's properly and securely attached to your vehicle's trailer hitch. For safety in case the hitch junction fails, run a chain between your vehicle and the trailer to keep them connected, but be sure there's no slack in it so the trailer hitch component can't drag on the ground after failure. Never drive a trailer anywhere without connecting its tail lights to your vehicle. Drive very carefully when using a canoe trailer to compensate for its added weight, wind resistance, and length and your reduced visibility. Be especially careful when turning, backing up, and passing other vehicles when towing a trailer.

Review of Tie-Down Procedures

In summary, the following is a chronological list of the steps you should take to secure a canoe to your vehicle.

1) Check that your roof support system (racks, blocks, etc.) and all attachment lines are in good working order. Replace or repair them if necessary.

2) Secure the support system to your vehicle (attach blocks to your canoe).

3) Get all tie-down straps untangled and ready for use.

4) Place the canoe(s) on your car.

5) Securely attach both cross ropes.

6) Secure bow and stern end lines.

7) Check to be sure all lines are tight and all knots are properly tied.

8) Shake the canoe vigorously to test its security.

LAUNCHING A CANOE

Launching a canoe is the process of putting it in the water. Improperly doing this can mar its outer appearance, damage its interior structure, make it difficult for you to get your gear inside and the boat afloat, and leave you with uncomfortable, wet feet. Always carry your canoe to the water and carefully set it in as described below. Simply dragging it across the ground and into the water is an indication of a raw greenhorn. It's best to launch a canoe *perpendicular* to shore when the water there is shallow or contains obstacles. A *parallel* launch is best done when the water next to shore is deep enough to float the canoe or when launching from a dock or in a strong current. A simple method of launching a canoe by carrying it out into the water and then dropping it in is self-explanatory in nature but not recommended for use in cold water or unsettled weather.

One-Person Perpendicular Launch

1) Use a one-person thigh carry (see page 91) to move a canoe from your car to the water.

2) Lower the canoe's far end into the water while standing in the thigh carry position with the boat perpendicular to shore.

3) Without moving your feet, "walk" your hands along the gunwale so the canoe slides farther and farther into the water (Example 5-13A).

Figure A

Example 5-13: Launching methods. One-person perpendicular (Figure A), two-person perpendicular (Figure B), one-person parallel (Figure C), and two-person parallel (Figure D).

Example 5-13 (Cont'd.)   **Figure B**

Two-Person Perpendicular Launch

1) Both people should stand amidships on different sides of the canoe with it resting on the ground perpendicular to the shoreline.

2) Simultaneously on command, both people grab the gunwales closest to them and lift the canoe off the ground.

3) In unison and with the canoe held above the ground, both people side-step to the water's edge, lower the far end of the boat, and pass it into the water hand over hand (Example 5-13B).

One-Person Parallel Launch

1) Stand at the water's edge with the canoe resting on your hips in a thigh carry position and parallel to shore.

2) Let the canoe slide down your thighs and into the water (Example 5-13C). Try to lower your body as you do this so you set the canoe on the water instead of dropping it there.

Example 5-13 (Cont'd.)   **Figure C**

Two-Person Parallel Launch

1) Begin with the canoe resting parallel to shore at the water's edge and both people standing slightly in from each end of it along its inland gunwale.

2) On command, both people hold the canoe's inland gunwale with both hands, lift the boat off the ground, take several short steps toward the water, and lower it in (Figure 5-13D).

Example 5-13 (Cont'd.)   **Figure D**

BOARDING A CANOE

Boarding a canoe is the process of entering it after you launch it. It's best to board a canoe when it's completely floating in water, since attempting to board a boat that's propped up on a rock or on shore could easily damage its hull and send you rolling overboard. You can board a canoe that's parallel or perpendicular to shore as described below or by wading out to it in shallow water and stepping in it. In any case, keep the following principles in mind when boarding and paddling a canoe:

1) *Keep your weight low in the boat.* The higher your center of gravity is (see page 121), the greater the chance of capsizing the boat.

2) *Spread your weight wide across the boat but keep it centered over its keel line* for the most lateral stability. For example, when entering a canoe, distribute your weight on your hands on its gunwales and then step into it directly on its keel line.

3) *Only one person should move in a canoe at a time*, since it can easily overturn if both paddlers shift positions at once. Always discuss your intentions with your partner before moving around in a canoe.

Several relatively minor points you should keep in mind when boarding a canoe are:

1) Clean your feet off on shore or in the water before entering your canoe to keep its interior clean.

2) Always place your paddle in the bottom of your canoe before entering or leaving it. It could fall into the water and float away if you simply rest it across its gunwales.

3) In most cases it makes no difference whether the bowman or sternman enters or exits a canoe first. However, you may have to vary your habitual boarding procedure to maintain maximum boat control in a fast current or on an obstacle-clogged stream.

Parallel Boarding

Procedure:

1) Hold the canoe's nearest gunwale at your paddling position with your right hand and with the canoe floating in the water next to shore. If you have a paddling partner, he should hold its shoreline gunwale at the opposite end of it.

2) Now hold the far gunwale with your left hand and then place your left leg in the center of the canoe (Example 5-14A). The instant it touches the boat, distribute your weight evenly between both hands and that foot. Be sure you place your left foot vertically on the keel line. If you plant it at an angle the canoe will drift away from the shore and leave you swimming.

3) Place your right foot on the keel line next to your left one (Example 5-14B). This position is quite stable as long as your hands support some of your weight on the gunwales.

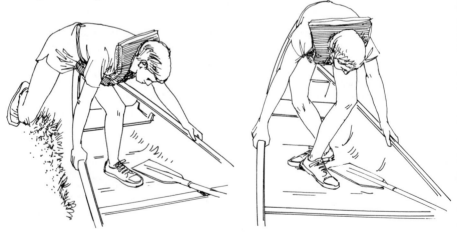

Figure A   Figure B

Example 5-14: Entering a canoe that's parallel to shore.

4) Get in your paddling position. Then stabilize the canoe with your hands or paddle braced against a nearby rock, the shore, or the river bottom while your partner enters the canoe like you just did.

Perpendicular Boarding

Procedure:

1) Place the paddles in the canoe at the appropriate bow and stern paddling position while the canoe is still on land.

2) Perpendicular-launch the boat as described on page 108. Then the bowman stands at the shoreline at the bow and locks the boat between his knees.

3) The sternman walks into the water and enters the bow near the bow seat or amidships if the water is still shallow there. He enters by following the steps outlined previously, being careful to balance his weight on the gunwales and to place his feet on the keel line.

4) The sternman *gunwale-walks* down the length of the canoe to his stern paddling position by sliding his hands along the gunwales and walking down the keel line with his feet (Example 5-15A).

5) The bowman walks the boat out into the water until there's enough draft at the bow. Then, while securely holding both gunwales, he places one leg in the canoe (Example 5-15B), pushes off with the other, and positions himself at the bow seat. While the bowman is hopping aboard, the sternman should brace the canoe with his paddle flat on the water or held against the bottom of the waterway for support if needed.

Figure A

Example 5-15: Boarding a canoe perpendicular to shore.

Figure B

Example 5-15 (Cont'd.)

LANDING A CANOE

Landing a canoe is the process of getting it to shore. *Perpendicular landings* are best done at obstructed shorelines and in shallow or calm water, while *parallel landings* work best when the water near shore is deep, the banks are unobstructed, or the current is fast.

When parallel landing in moving water, always beach the *upstream* end of your canoe first. If that's not possible, then downstream-brace while the current pivots the upstream end around the beached downstream end and parallel to shore. Back-ferrying to shore and eddy-turning behind an obstruction like a rock at the shoreline are two other safe methods of parallel landing in moving water. If there's no eddy where you want to land, simply pretend there is and eddy-turn right next to the bank. All these maneuvers are explained in detail later in the book.

Parallel landing a canoe on flatwater involves nothing more than paddling up to your landing area and getting out of it using the reverse procedure for parallel boarding discussed above.

To land a canoe perpendicular to shore, paddle it directly towards land until the bow almost runs aground, and then backpaddle to slow it down. Then the bowman should hop out of the boat, pull it towards shore until almost beached, and steady it while the sternman gunwale walks up to the bow and out of the canoe. Solo boaters may have to run their bow up on shore somewhat when landing perpendicular to shore, but this should be done with caution since it erodes the boat's hull and decreases its stability.

CHANGING POSITIONS IN A CANOE

Changing positions in a canoe, means switching your bow or stern paddling position with your partner's. Many people recommend never doing this while afloat because of the chance of capsizing and because it can safely be done at rest stops on shore. Without disputing those observations, the information that follows is included in case you ever decide to change positions in a floating canoe. You should know that there's a proper way to do it, even though many experienced boaters don't recommend it. For maximum safety, only proceed with this maneuver when your canoe is resting motionless on flat, calm water. Never attempt it in windy conditions or on moving water.

1) The bowman places his paddle amidships, while the sternman assumes a stable, kneeling, bracing position.

2) The bowman gunwale walks to the center of the boat with his hands on each gunwale and his feet centered down the keel line. If the hull is loaded with gear the bowman either walks or crawls on that gear or places his feet as well as his hands on the gunwales. He then crouches or sits in the bottom of the canoe amidships or where convenient.

3) Now the sternman passes his paddle to the bowman who transfers it to the bow. Then he gunwale walks up the length of the canoe over the bowman (Example 5-16) to the bow seat where he assumes a stable, kneeling, bracing position.

4) Finally, the bowman places his paddle at the stern and gunwale walks from amidships into position there.

Example 5-16: Changing positions while afloat in a canoe.

PACKING A CANOE

General Principles

When your gear is properly packed in your canoe, it will handle easier in the water, you won't have to dig through everything to find something you need, and you won't have to worry about losing anything if you capsize. Several principles govern how you should pack cargo in a canoe:

1) Always load a canoe while it floats freely in the water and never pull a loaded canoe up onto shore to unload it, so you don't damage its hull.

2) Pack a canoe so its load rides as low as possible in it, since the lower a canoe's *center of gravity* is, the more stable it will be. This important concept is explained further on page 121.

3) For maximum turning ability, pack heavy items directly on the keel line and lighter things along the sides of the boat.

4) For maximum lateral stability, be sure what you put on the port side of the boat balances the cargo stored on its starboard side.

5) A canoe must be packed to guarantee proper *trim*, which is simply how level it is when floating free in the water (Example 5-17). In most cases, canoes handle best when trimmed level, although situations exist where an uneven trim is desired (these are explained later in the book). Be sure you pack your canoe to compensate for significant differences in weight between you and your paddling partner. For example, if you have a very heavy bowman, pack heavier items on your half of the canoe to compensate for this weight difference.

6) The place where an imaginary line bisecting a canoe at its balance point intersects its keel line is called the *pivot point* (Example 5-17). Try to pack

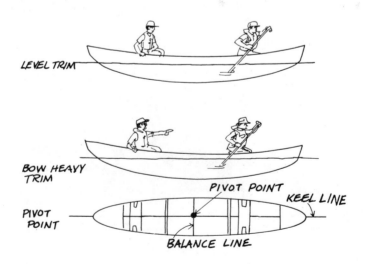

Example 5-17: Illustrating the trim and pivot point concepts.

heavier items close to the pivot point and lighter things like sleeping bags farther from it, since the closer an increment of weight is to the pivot point, the lighter a canoe's ends will be and the easier it can turn. Greater maneuverability without a loss of tracking ability is always a desirable quality in a canoe's performance.

7) Be sure your boat always has at least 6 inches of freeboard when fully loaded with its cargo and passengers to reduce the chance of swamping or shipping splashed water.

Miscellaneous Packing Suggestions

Generally it's easier to load a canoe when it's floating *parallel* to shore, although you may have to *perpendicular* load it in shallow water or from an overgrown bank. While you can often load a canoe floating parallel to shore from shore, you'll have to stand in the water to properly load a perpendicularly positioned boat, and this chould be uncomfortable or even dangerous in harsh conditions.

Carry frequently used or quickly needed items like snack foods, extra warm clothes, a raincoat, suntan lotion, sun glasses, camera, first aid kit, compass, and insect repellent in a small, easily accessible waterproof "travel bag" placed in a convenient spot in your boat. A fanny pack buckled to a thwart is especially handy for this purpose. Store your canteen in an accessible dry bag, backpack pocket, or day pack or tie it to a thwart with a short piece of cord. A convenient way to carry a map is to place it in a waterproof *map pouch* and shock-cord that to a thwart. When canoeing on rough water in wild areas, carry items like matches, a pocket knife, and a compass in your pockets on your body so you'll better be able to deal with a survival situation if you lose your canoe and its cargo in a spill. Consider carrying a small sheath knife on your belt when whitewater canoeing so you can quickly cut any ropes that got tangled around your body during a capsize. Some paddlers prefer packing their personal gear in someone else's canoe so there's a greater chance that it will remain dry if they capsize. When doing this though, be sure your gear is waterproof so it won't get wet if the other boat capsizes, and try to put it in a canoe paddled by people more experienced than you. Placing your equipment in a canoe paddled by greenhorns is risky at best.

Securing Gear to a Canoe

Always tie your gear to your canoe to prevent its loss or damage during a capsize, to keep it from shifting unexpectedly and throwing you off-balance, and to reduce the ugly mass of boating litter (sponges, bailers, gargage bags, etc.) accumulating in popular paddling areas. You can use thin nylon cord, shock-corded rope, bungy cords, nylon webbing, or other miscellaneous pieces of rope to secure your gear in your canoe. Since little strain will be placed on this line, the ease of securing it matters far more than its type, strength, or durability. In general, knots are a hassle to use, especially in cold and wet weather, while elastic shock cords are fast and easy to use though possibly less dependable in a capsize.

There are several ways to secure gear in a canoe:

1) *Tie each item in with separate ropes.* This involves securing many lines but provides flexibility in packing since you can remove any item you need without disrupting anything else.

2) *Use one long rope to secure all your gear.* This frees you from dealing with a mess of knots and a tangle of short lines but makes it difficult to remove something without untying everything else. With this method, simply tie one end of a long rope to a thwart. Then weave its other end through shoulder straps, handles, grommets, or frames on each piece of gear and secure it to a thwart when done.

3) *Construct a rope spider web.* With this method, you load your gear in the boat and then weave a spider's web of ropes over it and around and between thwarts and canoe tie down rings. Instead of securing each item separately, you tightly weave a mesh net above your gear so none of it can fall out. This method offers less security than the first two methods if not done adequately.

4) *Use elastic shock cords.* With this method, you load your gear into your canoe and either connect shock cords over it in a criss-crossed, spider web pattern or loop them through handles and straps on each item of gear as described earlier. The main problem with using shock cords to secure your gear is there are few good places to attach them on a canoe. You can overcome this problem by fastening eyebolts to your boat's thwarts and gunwales at strategic places.

Always carry a spare paddle in your canoe and always secure it so the sternman can access it quickly if he loses or breaks the one he's using to minimize the time the boat is out of control. This is especially important when canoeing in whitewater. You can secure a spare paddle to a canoe thwart with a thin piece of cotton string, heavier nylon rope, or a commercially available velcro strap. When using string or rope, tie the paddle handle to a thwart with a simple bow knot so you can remove it quickly in an emergency.

6

PADDLING A CANOE

GENERAL PRINCIPLES

Several factors determine where and how you position yourself in a canoe. The engineering concepts of forces and moments (turning effects) dictate the placement of the seats and how effective various paddling strokes are from them, and principles of stability determine how you should place yourself at each paddling position. The information presented here explains why subtle changes in paddling strokes and small shifts in paddling positions greatly affect how a canoe handles. It's important that you fully understand this material if you plan to do any serious canoeing. If you're new to the sport and are still concentrating on remembering which end of a canoe is the bow and which is the stern, skim over this section for now and return to it later after practicing several strokes for a while. It should make much more sense to you after you've had some experience in a canoe.

Forces and Moments

As discussed on page 116, the place where an imaginary line bisecting a canoe at its balance point (center of gravity) crosses its keel is called the *pivot point* (Example 5-17). Note that while a canoe's balance point can be exactly amidships, it's more frequently slightly off-center, especially in canoes with an asymmetrically shaped hull or with an uneven trim.

Almost all (the exceptions will be clear later) paddling strokes are designed to either make a canoe go straight ahead or make it turn. Strokes that make a canoe go straight act parallel to its keel line, while those that turn a canoe act parallel to that imaginary line perpendicular to the keel line and running through the pivot point. The farther a *turning stroke* is from that imaginary balance line, the greater its turning effect will be (Example 6-1), and the farther a *straight-ahead stroke* is from the keel line, the more it will tend to turn a canoe instead of propel it forward (Example 6-2). This is one reason why marathon racing canoes are extremely narrow. They

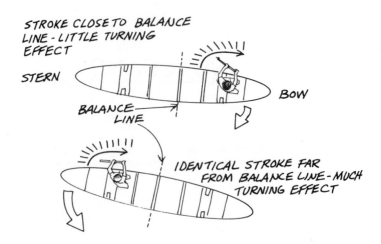

Example 6-1: A turning stroke's effectiveness increases with its distance from the imaginary line perpendicular to the keel line and running through the pivot point. (A reverse sweep is illustrated here.)

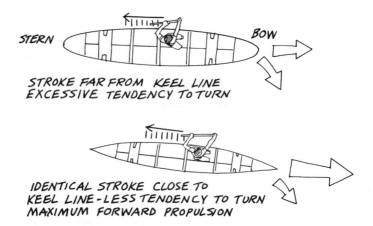

Example 6-2: A straight-ahead stroke's effectiveness decreases as its distance from the keel line increases. (A forward stroke is illustrated here.)

position the paddlers so their straight-ahead strokes are as close to the keel line as possible.

To complicate matters, the farther a straight-ahead stroke is from that imaginary amidships balance line, the greater it will tend to turn a canoe. Thus, a normal forward stroke performed at the bow of a long canoe will tend to turn it sideways more than an identical stroke performed at the bow of a shorter, but otherwise identical, boat.

If you didn't follow the theoretical points discussed above, just remember that you can greatly increase your paddling efficiency by performing the strokes *exactly* as described in this chapter. Minor variations in details like blade angles and paddling positions could greatly affect your paddling speed, boat control, and maneuverability.

Stability

An object's *center of gravity* is the point about which the entire object can balance. The 18-inch mark on a yardstick, for example, is its center of gravity. The *center of buoyancy* can be simplified to mean the center of gravity of the fluid that an object like a canoe displaces. The closer a fully loaded canoe's center of gravity and center of buoyancy are, the more stable it will be. While a canoe's center of buoyancy remains relatively constant no matter how much weight it carries or where it's placed in the canoe, its center of gravity can fluctuate wildly depending on the weight's location. As an example, the center of gravity shifts drastically when a paddler stands up in a canoe (Example 6-3).

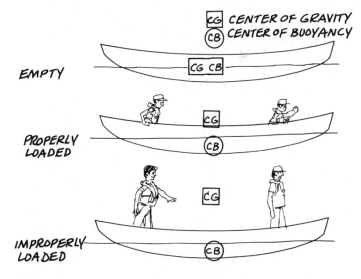

Example 6-3: How a canoe's center of gravity and center of buoyancy vary with changing loads.

PADDLING POSITIONS

Generally, it's best to paddle a solo canoe and a tandem canoe with a partner from their predetermined seat locations. Solo paddling a tandem canoe is best done from amidships (with no center thwart), from just behind or just in front of the center thwart, or from behind the bow seat when traveling stern first (symmetrical canoes only). Note that paddling solo from the stern of a tandem canoe is not recommended. When a solo paddler is positioned in the stern of a tandem canoe, its bow floats high above the water and easily catches the wind, its hull shape below the waterline is far from ideal, the boat tracks poorly because a great deal of its hull is above the water, and strokes have a great tendency to turn it since they're performed at its extreme end. Packing your cargo in the protruding bow to compensate for your weight in the stern eliminates the first, second, and third problems just mentioned, but not the last one.

You have a great deal of control over how you position yourself at a paddling position. *Sitting* is comfortable, which is valuable on long or relaxing canoe trips, but it raises your center of gravity which decreases your stability and encourages you to paddle inefficiently with your arms instead of with your entire upper body.

On the other hand, while *kneeling* can be uncomfortable, it significantly lowers your center of gravity for greater stability, lets you naturally paddle with your entire upper body for a more powerful stroke, helps lock your body in a canoe for better control of it, and permits effective leaning and bracing maneuvers in whitewater. Also, when kneeling, you have a much better "feel" of the boat and the water than when sitting. Because of these advantages, many experienced paddlers recommend kneeling at all times when canoeing and especially in rapids or rough water.

When *kneeling in a three-point position*, you rest your butt on the edge of a canoe seat or thwart and distribute your weight fairly evenly between it and both knees. Your legs should extend back under the seat or thwart you're leaning on and your knees should be placed wide apart for maximum stability. This is a reliable position because it offers a low center of gravity and great stability.

When *kneeling in a two-point position*, your weight is distributed only on your knees and your upper body is more erect than in the three-point position just described. Although this slightly decreases your stability, it increases your visibility and gives you a longer reach useful for performing technical whitewater maneuvers like braces.

Kneeling on one leg with your butt resting against a thwart and your other leg extended straight out in front of you is a powerful and efficient forward-traveling position. For added stability, extend the part of your leg below the bent knee diagonally across the boat's hull behind you. You can either extend the leg on your paddling side or the one away from your paddling side when canoeing this way. With this method, about 40% of your weight should rest on your bent knee, about 40% on your butt (on the edge of a seat or thwart), and the remainder on your extended leg.

Many people recommend never *standing* in a canoe since this raises its center of gravity far above its center of buoyancy. True, you're in a vulnerable, top-heavy position when standing in a canoe, but there are times when it's advantageous to do so. Standing just before entering rapids gives you a better view of them, standing on long trips gives you an opportunity to stretch your legs without leaving the boat, standing in a canoe can eliminate the blinding glare that occurs when sunlight reflects off it and the surrounding water, and standing is the only practical way to pole a canoe. Always let your partner know your plans before standing up in a canoe, never stand in rapids or rough water, and always balance your weight down the keel line when standing. Placing your feet wide apart in the bilge areas and distributing your weight evenly on them offers more stability than simply standing with both feet exactly on the keel line.

PADDLING PRINCIPLES

Bow and Stern Positions

Because the stern seat in a properly loaded canoe is farther from the pivot point than the bow seat, paddling strokes performed there have a greater turning effect than those at the bow. In other words, someone paddling at the stern can turn a canoe faster and easier than someone at the bow. Also, the sternman is in an ideal position to steer the boat since he can sight down its length to be sure it's on course. When sitting in the bow, it's real hard to determine if you're heading for your destination or are being pushed off-course by winds or river currents. In addition, the sternman always knows what the bowman is doing, can instantly compensate for any bad maneuvers a bowman makes, and can instruct the bowman while under way. For these reasons the person paddling in the stern is the "captain" of the canoe and is responsible for setting and maintaining its course. The only disadvantage of having the sternman direct the boat is that the bowman's body frequently obstructs his vision. Unfortunately, this can be a severe handicap when whitewater canoeing.

Although the sternman sets the ship's course, it's the bowman's responsibility to immediately change that course to avoid sudden, unseen obstacles in the way. This is especially important when paddling in rapids. When an obstruction suddenly appears in front of a canoe, its bowman must act quickly, decisively, without consulting the sternman, and without regard for what the sternman is doing at the time to avoid it. Then it's the sternman's duty to get the boat back on course again after passing the obstacle. In summary, when a collision with an obstacle is imminent, the bowman acts to avoid the danger and the sternman reacts to the bowman's actions. When traveling through rapids, for example, the sternman should instinctively draw if he sees his bowman suddenly pry.

It's best to position the most experienced paddler in each crew in the stern because of the skill needed to control a canoe's heading. When both partners are equally experienced, it's best to have the stronger of the pair paddle in the bow and the weaker of the two in the stern. One advantage of this is that a strong bowman can more powerfully propel a canoe forward, since that's the bowman's job in the first place. A second advantage is that a canoe will travel more efficiently if the stronger paddler is in the bow, since the sternman will have to make fewer wasteful course corrections to compensate for the greater turning effect at the stern.

Paddling Rhythm

Paddling *rhythm* is the cadence at which the bowman and sternman perform their strokes. There are two distinct possibilities:

1) *There is no rhythm.* According to this philosophy, the bowman and sternman simply perform their individual strokes without regard for when their partner is paddling. This method is ideal for people enjoying a relaxing, unpressured float trip and is usually necessary when canoeing through rapids or in large waves.

2) *Paddle in unison.* This means that both bow and stern paddles enter and leave the water and perform the power phase (see below) of each stroke at exactly the same time. Racers are advocates of paddling in unison because canoes track better and travel through the water more efficiently when paddled this way. A verbal command such as "Stroke . . . stroke . . . stroke . . ." sometimes is used to coordinate the efforts of people paddling in unison. With this method, the bowman should set the tempo, since the sternman can easily observe and follow him.

Switching Sides

In a sense, you have two sets of paddling muscles. If you paddle on one side of a canoe until tired, you'll feel almost totally refreshed if you begin paddling on its other side. Because of this, paddlers *switch sides* as needed to maintain a steady pace and rest their aching muscles. How often they should do this is subject to debate. Again, there are two philosophies:

1) *Rarely switching sides*, also known as *freestyle paddling*, involves switching paddling sides every hour or so for a change of pace. Casual canoeists prefer this method because they don't have to bother maintaining a constant switching rhythm, and some experienced paddlers prefer it because they claim that switching sides frequently is in itself tiring and inefficient. Advocates of this method must put a slight course correction in each stern stroke to travel in a straight line to their destination.

2) *Frequently switching sides*, also known as the *sit and switch* or *power paddling* methods, is preferred by high speed travelers like racers because every time they switch sides they get a new surge of power and because both sets of paddling muscles tire evenly throughout the day. Also, frequently switching sides eliminates the need for course correction strokes like the J-stroke that waste energy maintaining a straight heading. While canoes traveling with this technique tend to zig-zag to their destination, proponents of it claim that doesn't hinder them and believe they still travel faster than paddlers using standard course correction strokes. Experienced sit-and-switch tandem canoeists paddle 60–80 short, straight strokes per minute in unison with their partners and switch sides after every 8–12 strokes. Solo sit-and-switch paddlers should change sides every 3–6 strokes to maintain their heading.

The keys to perfecting this technique are switching sides *before* the canoe begins to drift off-course and switching sides so you don't lose your overall rhythm. For best results, make each switch a part of your paddling rhythm instead of something you do between each set of strokes. Many people believe the sternman should indicate when to switch, since he's in a better position to watch the canoe's heading. He should call "switch" at the beginning of a stroke and then both paddlers should switch at the end of it and begin the next stroke on the opposite side of the canoe.

With regard to switching sides in general, there are a few additional things to keep in mind. When canoeing tandem, bow and stern crew members must always paddle on opposite sides of the boat. Also, you should be able to confidently maneuver a canoe by applying the standard paddling strokes explained in this chapter on any one side of the boat. Switching paddling sides to make course corrections that your normal strokes should have done is inefficient and disrupts the natural balance that exists when partners consistently paddle on opposite sides of the canoe.

GENERAL PADDLING STROKES

The rest of this chapter describes a collection of paddling strokes useful on both calm and moving water. You'll use some like the forward stroke frequently and from all paddling positions, while others like the reverse sweep are designed for more specialized conditions. If you're primarily a recreational lake paddler, you can get by with just a handful of them, but you should master all the strokes presented here if you want to be a proficient whitewater canoeist.

Introductory Notes

1) If you're new to canoeing, begin with several basic strokes like the forward, J-stroke, draw, and pry, and then gradually learn the others as needed. It's best to learn a few strokes very well than to be inexperienced and confused with all of them.

2) Most canoeing strokes are exact opposites of other strokes. That is, if one stroke will move a canoe to the left in a certain manner, another will move it to the right the same way. Wherever possible, the strokes described in this chapter are paired with their opposing stroke for easier reference. You'll remember them better if you learn them in this paired order instead of in a random fashion.

3) You should practice these strokes until you can correctly do them at the bow and stern and on the left and right sides of a boat so you're not limited by who you canoe with and from what position you can paddle. At first, however, it may be a good idea to learn them well from just one position to prevent confusion.

4) All strokes explained in this section are useful for both solo and tandem canoeing, except where specifically noted otherwise.

5) Always grip a paddle in the standard way as shown in Example 2-1, except where noted otherwise.

6) The term *power face* is used in several of the following descriptions to indicate the blade's position in the water. By definition, the power face of a blade is the side of it that pushes against the water when performing a forward stroke (Example 6-4A, page 127). Note that the power face does *not* push against the water in some strokes (explained below).

A Note About the Illustrations

The following symbols are used in illustrations throughout this book:

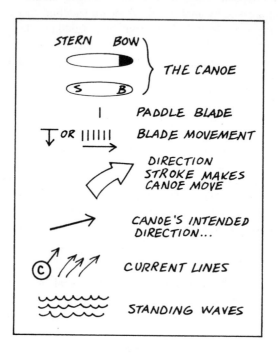

The closer the current lines are, the faster the current is (see page 170).

Note that we used a racing canoe in many of the following photographs. While you should kneel down in your boat for the greatest stability and control of it when paddling, the folks in the pictures had to sit in this one, since racing canoes are best paddled from a sitting position because of their extremely narrow width.

Forward Stroke

A *forward stroke* (Example 6-4) propels a canoe forward in the direction of its keel line. It's the most commonly used stroke in the bow, and variations of it (J-stroke, pitch stroke, etc.) are typically used in the stern.

Procedure:

1) Position the paddle next to your canoe so its blade enters the water in an almost vertical position (Example 6-4A). Both arms should be fairly straight.

Figure A

Example 6-4: The forward stroke.

Bend forward slightly at your waist and rotate your upper body toward your paddling side as necessary so you can "grab" the water with the paddle. Avoid lunging forward when beginning this stroke.

Your upper hand should be out over the water so the paddle enters it vertically and not at an angle (Example 6-4B).

Try to feel your entire upper body push down on the blade as it enters the water. Don't simply place it in the water and then pull it alongside the boat.

2) Move the paddle alongside the canoe by pushing its grip with your upper hand and pulling its throat back towards your body with your lower one (Example 6-4C).

Maximum efficiency occurs when your arms are fairly straight throughout this phase of the stroke, when the blade surface is vertical in the water (Example 6-4D), when the blade is completely submerged, when

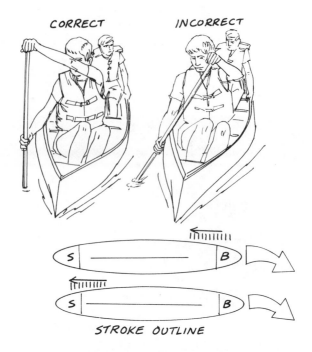

CORRECT   INCORRECT

STROKE OUTLINE

Example 6-4 (Cont'd.)   Figure B

Example 6-4 (Cont'd.)   Figure C

the blade travels parallel to the keel line (not the gunwales) (Example 6-4E), and when the stroke is fairly short and not stretched out along the length of the boat (Example 6-4F).

3) When your lower hand reaches your hip, remove the paddle from the water by dropping your upper hand to gunwale height and moving it back towards your waist. The paddle blade should cleanly slide out of the water and move into a horizontal position across the gunwales (Example 6-4G).

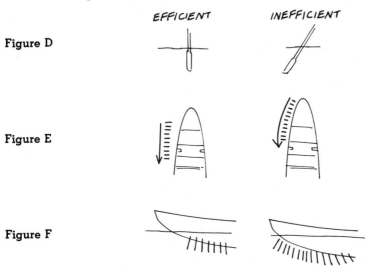

EFFICIENT   INEFFICIENT

Figure D

Figure E

Figure F

Example 6-4 (Cont'd.)

Example 6-4 (Cont'd.)   **Figure G**

4) Let your hands continue their natural swinging motion by pushing forward with your lower hand and raising your upper one until you move the paddle back into its starting position.

   When returning to the initial position, *feather* the blade by keeping it parallel to the water's surface so it travels through the air with minimum wind resistance.

Back Stroke

The *back stroke* (Example 6-5) is essentially the opposite of the forward stroke. It's used to reduce a canoe's forward speed or to travel backwards and is quite handy when maneuvering in rapids. When backpaddling, the bow—in effect—becomes the stern. However, because this is usually done for short periods of time, the sternman is still the "captain" of the boat and is responsible for steering it. He does this by using short draw and pry strokes at the beginning of each stern backstroke and by varying the angle and frequency of these according to how much directional correction is needed.

Method 1:

This is the backstroke in its pure form.

Procedure:

1) While you can perform the backstroke with your upper hand holding a paddle in its normal position, some people feel you'll get more power from this stroke if you reverse your upper hand grip on the paddle and hold it with your palm facing you as in Example 6-5A.

2) Position your paddle so it enters the water at a 65–70° angle to the waterline and slightly behind your body. Don't position the blade too far behind you or at too shallow an angle since then an excessive amount of the stroke's force will be directed down into the water and not horizontally as desired.

3) Move the paddle forward through the water by pushing it toward the bow with your lower hand and pulling its grip back towards the stern with your upper hand. You can lean backwards slightly at your waist to put more power into the stroke (Example 6-5B).

   Maximum efficiency occurs when the blade surface is vertical in the water, when the blade is completely submerged, when the blade travels parallel to the keel line (not the gunwales), and when the stroke is not stretched out along the length of the boat.

Method #1:　　　　**Example 6-5:** The back stroke.　　　　**Figure A**

Example 6-5 (Cont'd.)　　　　**Figure B**

Note that with this method, the paddle's power face is *not* the side of the blade pushing against the water.

4) When the paddle is slightly past a vertical position in front of you, remove it from the water by dropping your upper hand down along your body with the thumb on that hand pointing up in the air.

Then let your arms continue their natural rotation back into the initial starting position. For minimal wind resistance, feather the blade through the air when doing this.

Method 2:

This variation is useful when the sternman must put a directional component into his stroke to steer the boat or when he must turn around to see where the boat is going.

Procedure:

1) Hold the paddle in your hands as if doing a regular forward stroke (Example 6-4A, page 127).

2) Twist your upper body around to your paddling side, reach far back behind the canoe, and place the paddle as vertically as possible in the water (Example 6-5C).

At this point, your lower wrist should be twisted out away from the canoe and your upper arm should be next to your ear.

3) Pull the paddle towards you as if performing a forward stroke. With this method, the paddle's power face *does* push against the water.

4) Remove the paddle when it nears your hip, and repeat as necessary.

Method #2:   **Example 6-5 (Cont'd.)**   **Figure C**

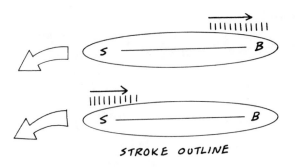

STROKE OUTLINE

Example 6-5 (Cont'd.)   **Figure D**

Draw Stroke

The *draw stroke* (Example 6-6) is a powerful turning stroke that moves a canoe toward the side the paddle is on. It's very useful in rough water because it provides quick maneuverability, acts like a brace for stability, and lets you rapidly shift into other strokes as needed.

Procedure:

1) Rotate your upper body to your paddling side, lean out as far as you can over the water without losing your balance, and plant your paddle in the water (Example 6-6A). The harder you need to perform this stroke, the farther you should lean out over the water. (Notice the pronounced lean in the picture.)

   When beginning, your lower arm should be almost straight, your upper arm should be slightly bent and held high in the air, the paddle should be as vertical as possible, and the paddle blade should be parallel to the canoe's keel line.

2) Pull the paddle directly towards you with your arms gradually bending as it nears the boat. Try to pull the canoe over to your paddle instead of pulling the paddle to the canoe.

   The power phase of the stroke ends when the blade is about 6 inches from the hull. Pulling it in any closer could pin it under the boat temporarily and leave you in a dangerously unbalanced position.

3) Slide the paddle out of the water by lifting up on your bottom arm and dropping your upper arm forward to just above the gunwale.

   Some experienced paddlers prefer making this recovery in the water instead of removing the blade from the water with each stroke. To do this, simply twist the paddle 90° so its blade is now perpendicular to the keel line and slice it through the water back to its starting position.

Example 6-6: The draw stroke.

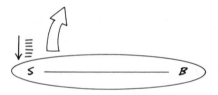

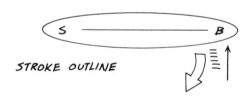

STROKE OUTLINE

Figure B

Example 6-6 (Cont'd.)

A bowman can abruptly turn a canoe under way by performing a modification of the draw stroke known as the *bow rudder* or *post*. While purists may claim that the draw, bow rudder, and post are three distinct strokes, this brief discussion highlights their similarities to prevent confusion and thus groups them together as one stroke. You execute these maneuvers by turning your paddle's power face perpendicular to both the current acting on your boat and its keel line (as much as possible), and performing a standard draw stroke as described above. This material is presented in a slightly different manner on pages 156 and 157.

Pushover Stroke

A *pushover stroke* (Example 6-7) turns a canoe away from the side the paddle is on. Unfortunately, it's a weak, inefficient stroke best used only when canoeing in a boat with a valuable or fragile finish. When possible, use pry or cross draw strokes which have the same effect on a canoe and are more powerful.

Procedure:

1) Rotate your upper body around to your paddling side. Stick the paddle vertically in the water right next to the gunwale and even with your hips (Example 6-7A).

Figure A

Example 6-7: The pushover stroke.

2) Push the paddle out away from the canoe (primarily with your lower
   hand) until you can't keep it vertical in the water anymore (Example
   6-7B).

Figure B

Example 6-7 (Cont'd.)

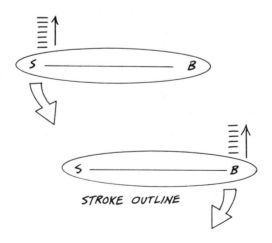

STROKE OUTLINE

Example 6-7 (Cont'd.)   Figure C

3) Drop your upper hand forward to about gunwale height and lift up and back on your bottom arm so you slice the paddle sideways out of the water. Then return to the initial position and repeat as necessary.

You can do this recovery phase with the blade completely submerged in the water by twisting the paddle 90°, pulling it through the water towards the canoe hull, and twisting it back 90° to its initial position against the boat.

Pry Stroke

With a *pry stroke* (Example 6-8) you rest your paddle against the canoe's hull and "pry" the water away from it. This turns the canoe away from your paddling side much faster and easier than the pushover stroke. Unfortunately, because the paddle acts like a lever against a canoe, prying can mar the finish on it. Another disadvantage with this technique is that the paddle could snag on an underwater rock and break or capsize the canoe in whitewater. Also, the pry restricts your ability to quickly perform other strokes and can't support your weight if you had to lean on it.

Procedure:

1) Rotate your upper body to your paddling side and stick the paddle in the water slightly past the vertical position with its blade angled under the canoe (Example 6-8A). Be sure the paddle blade is buried in the water and its throat is resting against the canoe's bilge.

    You may need to slide your lower hand up the paddle's shaft slightly to position the blade properly.

    The paddle's power face should be in against the canoe's hull, your upper arm should be out over water, and the thumb on your upper hand should be turned in towards your body.

2) Pull your upper hand in towards your body without breaking the contact between the paddle and the canoe.

3) Perform this "prying" maneuver until the paddle shaft touches the top edge of the gunwale, but don't let the blade get less than 30° from a vertical position (Fig. 6-8B).

4) Slide the paddle out of the water by dropping your upper hand forward and down and lifting your lower hand up and back. Then reposition it and repeat the stroke as needed.

    You can also do this recovery with your paddle completely submerged by feathering it through the water as described above for the draw and pushover strokes.

Example 6-8: The pry stroke.   **Figure A**

Example 6-8 (Cont'd.)   **Figure B**

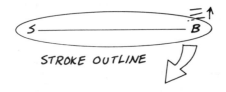

STROKE OUTLINE

Example 6-8 (Cont'd.)   **Figure C**

Stern Pry

A *stern pry* (Example 6-9) is a pry stroke performed at the extreme stern. It's very effective for evading obstacles in rapids and when correcting your course in heavy winds. When used properly, it will quickly and sharply swing the bow around toward the sternman's paddling side.

Figure A

Example 6-9: The stern pry stroke.

Procedure:

1) Position the paddle blade vertically in the water far to the rear of the canoe with its power face against the hull (Example 6-9A).

2) Pull the paddle grip back in towards your chest with your upper arm and push the paddle blade out away from the hull with your lower hand (Example 6-9B).

   The paddle blade needs to move only several inches or a foot at most during this stroke.

3) Remove the paddle from the water, reposition it, and repeat.

   As long as your boat has forward momentum, you can keep the paddle in the prying position as long as needed without repeating the entire stroke from the beginning.

Example 6-9 (Cont'd.)   Figure B

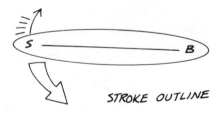

STROKE OUTLINE

Example 6-9 (Cont'd.)   Figure C

Sweep Strokes

A *forward sweep* turns a canoe away from the paddling side while a *reverse sweep* makes it move toward the paddling side. Both of these strokes should carve a 90° arc along a circular path next to the hull when tandem paddling and a full 180° semi-circle when solo boating. Because sweeps are surface strokes, they're extremely useful in shallow water where strokes like the draw and pry are ineffective. Several versions of sweep strokes are explained below and illustrated in Example 6-10. Note that few people perform a reverse sweep from the bow, since its close proximity to the canoe's pivot point reduces its turning effect.

Forward sweep (from the bow)

Procedure:

1) Extend the paddle low to the water and far in front of you with its blade vertically against the front of the canoe (Example 6-10A).

2) Swing the paddle in a wide arc away from its initial position. The stroke ends when the paddle is extended far abreast of you and slightly in front of your hips (Example 6-10B).

3) Remove the paddle from the water, feather it through the air, and repeat as needed.

Figure A

Example 6-10: Sweep strokes.

Example 6-10 (Cont'd.)   **Figure B**

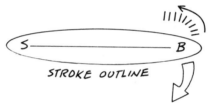

Example 6-10 (Cont'd.)   **Figure C**

Forward sweep (at the stern)

Procedure:

1) Extend your paddle low to the water and across from your hips with its blade vertical in the water and perpendicular to the keel line (Example 6-10D).

2) Swing the blade in a wide arc around towards the canoe's stern (Example 6-10E). The stroke ends when the paddle is extended far behind you and almost against the side of the canoe.

3) Remove the paddle from the water, feather it through the air, and repeat as needed.

Reverse sweep (at the stern)

Procedure:

1) Place the paddle's blade vertically in the water and far to the stern. Your upper arm should be out over the gunwale on the paddling side and

sharply bent. Your lower arm should be back behind your body and fairly straight (Example 6-10G).

2) Swing the paddle in a wide arc away from the canoe (Example 6-10H). The stroke ends when the paddle completes a 90° arc across from your hips.

3) Remove the paddle from the water, feather it through the air, and repeat as needed.

Example 6-10 (Cont'd.)   Figure D

Example 6-10 (Cont'd.)   Figure E

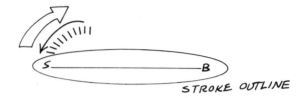

STROKE OUTLINE

Example 6-10 (Cont'd.)   Figure F

Example 6-10 (Cont'd.)   Figure G

Example 6-10 (Cont'd.)   Figure H

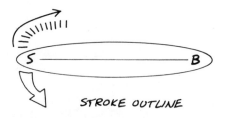

Example 6-10 (Cont'd.)   **Figure I**

Stern Course Correction Strokes

The *J-stroke* and *pitch stroke* (Example 6-11) compensate for a canoe's tendency to drift away from the side the sternman is paddling on. The J-stroke is basically a forward stroke with a "hook" added at the end of it; whereas, the pitch stroke is a forward stroke with a direction correction factor incorporated into it throughout its length. You need to vary the degree of this hook or correction factor with each stroke to keep your canoe headed on a straight course. Because developing this fine-tune control requires lots of practice, concentrate on mastering the art of paddling in a straight line and not on maximizing the power from these strokes when first learning them.

J-stroke:

Procedure:

1) Perform steps 1 and 2 of the forward stroke (see page 127).

2) As you near the end of that stroke, turn the wrist on your upper hand out away from the canoe and rotate the knuckles on your lower hand down towards the water so the paddle's power face turns away from the hull (Example 6-11A).

3) Pause in this position for a moment until the canoe swings to the desired heading, or give a noticeable push out away from the hull to emphasize the "hook" for added turning effect.

   Depending on the canoe's position, you can ignore this correction factor or can exaggerate it. In general, an exaggerated correction factor is needed when solo canoeing while little is needed when the bowman is much stronger than the sternman in a tandem canoe.

4) Remove the paddle from the water, feather it through the air, and repeat.

Pitch stroke:

The pitch stroke is best used on relaxing flatwater boating trips. Avoid it when paddling in whitewater since it doesn't allow the fast and powerful overcorrections possible with a J-stroke and useful when avoiding river obstacles.

Example 6-11: Stern correction strokes.   **Figure A**

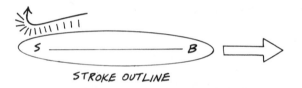

STROKE OUTLINE   **Figure B**

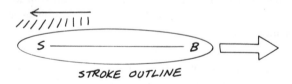

STROKE OUTLINE

Example 6-11 (Cont'd.)   **Figure C**

Procedure:

1) During the power phase of the forward stroke, curl your top hand around as if doing a J-stroke, but instead of performing the hook on the J, finish the rest of the forward stroke with the paddle slightly off-angle in the water and your upper wrist twisted out of its standard forward stroke position.

   The more you need to offset the canoe's drift away from your paddling side, the sooner you should begin to twist your upper wrist to angle the paddle's blade.

Rudder Stroke

If you're in the stern, you can use a *rudder stroke* (Example 6-12) to correct your course while paddling or to steer your boat when drifting with a river's current. This stroke should only be used when needed though, since it's a *passive stroke* that consumes a canoe's momentum. Beginning stern paddlers tend to rely on it far too much to compensate for their gross errors in maintaining a heading. Be sure your canoe has forward momentum before attempting this stroke. A rudder is absolutely useless when your canoe is resting motionless in calm water.

Procedure:

1) Position your paddle blade vertically in the water as far to the rear of the stern as comfortably possible (Example 6-12A).

2) Steer the canoe by moving your upper hand outward or inward to expose the two different sides of the paddle blade to the water.

Figure A

Example 6-12: The rudder stroke.

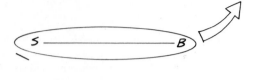

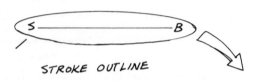

STROKE OUTLINE

Example 6-12 (Cont'd.)   **Figure B**

SPECIALIZED WHITEWATER STROKES

Cross-Draw Stroke

The *cross-draw* (Example 6-13) is a "once-and-done" stroke performed when the bowman must quickly avoid obstacles in the boat's path. This is an unusual stroke because it's done on the opposite side of the canoe from where you're normally paddling and you switch sides to execute it without changing your grip on the paddle. Many experienced paddlers favor a cross-draw stroke because it's more powerful and requires less water depth than a pry stroke. Disadvantages of a cross-draw are its relatively unstable "hands-crossed" position, the time lost switching the paddle back and forth across the canoe, and the fact that it's an isolated stroke that can't be combined with any other maneuver.

Procedure:

1) Let's assume you're paddling in the bow on the right side of your canoe and suddenly see a rock directly in front of you. You decide to detour around it to the left.

2) Without changing the position of your hands on your paddle, swing both arms and your paddle over your bow to the left side of the canoe. Rotate your upper body around to that side and plant the paddle in the water as far out from your hips as possible. Your lower hand should be extended straight and your paddle should be as vertical as possible when it enters the water (Example 6-13A).

3) Now perform a "draw stroke" by pulling the paddle blade in towards the canoe with your lower hand and pushing its grip away from the boat with your upper one.

4) Remove the paddle from the water when it's several inches from the canoe's hull and repeat once or twice as necessary.

Example 6-13: The cross-draw stroke.   **Figure A**

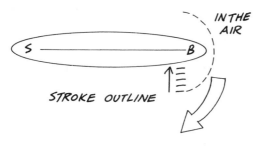

Example 6-13 (Cont'd.)   **Figure B**

Braces

Braces (Example 6-14) are stationary maneuvers you perform for added stability in rough water, to self-recover when capsizing, and when performing eddy turns. Because braces use water resistance for support, they work best when your paddle moves through the water or water moves around your paddle. Practice bracing in a tandem canoe by having your partner lean the boat to one side while you support it with a brace. When paddling solo, lean out over the water as far as you can and support that lean with a brace. Braces are powerful, reliable maneuvers, so don't hesitate to place a respectable amount of weight on your paddle blade when doing them.

There are two general categories of braces. You perform a *reaction brace* to prevent a capsize. It's a fairly weak maneuver since you're reacting to a problem and aren't in full control of the situation. On the other hand, a *planned brace* is strong and reliable because you prepare for it ahead of time and can then execute it with vigor. If it fails and you begin to tip, you can always do a reaction brace for emergency support.

There are two kinds of braces. A *low brace* is used to prevent capsizing when the canoe is leaning to the paddling side and as a precautionary, stabilizing stroke in rough water when you believe a capsize is imminent. A *high brace* is a useful recovery stroke when a canoe is rolling away from your paddling side and is useful when entering or leaving eddies. It's a much more dynamic stroke than the low brace, since you can quickly change it into a *power stroke* like a draw or a forward stroke if needed.

Low Brace—Method 1:

This method is useful when you need a great deal of immediate support to prevent capsizing toward your paddling side.

Procedure:

1) Rotate your upper body toward your paddling side and extend the paddle far out over and parallel to the water.

   The paddle should be perpendicular to the keel line and across from your hip, its blade should be almost flat on the water, and your lower hand should be pressing down hard on its throat (Example 6-14A).

   Don't hesitate to lean far out over the water and hard on the paddle for stability.

2) Maintain the paddle in this position as long as necessary, and scull it (see below) if you need more support.

3) Recover your initial position by pushing down on your paddle and lifting your body up and back into the canoe. Scull if necessary to do this.

Low Brace—Method 2:

This method is useful as a precaution against a capsize or when you want extra stability in rough water. It's a much more casual stroke than the first one.

Procedure:

1) With your body erect and facing forward, trail your paddle behind your canoe with its shaft horizontal to the water, its blade flat on it, and its power face up in the air (Example 6-14B).

Example 6-14: Braces.

Example 6-14 (Cont'd.)   Figure B

High Brace:

Procedure:

1) Position yourself and the paddle as if you were just beginning a draw
   stroke. Your upper arm should be high in the air and the paddle blade
   fairly deep in the water (Example 6-14C).

2) Instead of drawing the paddle and the canoe together like you would in a draw stroke, just maintain the paddle's position in the water exactly where you planted it. Think of the paddle as an immobile fencepost you're leaning on. Scull for additional support if needed.

3) Recover by drawing or sculling until you can pull yourself up to a stable position.

Example 6-14 (Cont'd.)   **Figure C**

Sculling

Sculling (Example 6-15) is a continuous stroke performed without removing the paddle from the water. When sculling, you keep the blade moving in a repetitive figure-eight pattern through the water with its power face constantly pressing against it. The angle of the blade in the water and how much you have to press on it will vary with the force of the water acting on it and with how much weight you want the paddle to support. You can easily combine sculling with other strokes like the draw or a brace for additional support in rough water or when capsizing.

COMBINATION STROKES

The preceding pages highlighted common canoeing strokes in their pure form. In reality, though, you often need to blend them together for greater control of your boat. For examples, a *diagonal draw* combines the draw and forward strokes into a stroke that moves a canoe both sideways towards the paddling side and forward at the same time, and combining forward and forward

Example 6-15: Sculling. Notice that the blade's power face always presses against the water.

Example 6-15 (Cont'd.)   Figure B

sweep strokes moves a canoe both forward and away from your paddling side simultaneously. Although you'll use many combinations of strokes when canoeing, it's best to master each one separately in its pure form as described above first.

PADDLING WITH THREE PEOPLE

When *three people paddle a canoe* (Example 6-16), the bowman should use a diagonal draw, the passenger positioned amidships should use a standard forward stroke, and the sternman should use a standard forward stroke on the opposite side of the canoe from the other two people. In most cases, no stern correction stroke is needed since the tendency for the canoe to turn away from the sternman's paddling side is offset by the two people paddling there.

Example 6-16: Paddling a canoe with three people.

SOLO CANOEING

As mentioned previously, almost every stroke described above is useful for both solo and tandem canoeing. When canoeing solo though, you either maintain your heading by paddling with a C-stroke (see next page) or by switching sides every 3–6 forward strokes using the sit and switch technique described earlier. Both methods have their disadvantages. Solo canoeists often must exaggerate the course correction factor when paddling to compensate for the canoe's tendency to turn away from the paddling side, and this can consume up to half the energy you put into each stroke. Likewise, switching sides every few strokes is annoying and possibly less efficient than staying on one side of the boat because so much time and effort are wasted moving the paddle back and forth through the air.

C-Stroke

The C-stroke (Example 6-17) is simply a J stroke with a diagonal draw attached to the beginning of it. How pronounced the beginning diagonal draw and ending "hook" are depends on how much course correction is needed with each stroke. Fine-tuning your C-strokes so that you can travel in a straight line without over- or underestimating these course corrections takes much practice.

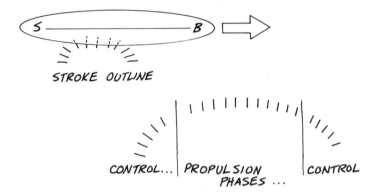

Example 6-17: The C-stroke. Note that the paddle's power face always pushes against the water and its blade travels partway under the boat for a while during each stroke.

PRACTICING STROKES

If you're a beginning canoeist, the three most important skills you should master as soon as possible are:

1) *Traveling in a straight line.* This is useful when you want to get from one place to another with the least amount of time and effort. Practice this skill by canoeing towards two aligned landmarks using the appropriate strokes described above. When learning to paddle in a straight line, don't switch sides to maintain your heading. Force yourself to keep paddling on one side of the boat and correct your mistakes with other strokes like the draw and pry. Avoid the temptation to correct your course by switching sides at all costs!

2) *Turning quickly.* The ability to quickly and decisively turn a canoe is useful when paddling in whitewater and on narrow streams and when landing or launching it. Practice this skill by pivoting in a complete circle when resting in the water, by playing "follow the leader" where you must duplicate every maneuver that a lead canoe makes, and by paddling around buoys set up in lakes and ponds.

Pivot turns are excellent practice maneuvers that help you become comfortable in a canoe and with the paddling strokes. Simply position yourself and a partner in a canoe in calm water and then practice spinning it in a complete circle around its pivot point. Ideal pivot strokes are draws, pries, and sweeps. Both partners can draw, both can pry, or both can sweep (forward sweep in the bow and reverse sweep in the stern). When paddling solo, a 180° forward or reverse sweep is the best way to turn around your pivot point.

3) *Balancing and leaning a canoe.* Being familiar with how your canoe balances and how far you can lean it before it capsizes will give you confidence when learning to paddle and is extremely important in whitewater. Practice balancing a canoe by rocking it back and forth while standing amidships in it as described on page 218. Practice leaning a canoe by performing your draws and braces with frequency and vigor until perfected.

ODDS AND ENDS

A few pointers to keep in mind when learning the paddling strokes are listed below:

1) You may notice that your canoe leans slightly to the side your paddle is on as you perform each stroke. While an excessive lean is not desirable, a slight lean is often unavoidable and is no cause for concern. If leaning is a problem for you, moving your lower hand several inches farther up the paddle shaft may help reduce it. For maximum efficiency when solo paddling, avoid any lean unless you're turning. Then lean the boat in the direction of your turn to lift its ends up out of the water so it can pivot easier. Many modern solo canoes are designed to turn promptly when leaned.

2) Try to paddle with a clean, flowing motion. Avoid jolting your boat with each stroke.

3) Strokes are designed for different purposes. Know when to use each stroke as well as how to perform them.

4) Paddle with your entire body. Use your upper body to move the paddle through the water and your lower body for support against the canoe. You should feel your back, side, stomach, and shoulder as well as your arm muscles tire when paddling.

5) Almost every stroke has two main components. The *power phase* is the part of a stroke that actually propels a canoe through the water, and the *recovery phase* is the ending part of it that returns the paddle to its initial, starting position.

6) The *ready position* is a resting position that allows you to perform any possible paddling action or stroke at a moment's notice. Variations of it include resting your paddle across the gunwales in front of you and holding it horizontally in the air in front of you. Your hands should always be gripping the paddle at their correct locations when in the ready position so you can react immediately to any need.

7) Usually your paddle blade must be perpendicular to the direction you're moving it for maximum efficiency. In many cases, though, strokes are more effective when the paddle blade is as perpendicular as possible to both the current

and the direction it's traveling through the water (because the greater the force acting against the paddle, the more effective that stroke will be). This concept can get very complicated, especially when paddling in whitewater. Example 6-18A illustrates a draw stroke performed in calm water; whereas, Example 6-18B portrays an identical stroke with a pronounced blade angle useful when performing eddy turns. Note that in this case the paddle's blade is angled somewhat to utilize a beneficial directional component generated by the current. It's important to realize that the actual draw stroke is performed exactly the same in both cases. Only the angle of the blade with respect to the canoe's keel line is changed.

8) Finally, when practicing your strokes and maneuvers, concentrate on mastering the proper techniques as described here instead of maximizing the power you put into and the speed you get from each of them. Increase the power you put in a stroke only after you have perfected it.

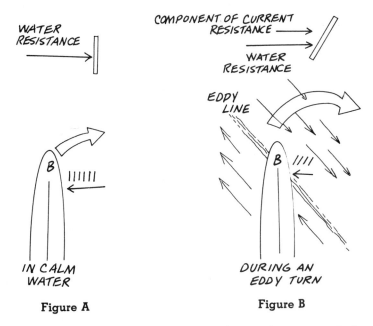

Figure A   **Figure B**

Example 6-18: Using the concept of diagonal components to properly position your paddle blade in the water.

7

FLATWATER CANOEING

FLATWATER is any waterway with no predominant moving current in it. Although you won't have to deal with the complicating effects of a river's current when paddling on flatwater, you often must contend with threatening waves and tricky currents stirred up by the wind instead. In addition, you won't have the beneficial push of a current to carry you along. Indeed, flatwater paddling does not imply consistently safe or easy boating conditions.

EFFICIENT PADDLING

You should paddle as efficiently as possible to avoid fatigue and to travel faster and farther with less effort. Suggestions for doing this are listed below:

1) Relax during the recovery phase of every stroke. Don't paddle with constantly tense muscles.

2) Pace yourself. Don't begin paddling fast and hard if you must paddle all day. The longer and farther you have to travel, the slower and more deliberate your paddling rhythm should be.

3) Use foot braces, contoured bucket seats, thigh straps, bent shaft paddles, a canoe with a sleek hull design, and related items of equipment specifically designed for efficient paddling.

4) Properly trim your canoe.

5) Cooperate with your partner instead of arguing with him.

6) Consider sit-and-switch instead of freestyle paddling. Many experienced canoeists feel it's the best method to use when traveling fast or for long periods of time.

7) Perform the canoeing strokes *exactly* as described in the preceding chapter. Particularly try to perfect your forward, pitch, and J-strokes since you'll use them extensively on flatwater.

8) Use the wind (or a river's current around a bend) to offset the tendency for a canoe to turn away from your stern paddling side. This way

you can use more powerful forward strokes instead of course correction ones there.

9) Switch paddling sides and rotate bow and stern paddling positions with your partner for variety throughout the day.

10) When possible, canoe immediately behind or on the leeward side of another boat because of the lesser wind and water resistance there.

11) Efficiently maintain your course by lining up two distant reference points in the direction of your heading, and then vary your stern strokes as needed to keep them aligned (Example 7-1). With this method, you'll know immediately if you're drifting off-course and can compensate for it with the next stroke. Skilled paddlers keep on course by subtly altering each stern stroke as needed instead of making gross alterations every few minutes.

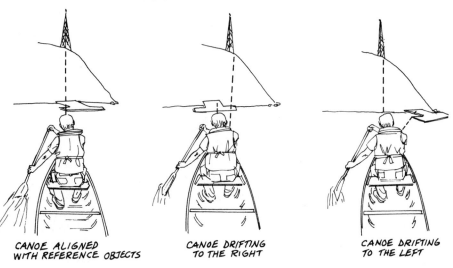

CANOE ALIGNED
WITH REFERENCE OBJECTS

CANOE DRIFTING
TO THE RIGHT

CANOE DRIFTING
TO THE LEFT

Example 7-1: Sighting on two distant objects to maintain your heading.

PADDLING IN WINDS AND WAVES

While rapids are the chief obstacle associated with moving water, winds are the bane of flatwater paddlers. Headwinds make you work much harder to cover distances, because it seems like they blow you back a foot for every 2 feet you paddle forward. Cross-winds play havoc with your navigation and threaten to capsize your boat. While tail winds can be an enjoyable treat, it's not difficult to swamp in the large waves stirred up by them.

Wind is nothing more than a river of air flowing over the land. Try to understand how surface conditions affect its flow, because this will help you when paddling in windy conditions (Example 7-2). Winds running down the length of a long lake create monstrous waves at its far end since all the energy

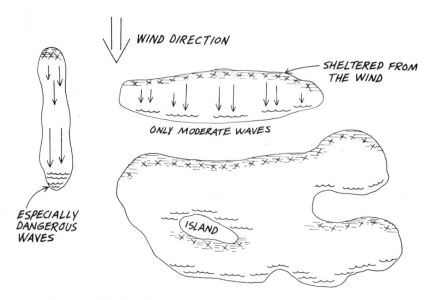

WIND DIRECTION

SHELTERED FROM THE WIND

ONLY MODERATE WAVES

ESPECIALLY DANGEROUS WAVES

ISLAND

Example 7-2: Landforms and wind effects. Note the rough waves on the windward side of landforms and the calm water on their leeward side.

from the wind is focused there. On the other hand, wind blowing across a long, narrow lake can't form very large waves along its windward shore, since relatively little water surface is exposed to it in the direction it's blowing. Even in a violent storm, fairly calm regions exist on the leeward side of islands, peninsulas, and other landforms, much like calm eddies exist behind obstacles in violent whitewater.

If you're new to canoeing, never launch your boat on a windy lake and head for shore immediately if threatened by a sudden storm when boating, since even mild waves can capsize or swamp your craft if you don't react correctly to them. Even experienced paddlers avoid canoeing in high winds, in large waves, or in approaching stormy weather. Be extremely careful when crossing large bodies of water, since conditions could change suddenly when you're far from shore. Avoid canoeing when a wind is blowing from land out towards the middle of a lake unless you're absolutely sure you can quickly reach shelter in an emergency. Chances are the conditions are far worse out there than you can see from shore. If you must paddle in winds, seek refuge behind landform obstacles and on the side of the water body nearest the source of the wind.

Maintaining proper canoe trim is very important when paddling in a wind. As a general rule, trim the end of your canoe away from the wind lighter than the end of it pointing into it to prevent it from catching the lighter, higher end of the boat and "weather-vaning" it around. For instance, when paddling into a wind, trim the stern lighter than the bow, and when running with the wind trim the bow lighter than the stern.

Paddling in Large Waves

Generally, paddle when you can with short, quick, commanding strokes in large waves. Chances are you'll have to discard your established paddling rhythm in this situation because there will be times when the water will come halfway up your paddle's shaft and other times when you can't paddle at all because it's far below your gunwale. When tandem paddling into or running with heavy seas, consider stowing your gear in the very center of your canoe, having the bowman paddle from behind the bow seat, and having the sternman paddle from in front of the stern thwart to lighten the ends of the boat and help it ride over the waves. The price you'll pay for this better end flotation is a slight loss of steering control and tracking, though. Quartering your canoe into oncoming waves also helps prevent swamping. This technique is explained below.

Paddling into the Wind

Slightly angle a canoe into a mild wind so you can use forward strokes on its leeward side at the stern and solo positions to offest its tendency to curve away from those paddling sides. In effect, use the wind as your course correction factor. In rough water, tandem paddlers should both use a forward stroke on the leeward side of their boat and should angle it into the wind and oncoming waves to maintain their course (Example 7-3).

Quartering (Example 7-3) a canoe is the process of angling it into the wind and oncoming waves stirred up by it. This quartering angle is frequently referred to as the *angle of attack*. When quartering in large waves, you need to accent this angle so they don't break over your boat and swamp it but not so much that you *broach* (turn broadside to them). Likewise, you should quarter your canoe

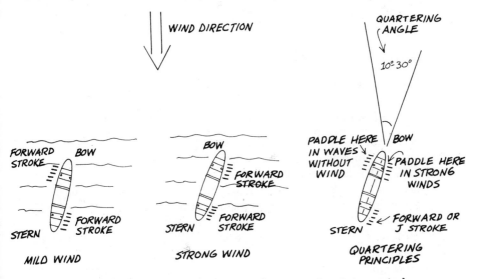

Example 7-3: Paddling positions when canoeing into a wind.

enough so the wind eliminates the need for stern course correction strokes but not so much that it blows you broadside. When quartering, the bowman should concentrate on propelling the canoe on its course while the sternman focuses on maintaining the proper angle of attack. Unfortunately, a canoe is somewhat harder to balance when quartered, since it's forever rolling from side to side with each passing wave, and you may need to *tack* (zigzag) across the water like a sailboat travels into the wind to get to your destination.

Paddling in a Cross-Wind

Stern and solo canoeists should paddle on a canoe's leeward side in a cross-wind. This way the wind negates the tendency for the canoe to turn away from their paddling side so they can use a forward stroke for maximum straight-ahead propulsion, and they can better over- or under-compensate (as necessary) for the wind's effects on their heading. There are two methods you can use when paddling in a cross-wind (Example 7-4).

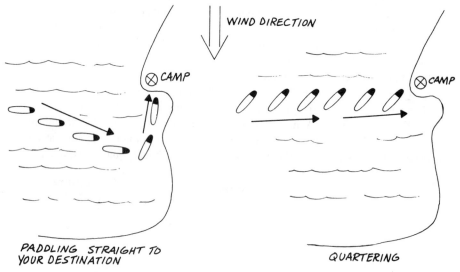

Example 7-4: Methods of paddling in a cross-wind.

1) *Paddle straight towards your destination.* With this method you make the most forward progress but are blown off course as you travel. Hopefully, you'll reach an island or shoreline that blocks out the wind so you can complete the final leg of your journey into it with relative ease. This method is not satisfactory in heavy seas because of the danger of swamping.

2) *Quarter into the wind to your destination.* With this method you in effect perform a forward ferry maneuver (see page 193) exactly as if the wind and waves were a river current. Quarter your canoe into the wind just enough so your forward progress into it balances its backward push on your boat and you travel at an angle across the water toward your destination. This quartering angle should

be far greater than the one used to paddle into the wind, since now you're traveling across it instead of into it. Maintain a maximum of about a 45° quartering angle when traveling in a strong cross-wind though, to help prevent broaching.

Running with the Wind

Paddling with the wind at your back is frequently called *running with the wind*. If the waves and wind are fairly mild, paddle just enough to keep the boat on course and enjoy the ride. Under those conditions, try rigging a sail (see below) for an even faster, more thrilling trip. Also, try *surfing* waves by seeing how long you can keep your bow riding on a wave crest. When running with a mild wind, you can lash two canoes together for greater companionship. While this gives you the stability of a barge, it reduces each canoe's ability to ride over waves and could lead to swamping if done in heavy seas. Also, be aware that stresses caused by the wind and water could damage canoes lashed together improperly in more than mild conditions.

Shipping water at the stern is the major problem associated with canoeing downwind, since waves always travel faster than a canoe. If the oncoming waves are moderately high, try slightly quartering the stern into them to help prevent swamping there but be careful not to quarter too much and encourage broaching. Avoid trimming your stern excessively heavy to avoid shipping water there, but don't forget that it should be trimmed heavier than the bow, as discussed above.

Before beginning a downwind run in large waves, rig a *sea anchor* to control your speed and keep your canoe lined up with the wind and waves. Simply tie about 20 feet of nylon line to the handle of your largest cooking pot or to a commercially available canoeing anchor. Then secure the free end of that rope to your stern painter attachment and store the anchor in the boat until needed. If you're caught in extremely rough water, rig a sea anchor and ride out the storm by sitting amidships in the bottom of your canoe to lower its center of gravity and lighten its ends.

PADDLING AT NIGHT

Canoeing at night can be a rewarding experience if you're prepared for its challenges or a deadly game of survival if you're not. Only paddle at night if you know where you're going, can see by moonlight, are on wide, calm, deep water, and have predictable, comfortable weather. Avoid canoeing at night on moving water, in waves, in narrow channels, in hypothermia-prone conditions, or in areas frequented by winds or powerboats.

SAILING A CANOE

Sailing a canoe is an exciting way to travel if the wind is moderate and at your back. There are several ways to do this with materials you'd probably have at hand on any trip:

1) In mild weather the bowman could simply hold a tarp, ground sheet, parka, paddle blade, or similar object in his outstretched hands, while the sternman keeps the canoe on course with a ruddering stroke. Wrapping the sail around a paddle and resting that on the bowman's shoulders or propping it up vertically in the boat will relieve the strain on his arms when sailing for a long period of time. Advantages of this method include the ease of setting up and taking down the sail. The primary disadvantage of it is the limited sail surface exposed to the wind.

2) You can easily rig a larger sail by rolling two long, skinny logs up in a tarp like an ancient scroll. When completed, the bowman simply holds these poles in position in the canoe, braces their bottoms against a thwart, or lashes them to the boat for greater permanence. Advantages of this method include the ability to regulate the sail's size by rolling or unrolling the poles and the greater sail area exposed to the wind. Disadvantages include the need to roll this on land before paddling, the possibility of a gust of wind capsizing the canoe or structurally damaging it if the sail is rigidly attached to it, and the damage rough poles could do to your tarp.

3) You can lash two canoes together and secure a sail between them when sailing long distances in mild winds. To do this, tie a pole completely across the bow thwarts of both canoes leaving a 3-foot gap between their gunwales at that point. Then tie a second pole across and to the stern thwarts of each canoe so they are about 4–5 feet apart there. (This difference in distance between the bows and sterns of both canoes provides additional floating stability.) Finally, rig a sail across the canoes using one of the methods just described. The main problem with this is the time needed to set up and the potential danger that a sudden storm will blow in before you can remove the rigging.

OCEAN CANOEING

Paddling a canoe far from shore along coastlines and across large bodies of water is extremely dangerous, though highly publicized accounts of adventurers' feats make it seem easy. Unpredictable currents, high winds, large waves, cold water, large ships, predatory and poisonous sea creatures, and isolation from help in an emergency all threaten ocean paddlers. If you have a desire to paddle along a coastline or to cross a large body of water, be sure your wilderness living, canoeing, and survival skills are honed with years of experience, your mind is psychologically prepared for the hardships you'll surely face, your body is in the best possible physical condition, your equipment is of the highest quality and most appropriate design, and every detail of your trip is planned with intense, extreme care. Then when you've done everything you possibly could do to avert disaster, kiss the ground one last time, cast off your stern lines, and paddle into the distant sun. A hundred thousand people too scared to do likewise will ride with you in their dreams.

8

READING A RIVER

READING *a river* is the art of understanding the behavior of moving water. Since all water, whether in the Mississippi River or in a tiny drainage ditch, reacts the same way to the pull of gravity, study its flow whenever you can and look for the features described in this chapter in it. Gaining a sensitivity to and understanding of moving water is essential for canoeing on rivers.

First, you should learn a few basic definitions associated with moving water:

upstream	the direction the water is coming from.
downstream	the direction the water is going.
left	the left side of the river when facing downstream.
right	the right side of the river when facing downstream.

JUDGING THE WATER LEVEL

Knowing if a river's water level is high, normal, or low is very important for a safe canoe trip. Generally, rapids become much worse at higher water levels since the current is faster and less predictable and obstacles close to the surface become harder to maneuver around. Also, at high water levels, rapids wash out and become sets of large roller coaster waves that can easily swamp a canoe. On the other hand, you must allow plenty of extra time to canoe a river during periods of low water, since its current is slower and sections of it could be too shallow to paddle effectively.

Signs of higher-than-normal water levels are . . .

. . . water flowing among trees on a riverbank.

. . . shoreline vegetation partly or entirely submerged.

. . . no gravel bars, or similar areas devoid of plant life between the waterline and the vegetation line.

. . . jagged, rough, unpolished rocks below the water's surface.

. . . islands partly or completely submerged. Bushes "growing" out of the middle of a river indicate a submerged island.

. . . muddy or turbulent water.

Signs of lower-than-normal water levels are . . .

. . . a large distance between the vegetation line and the waterline.

. . . prominent islands with no vegetation growing on them.

. . . exposed shoreline tree roots and steep, undercut banks.

. . . rounded, polished rocks exposed in the river and along the shore.

. . . exposed sand and gravel bars.

. . . clear water.

. . . an obvious water line on exposed rocks, bridge abutments, and similar obstructions above the present water level.

. . . an "aluminum coating" on exposed, above-waterline rocks in a river (this is caused by aluminum canoes scraping over them in higher water).

Also, rivers are generally much higher in spring than in autumn, especially in areas where the ground freezes in the winter or where melting mountain snowcaps drain into them.

KINDS OF RIVERS

There are several kinds of rivers:

A *pool-and-drop river* has long, relatively flat pools separated by steep, often dangerous rapids. The steep sections could be caused by the river bisecting hard rock layers, debris washed in from side canyons, or a general narrowing of the river gorge, as explained below.

A *staircase* river has a series of ledges and drops in it. It differs from a pool-and-drop river in that its rapids are not separated by long, relatively calm pools. Often "staircase" refers only to a small section of a river. The Shenandoah Staircase on the Shenandoah River in West Virginia is an example of this type of waterway.

A river with a *constant gradient* is the third kind of river you'll see when whitewater canoeing. This kind of waterway has a continuous, predictable loss in elevation from one end to the other and behaves in an ordinary, expected manner. Rapids in it tend to be more gradual than those in the previous two kinds of rivers since the loss in elevation is distributed throughout its course and not concentrated at a few severe bottlenecks.

In addition, by just looking at your map you can classify rivers as young, mature, or old. *Young rivers* travel through rugged, hilly country. They have a steep gradient, a fast current, and many difficult rapids. *Old rivers* are common in lowlands and plains and typically meander frequently. Expect a slow current and no rapids on them. *Mature rivers* have a moderate current and occasional, often mild rapids.

INDICATIONS OF RAPIDS

Predicting when you'll encounter rapids before getting dangerously close to them is a very useful skill to have. The guidelines that follow will help you estimate when you're approaching rapids and how severe they are.

1) *Side canyons.* Expect rapids slightly downstream from where every side stream enters the main channel. The larger the side stream is, the steeper its gradient, and the steeper the gradient of the main channel, the rougher the rapids will be. These rapids are caused by debris like logs and boulders washing down the side stream and piling up at its junction with the main river.

2) *Geologic features.* Expect difficult rapids when a river cuts into hard bedrock. Expect mild rapids when a river travels through a soft underlying material like shale or loose sedimentary deposits.

3) *Gradient.* The steeper the gradient, the more numerous and difficult the rapids and the faster and more unpredictable the current will be. You can predict when you'll be entering a section of river with greater-than-normal rapids and faster-than-normal current by recognizing changes in the river's gradient on your map (see page 170).

4) *River bottom surface.* Knowing the kind of surface present on a river bottom will give you an indication of what kind of rapids to expect there. Ignore deposition surfaces like sand, gravel, and small boulders which are dependent on the river's current. Instead, concentrate on the underlying bedrock. Smooth, flat rocks indicate the possibility of staircase rapids with dangerous ledges, while large boulders indicate the possibility of a maze-type of rapids with frequent eddies and interconnected channels.

5) *River bends.* Rapids occur much more frequently at river bends than on straight sections of water, and the sharper those bends are, the greater the possibility of rough rapids there.

6) *Shoreline features.* Steep banks dropping abruptly into a river at a bend typically portend sweeper trees, rough bank waves, and nasty overhangs battered by the river. Be extremely wary when approaching this situation. On the other hand, flat river bend shorelines indicate relatively shallow, safe riffles instead of pounding rapids.

7) *General topographic features.* Expect many rapids when traveling through rough, steep, mountainous terrain, a few riffles in flat countryside, and mild rapids in rolling hills and farmlands. Narrow canyons indicate long sections of often severe rapids, while wide river valleys indicate generally calm water.

8) *Obvious elevation drop.* Expect mean rapids if you look downstream and see a *horizon line* (Example 8-1) where the river disappears from view for a fraction of its course. On the other hand, expect moderate, consistent rapids with no large or abrupt drops if you can see down their entire length.

9) *Current.* Fast currents indicate a steep gradient and a greater chance of bad rapids. A calm pool indicates an obstacle is plugging a river's channel somewhere downstream.

10) *Water level.* Expect rapids at moderate, average water levels; expect rock gardens that may require intricate maneuvering skills and shallow sections requiring wading at lower water levels; and expect severe rapids and large waves at high water levels.

11) *White waves.* Distant, white, "dancing" waves guarantee some kind of obstacle or rough water ahead.

12) *Sounds.* In general, the louder the sound of a rapids and the farther you are from them when you first hear them, the worse they are. Remember though, that sounds are often muffled by vegetation, magnified in canyons, and vary greatly depending on prevailing weather conditions.

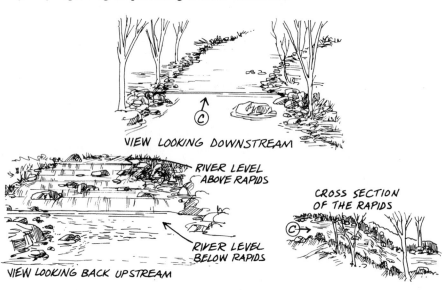

VIEW LOOKING DOWNSTREAM

RIVER LEVEL ABOVE RAPIDS

RIVER LEVEL BELOW RAPIDS

VIEW LOOKING BACK UPSTREAM

CROSS SECTION OF THE RAPIDS

Example 8-1: A horizon line at a rapids.

SEVERAL IMPORTANT CONCEPTS

A river's depth, speed, and current are all very much interrelated. With practice, you'll be able to tell which part of a river is the fastest, the slowest, the deepest, and the most shallow, and you'll understand much about why islands, beaches, and gravel bars are located where they are. You'll even be able to predict where you're likely to find these features on a river by just looking at a topographic map of the waterway. Most important of all, though, by mastering the concepts presented in this section, you'll greatly increase your paddling safety and efficiency on moving water.

Current

At first, you'll need a good understanding of *current*, which is simply the flow of the water. The current is fastest in the center and at the surface of a straight, uniform section of river, assuming it's not affected by events upstream. Thus, you can cover a greater distance with less effort when paddling down the center of a uniform, straight river because the current will be fastest and the water deepest there. The *main channel* is an imaginary line running down a river that indicates where most of the water is flowing. Usually it's the region with the dominant or fastest current. For example, the main channel runs right down the center of a uniform river because there's minimal resistance to its flow there.

When a river goes around a bend, however, the water in its main channel is affected by inertia and centrifugal force and no longer travels down the center of its bed. *Centrifugal force* is the tendency for any material to curve to the outside of an arc, while *inertia* tends to keep a substance traveling in its present direction unless acted on by a different force. A river's main channel hugs the outside of a bend because centrifugal force pulls its water there and because the resistance of the outer bank is the only force great enough to overcome the inertial tendency for the water to continue traveling in its initial, straight path.

Because the outside river bank is the only thing strong enough to counteract the effects of inertia and centrifugal force acting on a river, the main channel drifts toward the outside of a river bend and its water piles up there. *Bank waves* are waves caused by the water bumping into the bank on the outside of a bend, while *super-elevation* is the tendency for water to pile up on top of itself as it makes a turn. The outside shoreline on sharp bends tends to be highly eroded and even undercut because the full force of the river's current hits it, and trees on these outside bends often topple into the water as the ground underneath them wears away. In summary, the outside bend of a river is the best place to canoe because the water is deepest and fastest there, but it's the most dangerous because of the rough water and shoreline obstacles also present.

Additional variations in a river's main channel can also exist. For example, a main current tends to exist next to steep banks, since sharp drop-offs present above the waterline usually continue deep below the water as well and form a natural "brace" for it.

The significant points underlying this entire discussion are that the main channel doesn't always go right down the center of a river, and you must know where a river's main channel is for safe, efficient canoeing there. For instance, when canoeing at low water levels, you'll probably want to stay in the main channel because the water is fastest and deepest there, while you'll often need to avoid it at higher water levels and around river bends for greater safety.

Current lines are imaginary lines indicating the speed and direction of the current at various places in a river. It's important to note that current lines don't have to point downstream. For example, the current in eddies travels upstream opposite the main downstream flow, while current lines in diagonal bars often run perpendicular to the main river channel.

Depth and Speed

Water flowing in a river is very similar to water flowing in a garden hose. As far as canoeists are concerned, what goes in must come out. This means that virtually the same volume of water must flow through two nearby cross-sections of river during the same period of time. Several interrelated principles based on this observation are:

1) Calm rivers are deep and fast rivers are shallow.
2) Deep rivers have very little current and shallow rivers have a relatively fast current.
3) Water flows faster in narrow channels and slower in wide ones. The faster a channel narrows, the faster its current will increase.
4) Narrow channels are deep and wide ones are shallow.

Gradient

A river's *gradient* is how much it drops in vertical feet for every mile it travels. This is one of the most important general indicators of how rough a river is to paddle. Waterways with a gradient of less than 20 feet per mile usually have a fairly slow current and mild rapids, while those with a gradient greater than 50 feet per mile are probably quite difficult and dangerous. The two ways to measure a river's gradient are described next.

A river's *average gradient* is the vertical drop per mile along your entire route. Find it by using the following formula:

$$\text{A.G.} = \frac{\text{put-in elevation} - \text{take-out elevation (in feet)}}{\text{river length from put-in to take-out (in miles)}}$$

Note that a river's average gradient only indicates its general nature. A river can be as mellow as a sleeping kitten at one place and as vicious as a wildcat around a bend, and its average gradient will tell you nothing of these changing moods (Example 8-2).

Knowing a river's *specific gradient*—its gradient at a certain section of it—is far more useful than knowing its average gradient. You can calculate this for any section of river using the technique detailed in Example 8-3.

  1) Place a string along the waterway on your topographic map.
  2) Place a mark on the string everywhere a contour line crosses the river. Also, mark your starting and ending locations on it (Example 8-3A).

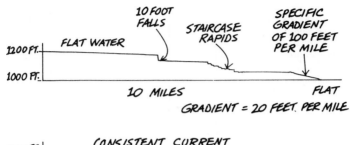
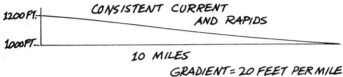

Example 8-2: Two rivers with the same average gradient. The dangers of relying on this gradient measurement should now be obvious to you.

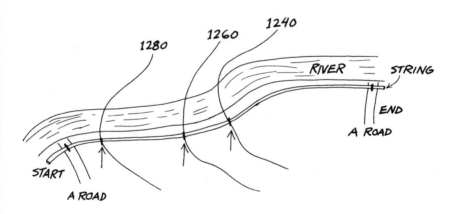

Example 8-3: Drawing a *river profile*.   **Figure A**

3) Straighten out the string and place it on a plain sheet of paper.

4) Place a mark on the paper everywhere there is a mark on the string.

5) Draw vertical lines through each of those marks.

6) Draw a grid pattern of evenly spaced horizontal lines to represent elevation levels. Label them with the appropriate elevation numbers.

7) Mark your initial and final elevations on the paper at the vertical lines

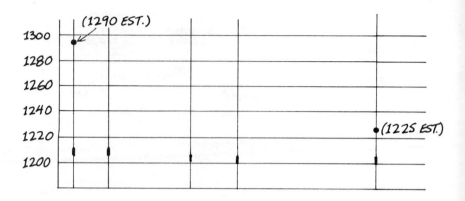

Example 8-3 (Cont'd.)   **Figure B**

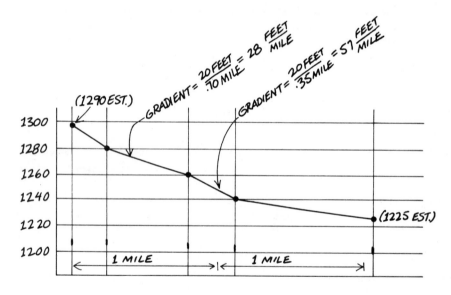

Example 8-3 (Cont'd.)   **Figure C**

representing them. Estimate if necessary (Example 8-3B). (1290 is the estimated starting elevation in the example.).

8) Beginning at your initial elevation mark, drop down one horizontal line, move to the right, and place a dot at the spot where the first vertical line crosses it.

9) Then drop down another horizontal line, work farther towards the right, and place a second dot at the next vertical line. Repeat for all vertical lines.

10) Connect the dots.

11) Using the scale at the bottom of the map, mark off 1-mile increments along any horizontal elevation line, beginning at your starting location.

12) Calculate the gradient at each section of river, as needed, by dividing the elevation drop there in feet by its length in miles (Example 8-3C).

RIVER OBSTACLES

In a sense, the previous discussion of kinds of rivers and river currents was just a primer for the material in the rest of this chapter. While that information explained how to read a river from an overall, "birds-eye" perspective, the information that follows analyzes each component in a rapids in great detail. Understanding the material that follows and applying it to the actual situations you'll encounter is of utmost importance when paddling in rough water.

Unfortunately, obstacles in a river rarely appear alone or in their pure form as presented here. Much more often they overlap each other or occur so frequently and with such confusion that you'll be at a loss to initially figure them out. Yet, this is precisely the challenge of canoeing in whitewater! With experience, you'll begin to see things like eddies and V's in what used to be just a mass of frothing, foaming, threatening water, and in time you'll be able to detect safe routes through even very difficult, lengthy rapids.

Upstream and Downstream V's

Imagine, for a moment, an idealized river with no obstacles in it. Its current lines would look like those in Example 8-4A. Now let's place a large boulder in the middle of it near the water's surface. In this case, the river's current lines would look like those in Example 8-4B. If you were in a canoe paddling down that river, you would see a V pointing upstream directly at you as in Example 8-4C. V's pointing upstream indicate an obstacle you must always avoid! This is one of the most basic rules for reading a river.

Now, let's place an identical boulder in the river close to the first one (Example 8-5). Here you can see two V's pointing upstream which you must avoid as explained above, but right down the center between them is a V pointing downstream. A second, very basic law of whitewater canoeing is that V's pointing downstream indicate a safe channel. (As you'll soon learn, there's a rather slim chance that rocks are close to the surface in these channels, but you should always aim for them unless you actually see an obstruction there.) Channels of water between two obstructions are called *tongues* or *chutes* and have a smooth, glassy, dark appearance indicating fast, deep, safe water.

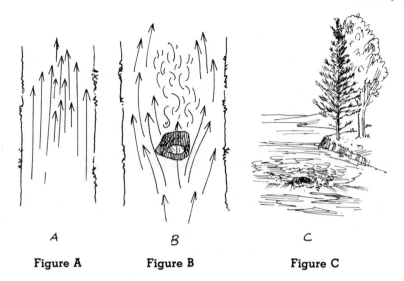

Figure A   Figure B   Figure C

Example 8-4: Current lines. In a uniform, unobstructed river (Figure A). Near a surface obstacle (Figure B). Your view of that obstacle from a canoe upstream of it (Figure C).

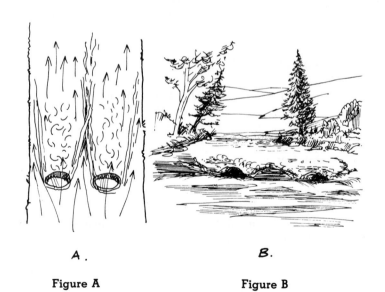

Figure A   Figure B

Example 8-5: One downstream and two upstream V's. Top view (Figure A). As seen from an upstream canoe (Figure B).

Standing Waves

Now, let's refer to another example illustrating a similar chute between two obstructions (Example 8-6). If you look closely at the far end of the chute, you'll see some large waves. These are called *standing waves* or *haystacks* and form when fast water flowing down the chute bumps into the slower water at the bottom of it. They indicate deep water and a safe passage free of underwater obstructions. You can easily identify standing waves by their roller-coaster appearance, repeated pattern at constant intervals, and regular, "standing" shape.

Haystacks are one of several kinds of *velocity differential waves* that form when fast water bumps into slower water. Bank waves on the outside of river bends and waves that form when two river channels converge are other examples. Velocity differential waves can range from small washboards of regularly spaced waves to huge Grand Canyon-sized monsters, depending on factors like the speed of the current. Velocity differential waves usually indicate an unobstructed route but you must be careful to prevent swamping in them.

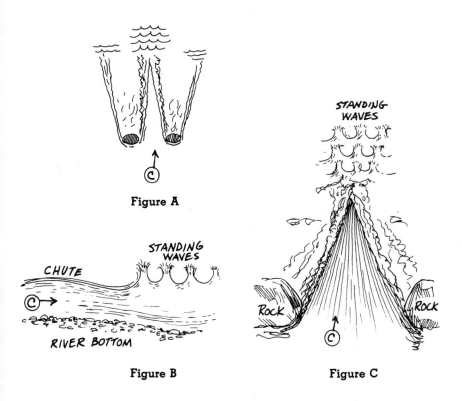

Figure A

Figure B

Figure C

Example 8-6: Standing waves. Top view (Figure A). Cross-section down the chute (Figure B). View from an upstream canoe (Figure C).

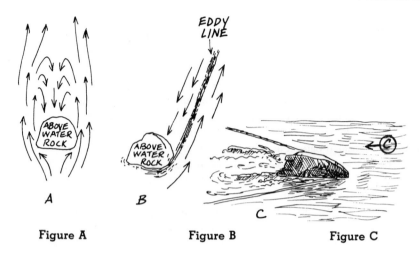

Figure A   Figure B   Figure C

Example 8-7: An eddy. Top view (Figure A). The eddy line (Figure B). View of an eddy from an upstream and slightly off-angle canoe (Figure C).

Eddies

Now let's return to the uniform river containing the one boulder we introduced earlier, but this time have it stick noticeably above the water as in Example 8-7A. Notice that behind the boulder, the current is actually flowing upstream! This region behind the obstruction is called an *eddy* and is one of your best friends in rough whitewater. You can use eddies to rest before continuing down a difficult rapid, as emergency harbors to avoid imminent obstructions, and as places from which you can unhurriedly scout the next section of rough water. In fact, proficient canoeists use eddies to help them maneuver from chute to chute in a rapids, to position their boat above a specific chute, to quickly land in a fast current, and even to travel upstream in whitewater. As you'll soon see, the greater the difference between the upstream and downstream currents at an eddy, the greater its use for whitewater canoeing. Since this difference increases as a river's main current increases, eddies become more and more useful as the difficulty of a river increases. Eddies vary in length from several inches to several hundred feet, depending on the width of the obstruction and the velocity of the current.

Example 8-7B shows a close-up view of the water at the edge of a boulder forming an eddy. Notice that there's a distinct line—called the *eddy line*— separating the upstream current in the eddy from the downstream current in the main river channel. In very turbulent water there's often a difference in height between the upstream and downstream flows as well, and in this case, the eddy line is called an *eddy fence*. It's important that you fully understand what an eddy line is and how water flows in and near one before attempting to learn the invaluable eddy turn technique discussed in the next chapter.

Figure 8-7C portrays your view of an eddy from upstream and slightly to the side. Notice that the presence of an obstruction sticking above the water is the best indication you have of an eddy's location. In fact, you can guarantee that an eddy exists behind every significant above-water obstacle in a river's flow, and the faster the current the more pronounced that eddy will be. Eddies can appear along the bank and on the inside of river bends as well as behind obstacles in the middle of the main flow. Example 8-8A illustrates a top view of the current lines in this kind of eddy, while Example 8-8B shows the same shoreline eddy as seen from an upstream and slightly off-angle canoe.

The eddies discussed above are "two dimensional" in nature, because they were caused by obstructions protruding above the surface of the water. "Three-dimensional" eddies exist behind submerged obstacles but aren't as useful as two-dimensional ones because water flowing over their obstructions dilutes the upstream current behind them.

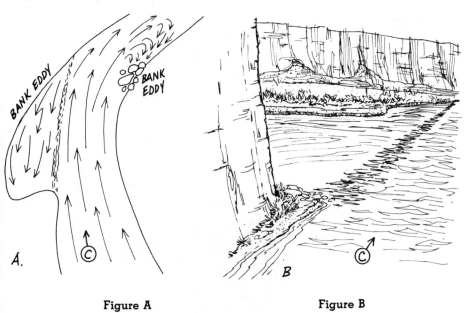

Figure A   **Figure B**

Example 8-8: Current lines in a bank eddy. Top view (Figure A). View from an upstream and slightly off-angle canoe (Figure B).

Holes

Let's return again to our idealized, unobstructed river with a large boulder slightly below its surface (Example 8-4). Notice that an upstream V and a hump in the water at the apex of that V are the only indications you have of that boulder's presence. If the rock is too close to the surface you must avoid it because your canoe will run aground on it or crash into it, but if it's deep enough below the surface, you can paddle directly over the hump without hitting the rock beneath it. Because this situation varies so much with the depth of the obstacle and the speed of the water (see Example 8-12), having a good feeling for how the current went over similar obstacles you've already encountered is the best way to determine if you can go over or must detour around this kind of obstruction.

While knowing whether you can or cannot paddle over a submerged obstacle without hitting it is important, what concerns us here is not so much the obstacle itself but what's after it. A large trough directly behind a submerged obstruction is called a *souse hole* or *hole* (Example 8-9). The wave that follows that is a velocity differential wave caused by the fast water flowing over the obstacle colliding into the slower, deeper water behind it. Typically this wave is called a standing wave, haystack, or *roller*. There are two problems associated with this standing wave. The first is the possibility that water will pour into your canoe and swamp it as you paddle through and over it. The second is that your canoe might not have enough power to climb the standing wave, since gravity is pulling you back down into the hole and the water in the wave itself is restricting your downstream progress. You can easily travel through small holes with small waves, but deep holes with intimidating rollers are quite dangerous and must be avoided.

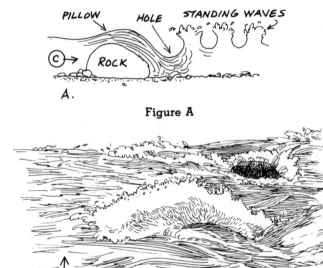

Figure A

Figure B

Example 8-9: A souse hole. Side view (Figure A). View from an upstream and slightly off angle canoe (Figure B).

Large, deep holes are called *keepers* because it's extremely difficult to get out of them once you're in. These are particularly dangerous when water from the following standing wave recirculates back on itself and forms a "whirlpool" type of current in the hole. Standing waves that do this are known as *reversals* or *stoppers*. Fortunately, though, keepers and reversals are almost always found on treacherous water frequented by experienced paddlers familiar with them. Beginning canoeists on mild whitewater streams will rarely if ever encounter them (except related dams and ledges; see below).

You should note that many boaters use the terms discussed here—including haystack, standing wave, roller, hydraulic, keeper, stopper, reversal, and hole—interchangeably and inaccurately. Be careful when discussing the "rollers" and "holes" on an unfamiliar river with an unknown canoeist.

Dams and Ledges

You should easily notice large dams and waterfalls in time to avoid them. However, small dams, ledges, and drop-offs are dangerous because they're hard to recognize from a safe upstream distance, they extend for a large distance across a waterway, and they form strong current reversals called *hydraulics* or *hydraulic jumps* (Example 8-10). In other words, some of the water going over this type of obstacle continues on downstream along the bottom of the streambed but some flows back upstream in an endless cycle to fill in the vacuum caused by the river's sudden drop over the edge. To see what could happen if caught in a hydraulic, toss a log into one and watch it spin around and around and around without leaving it. They're nasty.

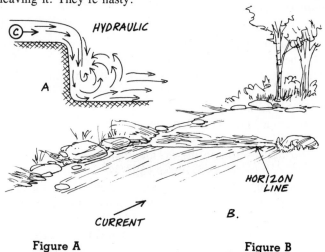

Figure A   Figure B

Example 8-10: A hydraulic. Cross section illustrating current lines (Figure A). View from a canoe directly upstream (Figure B). Note the horizon line in Figure B.

Several—though often difficult—ways to identify a downstream dam or ledge include:

1) Look for sharp drops in the shoreline or in vegetation lines along the shore. Since vegetation lines are often less distinct than shorelines, a significant drop in the river level (often 5 or 10 feet) usually occurs when the vegetation line drops noticeably.

2) Look for a *horizon line* running part way or completely across the river. The river will appear calm and glassy in front of this line and will seem like it disappears behind it for a fraction of a second. Foaming whitewater or rapids next to a horizon line extending partway across a river guarantees the existence of a ledge or similar drop-off there. Note the difference between a horizon line at a rapids (Example 8-1) and a horizon line at a hydraulic jump (Example 8-10).

3) Listen for the sound of cascading water in an otherwise calm section of river.

4) Indications of a hydraulic include nonexistent standing waves following a barely submerged obstacle in a moderate current and pieces of driftwood that disappear underwater for a few seconds, reappear again a short ways downstream, and then drift back upstream again in cyclic fashion. These two signs are best observed when scouting a rapids from shore.

5) Dancing white waves just downstream from a glossy section of water indicates a sharp drop and a possible hydraulic.

Miscellaneous Obstacles

Rock gardens are mazes of above-water rocks common in rapids at low water levels. The greatest problem associated with them is the time and care needed to maneuver around and between the obstacles in them.

Riffles are very small waves that indicate shallow water and the chance that you'll have to walk or wade your canoe.

Diagonal bars are gravel bars running diagonally across a river. It's best to paddle parallel to the current through them, even though your canoe may be perpendicular to the shore or to the main current when doing this (Example 8-11).

Be on the lookout for *fences* running across smaller streams in ranching and farming country. Some will be marked with colored rags, surveyor's tape, or signs, while others will not. A rare few could be electrified.

Always portage your canoe around *low bridges* and *drainage culverts*. They frequently contain debris and obstructions you can't see from outside.

Be careful when paddling near *bridge abutments*, *fill areas*, *dams*, and other developed areas. It's easy to wrap a canoe around a bridge pillar in moving water, and the river bottom near these obstacles often contains a jumble of sharp concrete blocks, railroad ties, metal posts, and similar deathtraps.

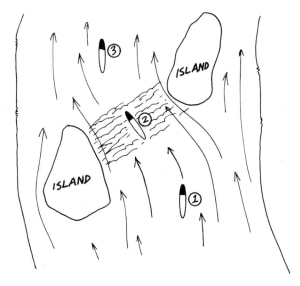

Example 8-11: Paddling parallel to the current over a diagonal bar.

Boils are regions of foaming water with a flowery, bubbly generally flat surface appearance. They warrant some caution since your paddle will grip less in their aerated water and because of their tricky currents. Be extra careful when paddling through the deep, white, violently bubbling foam you see in the midst of rough water, since it contains so much air that your canoe, your paddling strokes, and your braces will have little support there.

Trees submerged in a river or hanging low over it from shore are extremely dangerous. When you hit other obstacles like rocks there's a good chance the current will push your canoe off them as it rebounds from them or that your boat will bounce off them after a collision, but when you hit a downed tree the current can pin you to it while it freely goes through. For this reason trees floating or submerged in the water or hanging over it from shore are called *sweepers* or *strainers*. It's extremely difficult to extricate yourself when pinned against a tree or logjam because there's nothing solid to hold onto and because you simply can't let the river carry you away from the problem as you always can do when you hit a rock. For safety, always steer wide around these obstacles and be especially on the lookout for them around river bends and in front of bridge abutments.

You may occasionally have to detour around a commercial or private *fish trap* or *weir*, partway or completely across a stream. These obstacles vary in design from simple piles of rocks that channel fish into boxes placed in the stream to major wood and metal contraptions. Recognizing and avoiding them is usually not difficult.

OBSTACLES AND WATER LEVELS

Now that you know the basic obstacles confronting you in moving water, you should get a feeling for how they vary with changes in a river's depth and current. Figure A of Example 8-12 portrays two cross-sections of a large rock completely submerged in water of equal depth. In the left column, the current is relatively slow and in the right column the current is relatively fast. Canoeing over the rock in both Figure Aa and Ab is simple because the rock is so far below the water's surface. Note that the rock causes virtually no surface disturbance in fast water and absolutely no disturbance in the slower current.

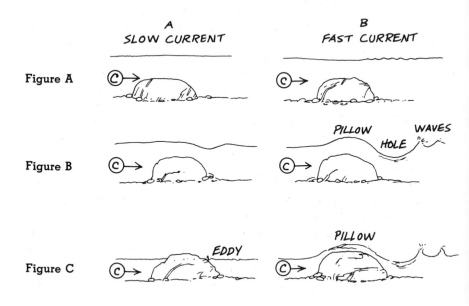

Example 8-12: The same obstacle at different water levels and current speeds.

In the second row of Example 8-12 illustrations, the water level is noticeably lower (Figures Ba and Bb). Note that in this case the rock causes a slight surface disturbance in slow water and a much more pronounced one in faster water. Also, note that the disturbance appears farther downstream behind the rock in the faster current. These two concepts, the amount of surface disturbance and the distance it occurs downstream behind an obstacle, are the major indicators of whether or not you can safely float over a submerged obstacle without hitting it. This is a complicated thing to understand, however, because they depend on the river's speed, the size of the obstruction, and its depth below the surface, all of which vary greatly and independently of each other. Two extremes are useful for comparison. A rock located an inch below the surface will cause *no* surface disturbance in calm water (these are called *sleeper* rocks), while an identical rock can cause a large disturbance in very fast, moderately deep water. Frequently comparing the depth of rocks below the surface, their size, the disturbances they cause, and the current's speed is the best way to become proficient at this complicated river reading skill.

In the third row of Example 8-12's illustrations (Figures Ca and Cb), the water level is even lower. The rock sticks above the surface of the slower water and creates an obvious though short (due to the slow water) two-dimensional eddy behind it. The rock in the fast current is submerged, though, because gravity pulls the upstream water into it and forces some over it. This creates a *pillow* of water above the rock which indicates an obstruction.

A HELPFUL RIVER READING TIP

By now you should have a basic understanding of how to read a river and some appreciation for how the features in a river change with varying water levels and currents. The next thing you should do is take this guide outdoors and practice reading an actual rapids with it. At first you'll probably be quite confused, because it will seem like just a confusing mixture of foaming whitewater. Don't let the length, width, or apparent complexity of a rapids intimidate you, though. Study one small section of rough water at a time and you'll soon be able to identify the features discussed in this chapter with ease.

Study a rapids from all possible angles and distances to get the best perspective of it. Observe it from upstream, since this is the way you'll have to approach it when paddling through it. Study it from the side along the shore to determine the size of its waves, the depth of its holes, and the height of its drops. Looking upstream at a rapids is particularly helpful for identifying ledges, drop-offs, and pillow rocks in it. Finally, you can usually get a good perspective of entire routes through rapids when looking down on them from a bridge or a hillside.

9

RIVER CANOEING

Being somewhat scared or uneasy when in moving water is a *healthy* feeling, especially if you're a beginning canoeist. Having no respect for the power of moving water (see Chapter 12) is one of the fastest ways to get in trouble on a river. However, there's a big difference between respecting a river and being totally frightened of it. River canoeing is a safe sport, especially when you follow the standard safety precautions stressed throughout this book. Injuries, damaged equipment, and survival situations are very rare and usually occur to those not prepared for them.

If you're a beginning canoeist, you need to eliminate your unwarranted fears of whitewater canoeing and cultivate a healthy respect for the real dangers that await you on a river. Learn to "feel" the water under and through your canoe. Think of yourself as floating *in* the water and not *on* it. Get used to the stability your canoe offers by practicing just how far you can lean it in a river current and how much weight a brace will support. Practice the strokes discussed previously and the whitewater maneuvers explained in this chapter. Get used to the feeling of going overboard, of swimming in cold water, and of swimming with your life jacket on through rapids. Be prepared for all possible emergencies. A river is your friend if you understand it and are prepared for its challenges, but it's unforgiving when you make a mistake.

GENERAL SAFETY GUIDELINES

A list of important safety precautions for river canoeing follows:

1) A minimum of three canoes is required for safety in whitewater. In case one canoe gets "hung up" on an obstacle or capsizes, other canoeists are nearby who can help rescue swimmers and retrieve abandoned equipment. Canoeing alone through rapids is asking for trouble. If you do canoe

alone in whitewater, may luck ride as your bowman, danger lie in your wake, and wisdom be your reward for attempting such a foolish venture.

2) A *lead canoe* should be the first canoe and a *sweep canoe* the last canoe in your group. Experienced paddlers familiar with the river should be in the lead canoe, while experienced paddlers trained in first aid and rescue techniques should follow in the sweep boat. Both canoes should contain rescue equipment like a first aid kit and throw lines so the lead canoe can help anyone who capsizes and floats down through a rapids, while the sweep canoe can help anyone with problems farther upstream. It's imperative that all other paddlers stay between the lead and sweep canoes at all times and that everyone in your group understands this before entering the water. Nothing's more scary than watching a boatload of beginners go paddling downstream out of sight, while the lead canoe waits to be sure everyone safely negotiates a set of rapids.

On long stretches of flat water, it's okay if everyone on your trip paddles together as a group for conversation, but the lead and sweep canoes must not forget their *responsibility* for being sure no one is in front of them or behind them respectively. They can keep those responsibilities even though they don't maintain the exact first or last positions in the group. Likewise, the other boaters should not flaunt this more relaxed atmosphere on calm sections by wandering downstream or delaying upstream from the group as a whole. When paddling in moving water, though, the lead canoe must be the first canoe and the sweep canoe must be the last canoe in position as well as in title.

3) Canoeists should use prearranged paddle signals in rapids to help following boaters avoid obstacles not seen from upstream of them or from the preliminary scouting trip on shore. Avoid verbal signals which are useless in violent, noisy rapids. Popular signals include "go left," "go right," "slow down— congestion ahead," and "trouble—head for shore."

4) Everyone in your group should closely watch the lead canoe's trip through rapids and alter their intended route as needed based on it. The paddlers in that lead canoe should signal the remaining boaters if they notice unusual dangers not observed earlier.

5) Canoes should follow each other at a respectable distance in rapids for maximum maneuverability and safety. Avoid situations involving several canoes in close formation bearing down on another one hung up on a rock in a narrow channel. A minimum of five to eight canoe lengths between boats is required in moderate rapids or narrow channels, assuming eddies and other sheltered spots exist throughout them. Canoes should run severe rapids one at a time for maximum safety. River traffic congestion will always occur above a set of rapids when paddlers are discussing possible routes and waiting their turn to go, and below them when waiting for the remaining boats to negotiate the rapids. By all means, avoid congestion in rapids themselves.

6) When paddling in moving water and especially around river bends, know who is in front and who is behind you at all times. Also, you are responsi-

ble for maintaining a comfortable distance between your canoe and the boat in *front* of you, and you must never let the canoe *behind* you get out of sight. Finally, always be ready to rescue anyone upstream or downstream near you if they capsize or get hung up on an obstacle. This is especially important when your group is strung out in a long set of rapids or when paddling on narrow, meandering streams.

7) Never carelessly paddle on a river you aren't absolutely sure is safe. You can have prior experience in a section of river, know its rating classification, and read a guidebook description of it to *get an idea* what to expect there, but the only way you'll know *for sure* it's safe for you to travel at your ability level is to proceed cautiously down it and scout all its rapids from shore. This is especially important on rivers greater than II in difficulty, on narrow streams where trees could have recently fallen into and blocked the channel, and on rivers with sharp bends obstructing your downstream vision. In general, the wider a river is, the lower its rating classification, the fewer bends it has, the lower its water level, the less gear you're carrying, the greater your experience, and the closer you are to civilization, the less you'll need to scout a set of rapids before running them.

8) Beginners should follow experienced canoeists through rapids so their inferior river reading skills won't hinder them as much. Also, they should paddle in the middle of a group of boaters so others are nearby who can help them when needed. Experienced paddlers should always accompany beginners on their first few river trips and should be paired with beginning canoeists in tandem canoes whenever possible.

9) It's a good idea to position several people with rescue lines on shore or in canoes sheltered in eddies in particularly difficult sections of rapids to help anyone in trouble there.

10) Never paddle past a point where you can safely land without knowing where the next downstream landing site is, and be sure you can negotiate the section of river between those landing areas without difficulty.

11) Be more cautious at the beginning of a set of rapids than near the end of them. If you capsize early in a rapids you'll have to deal with a long, potentially dangerous swim through or difficult rescue in them. Those problems are lessened considerably if you capsize near the end of a section of whitewater. Likewise, practice unfamiliar maneuvers like eddy hopping at the end of a rapids for greater safety.

12) Learn to identify a difficult section of rapids before actually getting to it on rivers you frequent. Reliable upstream landmarks include bridges, shoreline cliffs, side canyons, farms, and communities.

13) When beginning a trip, observe how the river's current, depth, and width interact at various places to determine the best route down the waterway. Also, study how the current, water depth, size of obstacles, and the disturbances they cause interact, since a good understanding of these factors will help you decide when you can safely pass over specific obstacles and when you should detour around them.

14) Be extra careful when running rapids in remote areas, physically tired, carrying nonswimmers or children, in a hurry to get to your destination, paddling in poor late afternoon light, in dangerous hypothermia conditions, in a fragile or valuable canoe, carrying cargo, and when few safe landing spots exist before, during, and after the rapids.

15) Avoid paddling in rapids you've seen others navigate, unless you're sure you can safely handle them *at your own ability level*. Prudence, not the quest for adventure, should dictate your actions in whitewater.

16) Don't advance yourself from one class of river to the next too quickly. It's best to paddle at least three or four trips on class I rivers before attempting more difficult class II ones, and to have plenty of boating experience under your belt before trying class III rivers. Most experts feel there's a surprisingly large gap between class II and class III water.

MAINTAINING YOUR HEADING

If you're just learning how to canoe, paddle easy class I rivers until you're familiar with the behavior of moving water and can maintain a constant heading because you'll never be able to avoid obstacles confronting you in difficult rapids if you can't keep on a set course. As you graduate to more challenging class II and III water, you must be able to respond faster and more decisively to deal with their obstacles without focusing on maintaining your heading in the process.

Having complete control of the course your canoe is taking is very important for efficient and safe river paddling. Unfortunately, one moment your canoe could be heading straight for your destination and during the next moment an unexpected river current could catch it and push it off course into an obstacle. *Drift* is the term that describes a canoe veering off course. You know you're drifting off course when two river obstructions or a river obstacle and a shore marker don't remain aligned (Example 9-1A), when submerged rocks don't pass under your boat parallel to its keel line (Example 9-1B), or when your heading sighting markers no longer line up with each other (Example 9-1C).

Example 9-2 illustrates how drift can play havoc with your river running plans if you're not careful. In Example 9-2A a canoe is headed directly for a rock, which is a safe distance away and is no cause for alarm. The sternman decides to detour to the right of it to avoid the large standing waves in the left channel. He makes course corrections in his strokes and continues paddling downstream, reasoning that the slight modifications in them will carry the canoe around the rock (a correct assumption in this case because of the large distance between the canoe and the rock—see below). In Example 9-2B the canoe is much closer to the rock. Now the bowman warns the sternman that there's a rock in front of them. The sternman responds by telling the bowman that they're going to the right of the rock and that he should draw in the bow while he pries in the stern to sideslip around it in that direction. In Example 9-2C the canoe is almost directly in front of the rock, despite their efforts to avoid it.

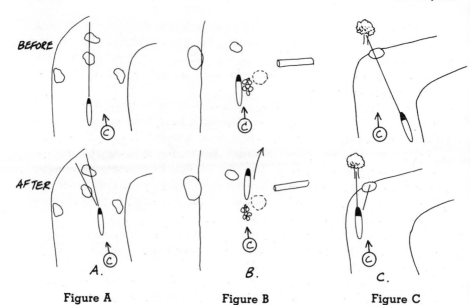

Figure A   Figure B   Figure C

Example 9-1: Ways to detect drift. Two river obstacles no longer remain in line with each other (Figure A). Underwater rocks don't pass parallel to your keel line (Figure B). Your heading reference points no longer line up (Figure C).

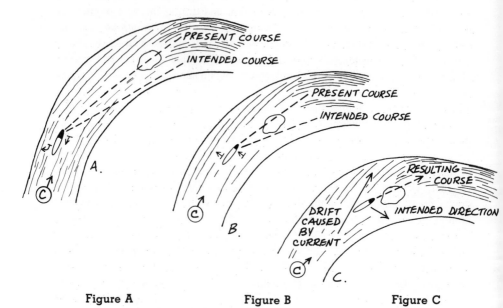

Figure A   Figure B   Figure C

Example 9-2: How drift can affect your river-running plans.

We'll stop here with this illustration because the point of this discussion has already been made. No matter how hard the two people tried to get to the right side of the rock, the current was pushing their canoe to the left of it towards the outside of the bend. While they were working to get to one side of the rock, they were drifting towards the other side of it in the strong current.

In summary, almost every time you're faced with an obstruction in your path on a river, you'll have to deal with drift. In very few cases can you simply steer your canoe around the obstacle without regard for the current. Drift is an especially challenging problem around river bends, at the junction of two streams, at the junction and separation of two river channels, and near major river obstacles like boulders and gravel bars.

MANEUVERING TECHNIQUES

In difficult water you must maneuver your canoe around and between obstacles, instead of simply selecting a channel through them and maintaining your course in that channel. The next sections describe common techniques for doing this.

Speed

The slower you travel through a set of rapids, the more time you'll have to choose a route through them and the less chance you'll have of swamping in large waves. However, going slow is not always the best way to negotiate rough water. You'll need speed to punch through holes, perform eddy turns effectively, and scrape over obstacles and gravel bars without sticking to them. You should become skilled at quickly varying your speed as needed in rough water to negotiate around or over the hazards confronting you there. For example, backpaddle through standing waves to slow down and prevent swamping, but then immediately afterwards charge forward to aggressively eddy turn.

Some people claim that you must go faster or slower than the current for maximum maneuverability, but this isn't entirely correct. True, *passive strokes* like the rudder need forward speed to be effective, but *power strokes* like the forward or draw work well no matter how fast or slow you're traveling and these are the ones you'll use most often in rough water. Thus, your maneuverability in rapids depends much more on which strokes you use than on how fast you travel.

Power paddling (Example 9-12) is forcefully charging through rapids with your canoe out of alignment to the current, as needed. Generally this technique is useful only when wide distances separate obstacles because it reduces the time you have available to avoid them and only when the waves confronting you are mild to prevent swamping.

Steering

One of the most important things to understand about canoeing on a river is that you should keep your canoe lined up with its current (almost) all the time for greater control of it and so less of it is exposed to downstream obstructions. You can have up to seven times more canoe area exposed to obstacles when traveling across a river than when traveling with your canoe in line with its current. The few exceptions to this rule include ferrying and eddy turning which are specifically discussed later.

Example 9-3A illustrates a common way to maneuver around an obstacle on flat water. In it, the sternman emphasizes and ignores the hook on the end of his J stroke to turn the boat while it travels forward. Example 9-3B depicts what could happen if you tried the same method in a river. In this case, the river's current carries the canoe into the obstacle even though the canoeists paddled just as hard as in the previous drawing. Example 9-3C illustrates the proper way to detour around a nearby obstacle in your path in moving water. Here the bowman pries (or draws) and the sternman draws (or pries), which slides the canoe sideways across the river so its keel remains parallel to the current. On moving water, paddling forward toward an obstacle reduces the time you have to avoid it, and steering around it instead of positioning your canoe around it as just described increases the canoe's exposure to the obstacle and the chance of hitting it.

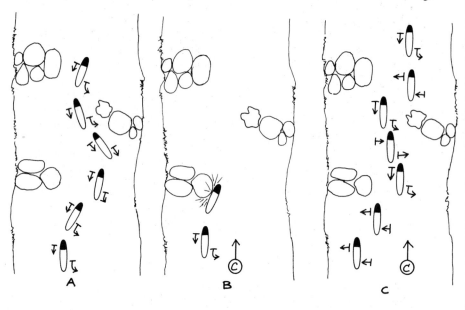

Figure A   Figure B   Figure C

Example 9-3: Avoiding an obstacle. Steering in flat water (Figure A), steering in moving water (Figure B), and positioning your canoe with the parallel sideslip method (Figure C).

In summary then, when paddling in moving water you *position* your canoe around an obstacle as often as possible instead of *steering* around it. Here positioning is defined as moving a canoe sideways across the river with its keel remaining parallel to the current. Parallel sideslipping (illustrated above) and back ferrying are the two most powerful ways to position your canoe in a river, and both are explained in detail below. Steering, on the other hand, is defined as turning a canoe with stern course correction strokes. This is only useful in moving water when you have *plenty of distance* between your canoe and an obstacle.

Before proceeding with our discussion of running rivers, there's a point about steering a canoe you should know. While I've stressed keeping your canoe lined up with the current throughout this section because it's an extremely important whitewater principle, some experienced boaters recommend *not* paddling through rapids with your keel line parallel to the current to improve the sternman's visibility. You'll have to decide if greater stern visibility is worth the risk of exposing more of your canoe's hull to oncoming obstacles. In tricky rapids, you may want to move your stern out of alignment with the current as needed for visibility but then quickly align it again for greater safety.

Sideslipping

Parallel sideslipping (Example 9-3) is one of the safest ways to detour around a nearby downstream obstacle. This involves using turning strokes simultaneously in the bow and the stern so the canoe moves across the river while its keel line remains parallel to its current. For example, if the bowman draws and the sternman pries, a canoe will move sideways across a river and yet remain in line with the current as desired. As a word of caution, the person drawing tends to overpower the person prying, and this could move the canoe out of alignment with the current if you're not careful.

Sideslipping is a very powerful technique to use when making an emergency detour around a rock directly in front of you (Example 9-4). In Example 9-4A, a canoe is bearing down on an unseen obstacle directly in its path. Suddenly the bowman notices it and instinctively draws to avoid it (Example 9-4B). The sternman immediately reacts to the bowman's actions by prying the stern around to keep the canoe lined up with the current (Example 9-4C). In that instant, the canoe slid a foot or two sideways through the water and avoided the rock. With practice, this maneuver becomes second nature and requires no communication between partners. The bowman either draws, pries, or crossdraws, depending on which side of the rock he thinks is the best way to go. Then the sternman draws if the bowman pries or crossdraws, and pries if he draws to keep the canoe parallel to the current.

Backpaddling

Backpaddling means paddling with a back stroke to delay your forward progress down a river. Unlike back ferrying (see page 193), it has no horizontal component that moves you sideways across the waterway. Backpaddling is useful in large waves where you must reduce your speed to prevent swamping, when

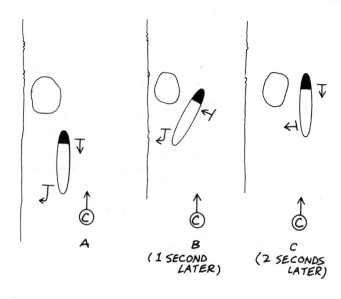

Figure A   Figure B   Figure C

Example 9-4: Emergency sideslipping to avoid an obstacle.

improvising your route through difficult rapids or in a fast current, and when delaying your progress down a set of rapids to give the boat in front of you more room. In addition, if a collision with an obstacle is imminent and unavoidable, backpaddling until you hit it will soften the blow and could prevent significant damage to your canoe.

Ferrying

A *ferry* is one of the most important maneuvers used when river canoeing. When ferrying, your canoe travels directly across a river without drifting down it; whereas, when sideslipping your strokes propel you across a river while the current carries you downstream. Ferrying is useful when maneuvering from the end of one chute to the beginning of another one in intricate rapids, when positioning your canoe in the correct channel to begin a set of rapids, when eddy hopping (see below), when trying to reach a landing area abreast of you, and as an emergency maneuver to avoid an obstacle directly downstream from your canoe. It's also useful for counteracting drift and maintaining a constant position on the inside of river bends to avoid rough waves on the outsides of them.

When ferrying, select a shoreline reference point and angle your canoe into the current just enough so that your strokes both propel it sideways across the river towards that point and counteract the current's tendency to carry you downstream. In other words, the faster a river's current is, the smaller your *ferrying angle* (Example 9-5) must be, and the slower the current the larger this angle must be. This means that when ferrying across a fast river, most of your

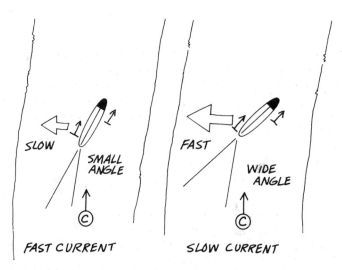

Example 9-5: The relationship between ferrying angle, current, and traveling speed.

energy is needed to fight the current, so only a small amount of it propels you across the river and a relatively large amount of time is needed to traverse it. Conversely, when ferrying across a slow river, only a little energy is required to negate the current so most of your energy propels you across it and you need a relatively short amount of time to travel to the other side. Unless the current is very slow and the river contains few obstacles, try to keep your ferrying angle smaller than 30–45° to reduce the chance of broaching in the current and broadsiding into a rock.

Note that the ferrying angle is the angle of the upstream end of the boat with respect to the current, not the shoreline. While selecting and maintaining a proper ferrying angle is difficult but fairly straightforward in a river with uniform current lines, it can be quite challenging in the midst of a rapid or a river bend where the current lines are not constant and usually don't point directly upstream.

There are two ways to ferry your canoe. A *back ferry* is performed by backpaddling with your stern pointing off-angle upstream (Example 9-6). In this maneuver, the bowman paddles a pure backstroke while the sternman blends draws, pries, and diagonal backstrokes with pure backstrokes to maintain the proper ferrying angle. This maneuver is somewhat difficult to do since the sternman must keep looking over his shoulder to see where he's going and since he's in an awkward, backward position to steer the canoe and set its course. Several uses of backferrying are illustrated in Example 9-7. Note that backferrying to avoid a nearby downstream obstacle (Example 9-7A) is often safer than parallel sideslipping around it in fast water since it delays your progress down the river as well as moves you sideways in it.

A *forward ferry* (Example 9-6) is more powerful and easier to perform than a back ferry since you're in the stronger, more comfortable forward paddling

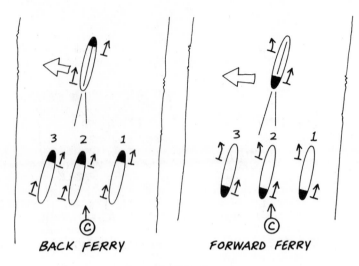

Example 9-6: Ferrying.

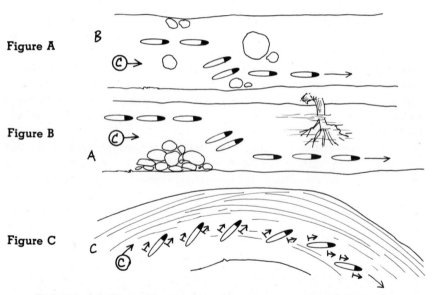

Example 9-7: Several examples of backferrying. To avoid an obstacle (Figure A). To reposition your canoe in a different channel (Figure B). To stay on the safer inside bend of a river (Figure C).

position and you travel bow first so you can see where you're going. In fact, solo paddlers frequently prefer forward and not back ferrying because of the greater power available to them with it. While forward ferrying is useful when crossing a river from one side to another or when hopping from one eddy to another, it's almost useless for avoiding obstacles or when traveling downstream, since you'll have to turn your canoe around so its bow points upstream into the current to do it properly, and then you must turn your canoe around again before continuing downstream through the rest of the rapids. When forward ferrying, the bowman should only paddle forward strokes, while the sternman should paddle forward and course correction strokes as needed to maintain the proper ferrying angle. Also, the stern paddler will have more power available to him and can better regulate the force of the current on the boat if he paddles on its downstream side during this maneuver.

Switching Sides

Occasionally partners should consider switching paddling sides for greater turning power and boat control when maneuvering around an obstacle in rough water. This concept is illustrated in Example 9-8. In Example 9-8A a canoe needs to make a particularly sharp turn around a dangerous ledge at the bottom of an intricate rapids. There are two ways to do this. In Example 9-8B both paddlers approach the ledge with strong forward strokes using the power paddling technique described earlier (to round the ledge before the current sweeps them into it). Then, they both simultaneously draw to pivot the canoe around and into the chute. The dangers with this method are that the stern will drift into the ledge because it didn't swing around in time or that the boat will broach because it continued to pivot around after making the turn. The second method is illustrated next. In Example 9-8C the paddlers approach the ledge with strong forward strokes as before. Then, just before turning, they quickly and simultaneously switch sides so the sternman can paddle on the inside of the upcoming turn. At the precise moment the canoe must pivot around into the chute, the bowman continues his forward strokes while the sternman vigorously applies a stern rudder. If done properly, the canoe will cleanly pivot around and into the chute with the sternman's rudder fully controlling its heading.

As a reminder from Chapter 6, you should only switch paddling sides when truly needed. Beginners tend to switch sides far too often to compensate for their weak course correction strokes and poor maneuvering techniques.

Eddy Turns

An eddy is one of the safest places to be on a river, and an *eddy turn* is the maneuver you use to get there. Because the ability to perform an eddy turn quickly, instinctively, and with confidence is extremely important in whitewater, you should practice this technique often until it becomes second nature to you. There are two ways to eddy turn:

1) *The backpaddling method.* With this technique you paddle your canoe slightly downstream of an obstruction and then backpaddle upstream into the eddy behind it. Backpaddling into an eddy is satisfactory in mild water but useless in crashing rapids because its strong current can easily overpower your inherently weak back stroke. While this method is safer than the leaning and

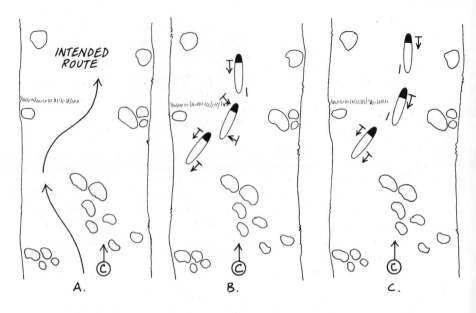

INTENDED
ROUTE

Figure A   Figure B   Figure C

Example 9-8: Switching paddling sides for greater turning leverage. Overall view (Figure A), standard pivot turn (Figure B), and switching sides before pivoting (Figure C).

bracing technique that follows, experienced paddlers familiar with that maneuver greatly prefer it because of its reliability in rough water. In fact, backpaddling eddy turns are performed so infrequently that the words "eddy turn" imply the lean and brace method described next.

2) *The lean and brace method.* This technique requires lots of practice but is so useful in rapids that you should be familiar with it before paddling class II water and must master it before canoeing on class III rivers. This method may appear complicated at first, but it will begin to fall in place if you closely study the following procedures and then practice them frequently on a river. Eddy turns for tandem canoes are explained in detail first, and then a section describing solo eddy turns follows.

Before learning the procedural details of a lean-and-brace eddy turn, you should understand the principles behind why they work. As explained in Chapter 8, there's a downstream current in a river's flow and an upstream current behind above-water obstructions in it. This current differential is precisely what makes lean-and-brace eddy turns so effective. In Example 9-9A, a canoe is traveling down a river near an eddy. At this point, the river's downstream current and the boaters' paddling strokes are the only forces acting on it. Example 9-9B portrays that canoe after its bow sliced through the eddy line. Notice that as soon as this

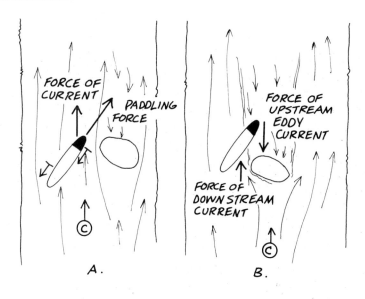

Figure A   Figure B

Example 9-9: The mechanics of an eddy turn.

happens, the current in the eddy tries to push it upstream while the main current continues driving the rest of the boat downstream. (The paddling force is now negligible, as you'll soon find out.) When properly positioned as shown in Example 9-9B, a canoe will actually pivot around with little help from the paddlers, and the greater the current differential, the quicker and more effortless this turning effect will be! Thus, when performing a lean-and-brace eddy turn, you should be primarily concerned with maintaining a proper entry angle, leaning and bracing the boat so it doesn't capsize, holding the boat in position relative to the obstacle as it swings around, and propelling it into the eddy when aligned with the current behind it. The current differential will turn your boat around into the eddy with little assistance from you.

When performing this kind of eddy turn, it's imperative that you lean and brace on the *inside* of each turn to compensate for the canoe's tendency to roll to the *outside* of it. The greater the current differential, the greater you'll have to lean the boat and the more weight you must put on your braces to support that lean. This leaning technique can be confusing, especially since it's popularly described in several different ways. Many people believe it's easiest to remember to lean into each turn (as described above and below), just as if you were riding a bicycle around a corner or skiing down a mountain. Describing this lean as a downstream or upstream one can be confusing since the water is going downstream in the main channel and upstream in the eddy and your boat is in both currents at the same time for much of the turn.

The four aspects of a lean-and-brace eddy turn are now described.

a) Entering an eddy—bowman's paddling side is next to the obstruction.

Procedure:

1) Initially you should be upstream from the obstruction causing the eddy and forward paddling towards a point slightly downstream from it at about a 30° angle to the river's main current.

   Your goal is to drive the bow through the eddy line close to the obstruction so you can use the strong current differential there and so you'll have maximum use of the eddy's length for maneuvering.

2) As soon as the bow pierces the eddy line, the bowman plants his paddle in a high brace far out from the canoe *in the upstream current behind the obstacle*, *leans hard on it*, and *leans the canoe into the turn*. As soon as this is done, the canoe should begin pivoting sharply around his paddle blade (Example 9-10A).

   Simultaneously, the sternman performs a forward sweep to initiate the turn and propel the canoe into the eddy.

3) The sternman paddles forward to drive the canoe into the eddy, while the bowman maintains his brace until the canoe finishes its arc and then forward paddles as needed until the boat is safely behind the obstruction.

   As soon as the stern crosses the eddy line, the canoe will tend to roll to the outside of the turn. The sternman should briefly use a low brace as needed to control this rolling action.

b) Entering an eddy—bowman's paddling side is away from the obstruction.

Procedure:

1) Identical to #1 in Method a) above.

2) As soon as the bow pierces the eddy line, the bowman plants a cross draw away from the canoe and *in the eddy's upstream current*, while the sternman pries to initiate the turn and then *leans hard to the inside of it* and braces for stability (Example 9-10B).

   Entering an eddy with the bowman's paddling side away from the obstacle is somewhat more difficult because the sternman can't propel it into the eddy.

3) After the canoe completes its turn or when it begins to stall, the bowman forward paddles or forward sweeps as needed and the sternman forward paddles to propel the canoe up to the obstacle.

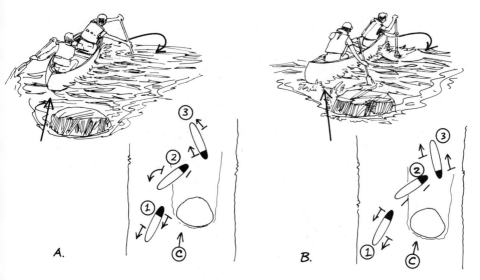

Figure A   Figure B

Example 9-10: Entering an eddy with the lean and brace technique.

Note that the sternman may have to high brace to keep the boat from rolling to the outside of the turn after its stern enters the eddy.

c) Leaving an eddy—bowman's paddling side is away from the obstruction.

Procedure:

1) Initially your canoe should be motionless and facing upstream in the eddy and parallel to the river's main current.

2) The bowman does a diagonal draw to angle the bow off-center and then forward paddles, while the sternman forward sweeps to nudge the bow out of the eddy and help initiate the turn.

   Cut the eddy line at about a 30° angle and with some speed for a more responsive turn.

3) Very soon after the bow cuts the eddy line, the bowman high braces *in the river's main downstream current* and *leans the canoe strongly into the turn* (Example 9-11A).

   Meanwhile the sternman forward or forward sweeps to move the canoe out into the main current and then low braces as needed for stability.

4) This maneuver ends when the canoe is parallel to the main current. Then the bowman forward paddles while the sternman braces as needed to offset the canoe's tendency to roll to the outside of the turn.

d) Leaving an eddy—bowman's paddling side is next to the obstruction

Procedure:

1) Identical to #1 in Method c) above.

2) The bowman pries to angle the canoe off-center, and then both canoeists forward paddle to propel the bow out of the eddy.

   Cut the eddy line at about a 30° angle and with some speed for a more responsive turn.

3) Very soon after the bow cuts the eddy line, the bowman cross-draws *in the main downstream current* (Example 9-11B).

   Meanwhile the sternman forward paddles a little more to propel the canoe out of the eddy and then braces in a *strong, stabilizing lean into the turn*.

4) Finally, the bowman resumes forward paddling and the sternman braces and draws as needed to offset the canoe's tendency to roll to the outside of the turn.

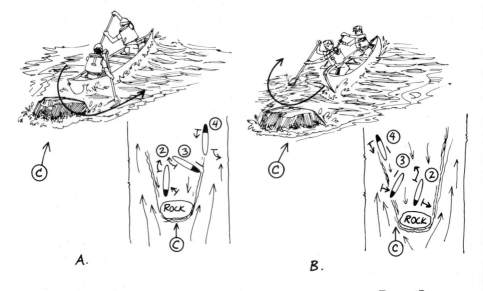

Figure A   **Figure B**

Example 9-11: Leaving an eddy with the lean and brace method.

Solo eddy turns are similar in principle to those just described for tandem canoes. For example, concepts like cutting the eddy line close to the obstacle when entering the eddy and leaning into the turn are the same in both cases. When solo canoeing, though, you should drive your canoe a little farther and harder into or out of an eddy before initiating the turn, and you should paddle on the inside of it so you can use the strong high brace stroke instead of the weaker cross-draw. Don't hesitate to switch paddling sides, if necessary, before performing a solo eddy turn.

Eddy hopping (Example 9-12), or maneuvering downstream from eddy to eddy, is an advanced technique useful for working your way down a difficult rapids, when positioning your canoe in different river channels, and when carefully navigating a waterway that was difficult or impossible to scout from shore. If you're a beginning canoeist, you can practice eddy hopping on easy rivers by *eddying in* (entering an eddy) and *peeling out* (leaving an eddy) behind every obstacle along your route.

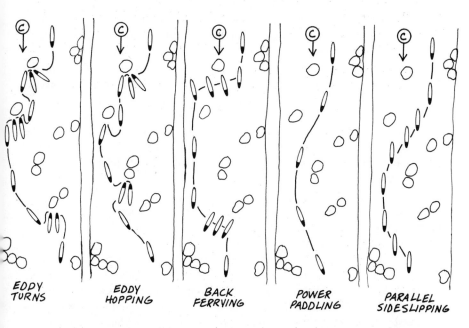

EDDY TURNS   EDDY HOPPING   BACK FERRVING   POWER PADDLING   PARALLEL SIDESLIPPING

Example 9-12: Comparison of downstream river running maneuvers. Each boat symbol in the drawings represents the location of a canoe at five-second intervals.

Surfing

Surfing is the art of riding a wave with your canoe. This is more of a recreational pastime than a technical whitewater canoeing maneuver, although skilled paddlers can use it instead of a forward ferry to travel across a rapids. To surf on a wave, position your bow at its base and pointing into the current as if beginning a forward ferry. Then paddle up onto the wave with a slight ferrying angle until you feel the canoe balance on its crest. The faster the current and the higher the wave, the smaller this angle should be. From the balanced position on the wave, you can easily travel sideways with a few properly placed strokes.

When surfing, always be ready to lean and brace downstream in case your angle isn't correct or in case you overshoot the wave, and be sure you have a clear channel below you so you don't crash into a downstream obstacle if you make a mistake and lose control of the canoe.

AVOIDING MAJOR OBSTACLES

Scouting Rapids

Scouting means studying rapids before actually traveling through them. For safety, scout any rapids you aren't definitely sure are navigable at your ability level. Avoid relying entirely on guidebook or difficulty ratings, since river conditions fluctuate widely with changing water levels. Often you can scout rapids on mild rivers from a canoe positioned just upstream of them. Having one person in a tandem canoe stand up at his paddling position helps with this. Rapids around a blind turn, in a narrow canyon, with few safe landing places, on some class II, and on almost all class III or greater rivers, must be scouted from shore. To do this properly, land your canoe a safe distance upstream from the rapids so you'll have the time to position it in the proper channel after scouting them. Then hike downstream along the shore as far as necessary to get a clear, closeup view of every part of the rapids and of the river below them. Many boaters ignore this latter point in their haste to run the river.

Dangerous river obstructions, like trees, keeper holes, dams, and drop-offs, are the first things to look for when scouting a rapids. Consider portaging around these specific dangers or around the entire set of rapids if you can't keep your canoe far away from them.

Safe landings are the second things to look for when scouting a rapids. Always be sure there's a calm section of water below a rapids and several reliable landing places like eddies in the middle of them where you can wait for the remainder of your group, rescue people and gear that capsized upstream, pause for a rest before proceeding, and bail shipped water out of your boat. Canoeing through interconnected sets of moderate or difficult rapids with no intermittent landing spots in them is extremely dangerous.

Finally, look for runnable *river channels* extending the length of the rapids. There are two ways to do this (Example 9-13). You can select and follow a *direct line* through rapids if they're relatively short and contain comparatively few obstacles. With this method you travel primarily downstream with little or no sideways maneuvering. When following an *indirect line* you maneuver back and forth across the river a great deal to run the best route through each section of whitewater. This is the method you'll probably have to use when negotiating long or difficult rapids.

When scouting, look for channels forming as direct a line as possible down a rapids. If it's not possible to run the rapids on a direct line, try to interconnect passageways so you have at least one clear—though indirect—path from the

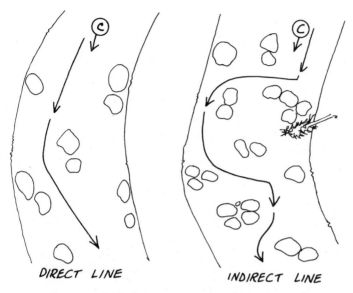

DIRECT LINE   INDIRECT LINE

Example 9-13: Selecting a route through rapids.

beginning to the end of them. As a last resort, try to find several separate routes you can connect by backpaddling, sideslipping, ferrying, or eddy hopping, if you're capable of performing those skills. If the rapids are long or difficult, draw a sketch map of the best route through them, mark major obstacles and landmarks on it, and fasten that to a canoe thwart before proceeding down the river. As a word of caution, routes you can identify on a scouting trip are often difficult to find when in a canoe careening through whitewater. Be especially careful to remember your route as if you were in a boat looking downstream at it from just above water level. Finally, station someone at particularly difficult places in a rapids to guide each canoe through there.

Lining a Canoe

If a section of river is too dangerous or too shallow to paddle, you'll have to either line your boat through it or portage around it. *Lining* is the process of using a rope to guide or pull a canoe up or down a waterway. (Technically, *lining* is guiding a boat downstream, and *tracking* is pulling it upstream.) Lining is useful on sections of rivers that are too dangerous or too shallow to run yet aren't so bad that they warrant a complete detour. Usually you can keep all your gear in a canoe when lining it through rapids, especially if they are short and relatively mild. However, don't hesitate to carry your cargo around and line your empty canoe through rougher whitewater or to portage all your equipment including the canoe around particularly dangerous rapids. Try to avoid lining a canoe in rivers with strong, unpredictable currents, numerous obstructions, overgrown shorelines, or steep banks, or when you have to risk getting hypothermia wading in the water near shore.

When lining a canoe, its upstream end must stick out into the river farther than its downstream end so the current can tighten the lines and keep it away from shore. Selecting and maintaining this *lining angle* requires much practice, though. You'll fight the current too much with a lining angle that's too large, yet one that's too small will let it readily swing your boat in towards shore and beach it. To complicate matters, this angle must be adjusted constantly as the canoe travels sections of rapids with varying currents. The faster the current, the smaller the angle you must use, and the angle must be in reference to the current affecting the upstream end of the boat, not the main river current or the shoreline. Typically, lining angles range from 15 to 45°.

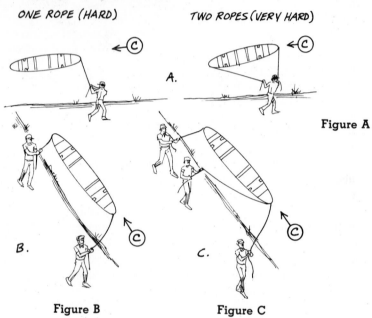

ONE ROPE (HARD)   TWO ROPES (VERY HARD)

A.

Figure A

B.

C.

Figure B   **Figure C**

Example 9-14: Lining a canoe. With one person (Figure A), with two people (Figure B), with three people (Figure C).

When lining a canoe, attach 20- to 40-foot sections of strong rope to its bow and stern painter attachments. For safety, never wrap a lining rope around your hand. If the canoe is suddenly caught in a fast current, it could pull you into the water and drag you downstream. By simply holding a small coil of rope in your hands you'll have better control over it and can let go of it immediately if the canoe pulls you off-balance. Lining a canoe with one person (Example 9-14A) is difficult to do in anything but ideal conditions. Lining with two people and two lines (Example 9-14B) gives far greater control over the canoe and added security in case you must release one line. For example, if you lose control of your lining angle and the canoe begins to broach, release the upstream line, let the boat swing to shore on the downstream line, and begin lining again with the ends of the boat reversed. Lining with three people and three lines (Example 9-14C) is useful when the rope controlling the lining angle must be passed around or over shoreline obstacles. With this method, the two lead people alternate control of the upstream end of the canoe as needed when detouring around obstructions so that one person is always in full control of the boat's lining angle.

Portaging

Portaging is the process of carrying your gear around an obstacle in a river or across a watershed divide. Because portaging is tiring and time consuming under ideal conditions and extremely slow and difficult in overgrown or hilly terrain, carrying a light complement of gear and being in top physical condition are important qualities to have before attempting it.

The process of portaging generally goes something like this. Scout a set of rapids as described above to determine if you can navigate them safely. If they're mild and have reliable landing spots during and below them, you can get back in your canoe and continue down the river on your journey. If they are more difficult, you can carry your gear around and paddle the boat through them unloaded, you can line your loaded canoe down the stream, or you can carry your gear around them and line the boat down empty. If the rapids are nasty, you should portage all your equipment around them for safety.

If you must carry equipment around the rapids and you did not land at a trailhead, spend some time looking for a trail or suitable portage location. Carrying gear cross country through an overgrown forest is not an enjoyable thing to do. Trails usually *contour* (stay as level as possible) around the inside of a bend or along the shore slightly away from the water. Even in wilderness areas, there's a good chance that a portage trail detours difficult rapids, since most waterways were used extensively by Indians, early explorers, and trappers.

Experienced boaters recommend hiking briefly along any "portage trail" you find to be sure it actually skirts the rapids. Many animal trails, old logging roads, and hiking paths parallel or bisect waterways, and you must be sure you don't get sidetracked on one of them by mistake. Also, hiking on a trail for a while without your gear gives you a chance to exercise your stiff, inactive leg muscles and to check and improve the trail's condition as needed. It's a good idea to mark any trail junctions you pass with sticks or rocks so you know which way to return. When planning to carry your canoe in an overhead carry, remember the location of a few trees with conveniently located horizontal branches you can use to prop the boat against and rest your shoulders. Finally, before portaging, consolidate all your gear in as few packs as possible to reduce the number of trips you'll need to make and cover yourself with insect repellent in infested areas to help preserve your sanity as you walk.

There are many ways to actually move equipment on a portage. Some people recommend carrying your gear first so you can look for and remove obstacles like downed trees before transporting the more awkward canoe. A boating crew can carry their canoe together and then return for their gear, or one person can carry the boat while his partner takes the gear if they are strong and are traveling light. Consider carrying the canoe first if you must make one more trip, so your partner can begin packing it again while you return with the remaining equipment. It's best to break a long portage up into several, shorter ones, for physical and psychological relief from your task, and camping in the middle of a long portage will make it seem more manageable. Some hardened solo travelers carry both their pack and canoe so they can complete a portage in one trip. They claim that supporting some of the canoe's weight on their pack helps transfer that load directly to their leg muscles for easier carrying. This method is best done on flat, smooth trails in fairly open terrain. Avoid it on steep, rocky, or undefined routes. Other people who are less physically fit allow one trip for their canoe and at least one or two trips for the rest of their gear.

When portaging heavy equipment like a canoe, walk with gentle, shock-absorbing steps and a slow, steady, comfortable pace, and rest as often as needed to avoid fatigue. Avoid hurrying or racing others in your group. Walk over obstacles like rocks and logs instead of stepping on and then over them, and be especially wary of low branches, slippery footing, and obstacles in your path. When portaging any distance at all, dry your feet and change into hiking boots for the most support and comfort.

Canoeing Upstream

You may have to travel upstream on occasions such as extended wilderness canoe trips. Lining or portaging your canoe may be the best way to do this in rough water, but in mild rapids or shallow water you may be able to wade or paddle it safely around obstacles. For maximum safety avoid wading in water deeper than your knees, and for maximum efficiency travel a route with the least current resistance. Try to stay near shore and on the inside of river bends where the current is slower, and stay in eddies where the current actually flows upstream. Poling is an excellent way to travel upstream in shallow water and is described in detail in Chapter 10.

AVOIDING COMMON OBSTRUCTIONS

Large Waves

Swamping (shipping excessive water over the gunwales) and *broaching* (turning perpendicular to the current) are the two primary dangers associated with canoeing through large waves. While skirting the edge of large waves or detouring around them altogether is safer than plowing through the middle of them, it will often be impossible to completely avoid these obstacles in whitewater. There are several ways to canoe through standing waves:

1) Backpaddling through waves helps prevent swamping but your canoe will flounder in the troughs between them or on their upstream sides if you paddle through them too slow.

2) Slightly quartering into haystacks at medium speed helps your bow ride over them easier but encourages broaching since your canoe is off-center in relation to the current.

3) Concentrating your weight in the center of a canoe helps lighten its bow and stern so they ride over waves easier. Unfortunately, this is impractical to do halfway through rapids, and it's inconvenient at best to paddle the length of a rapids with both you and your partner in an almost-amidships position.

4) Another, more difficult, strategy to use when canoeing in a series of standing waves is to maintain a slow speed when the bow is on the downhill, downstream side of each wave so it doesn't burrow into the following one, and then to paddle fiercely in the trough so it can climb over the next oncoming one. While this is great in theory, river waves often come at you so fast that it's hard to coordinate this method with your partner and with the oncoming waves.

5) Finally, you can simply enjoy a ride right down through the middle of them! Chances are you'll get a boatload full of water and may even capsize, but this isn't particularly dangerous when your gear is waterproofed and secured in your boat, the water is warm, the weather is comfortable, and a calm section of water awaits below the waves.

If your boat swamps in rapids, remain in it and paddle as necessary to keep it aligned with the current. Avoid jumping out of it, since you're far safer in it than swimming unprotected in the water. (Carol B., this paragraph is dedicated to you . . . and to those waves on the San Juan River!)

A Nearby Downstream Rock

If there's a rock or similar obstruction directly in your path, try to avoid it by backferrying or sideslipping and then canoeing in the chutes of water immediately to its left or right. If you're very close to a rock and have no time to sideslip around it, backpaddle to reduce your speed and then fend it off with your paddle. Though this is poor technique, it's better than risking getting stuck on the rock or being swept broadside into it. Immediately before you hit a rock, brace the canoe with your paddle blade on the water, the rock, or the river bottom to prevent tipping. Beginners tend to grab their canoe's gunwales for stability in a collision, but this is the worst possible thing to do since they offer no support from rolling over. Many times when a collision is imminent, all you have to do is brace the canoe enough so the water bouncing off the obstacle (called the *hydraulic cushion*) shields you from it and carries you downstream. Finally, if you do hit an obstacle, the current will try to push the upstream gunwale under water, so be prepared to aggressively lean and brace *downstream* to counteract this.

Snagged on a Rock

While just hitting an obstacle like a rock will usually damage nothing but your confidence and hurt only your pride, actually pinning a boat to one will scar your reputation and may even destroy your canoe. A canoe that's *pinned* to a rock is firmly stuck on it, and you must remove it as fast as possible to reduce the damage to it. As with everything else in life, an ounce of prevention is worth a pound of cure. The next several pages list ways to prevent a pin, while Chapters 11 and 12 describe its cure.

If your canoe hits a rock in a river, it could bounce off it, it could snag on it, or the current could swing it broadside and pin it there. General principles you and your boating partner should follow to free a stuck canoe are listed below. Exactly what you should do, of course, will vary with each situation.

1) *Brace* your paddle on the rock, the water, or the river bottom for support while the hydraulic cushion or the main current frees you, as described above. Holding onto a rock with your hands can work but is more dangerous.

2) *Lean downstream* to prevent the river from pouring into the exposed upstream end of the canoe. While leaning downstream often won't free your stuck canoe, it will definitely keep your predicament from getting worse.

3) If the obstruction is near your end of the canoe, quickly *hop out of the boat* onto it if it's large enough or place one foot on it if it's not. This will lighten the end of the canoe near the obstruction and help the current pivot the other end around it. Consider stepping into the water to free the stuck end of the canoe only if it's less than knee deep and then only on the *upstream* side of the boat.

4) *Use the water's force to help you* release your boat from the rock. For example, if the canoe's bow is stuck with its stern angled downstream, push the bow back upstream against the current. In this case, pulling the stern back upstream will be a lot more difficult because its larger area is exposed to the downstream current.

5) *Shift your weight* inside the canoe to lighten the part stuck on the obstacle. For example, if your stern is snagged on a rock, try freeing it by moving from the stern paddling position to amidships.

6) *Rock the canoe* back and forth to jiggle it free from the obstacle. Do this in unison with your partner for maximum effect.

The following paragraphs explain how to deal with specific collisions when traveling downstream in a bow-first canoe.

1) *If your bow sticks on an obstacle*, the current will try to pivot the stern around and position the canoe bow upstream behind or to the side of the obstacle. Sometimes this pivoting action will free the bow so the boat drifts downstream backwards and other times the current will capsize the canoe or broadside it into another nearby obstacle. The bowman should encourage this pivoting by standing on the obstacle, holding the bow deckplate, and swinging the canoe downstream into the eddy below the obstacle, if he thinks it will free the canoe without capsizing it and if there are no obstacles immediately downstream. If the bowman cannot stand on the obstacle, he should position himself in the river behind and downstream from it, push on the obstacle with his paddle, or shift his

weight amidships and then encourage, regulate, or restrict the pivoting as needed in his particular situation. The sternman should downstream brace throughout this maneuver for more stability.

2) *If your stern sticks on an obstacle*, the sternman should shift his weight amidships, hop out onto the obstacle, push off of it with his paddle, or stand in the water upstream of the canoe to free his end of it. Exactly what he does, of course, will depend on his particular situation. If possible, the sternman should then hold the deckplate or painter and swing the canoe into the eddy behind the obstacle where he can board again with ease. If the canoe drifts downstream again when freed, he should carefully but quickly leap into it before it drifts away. Meanwhile, the bowman steadies the canoe throughout this procedure as best he can with a downstream brace.

3) *If you broadside into an obstacle*, quickly lean downstream to prevent the river from pouring into the open end of the canoe. Then, try shifting your weight to the end of the boat most likely to float downstream, hopping out onto the obstacle to lighten one or both ends of it, and pushing, pulling, or lifting the canoe off the rock so it drifts downstream on the side with the most canoe length exposed to the downstream current.

Abandon your canoe and consider it pinned if you're in a dangerous, threatening situation or if you've tried the methods recommended here without success. Then return with a rescue party as quickly as possible to salvage it before the current tears it to shreds (see Chapter 12).

RIVER RUNNING SUGGESTIONS

Selecting a Route

Much of successful river canoeing depends on how good you are at selecting a safe, efficient course. General guidelines to help you do this follow:

1) *Approach river bends from the inside*. In rough water this gives you the options of staying on the inside of the bend where the water is shallower and slower, of heading for shore on the safer inside bend to scout any rapids, or of letting the current carry you to the faster and more treacherous outer side of the river if the rapids there aren't as bad as they initially appeared to be. Remember that once you're in the main, outer channel, it's hard to get out of it in an emergency. In calm water, cut your turns around river bends as sharp as possible to reduce the distance you'll have to paddle.

2) When possible, *follow the main channel* so you travel faster and with less effort to your destination. This is especially useful during periods of low water when you'll need extra depth to prevent grounding.

3) Always *keep parallel to the current* to reduce the chance of hitting an obstacle or broaching in large waves. Remember that the current and the shore often aren't parallel with each other.

4) If the river forks around an island, take the channel with the largest waves at low water levels, since they indicate the deepest channel. Also, the widest branch often (but not always) has the deepest water and fewest obstructions at low water levels. At normal or high water levels, take the channel that drops first so you're not surprised by a hidden ledge or rough whitewater on the far side of the island.

5) Hug the leeward shore to avoid winds. If you have a tailwind, however, get out in the middle of the river where it can best push you along.

Launching and Landing Sites

There are several things to keep in mind when launching or landing a canoe in a river:

1) When possible, pick a launching and landing area that's not overgrown, rocky, excessively shallow, or too small for your party. If possible, launch or land in areas with a clean, distinct flow. Stopping in a stagnant eddy can be depressing. In hot weather, try to launch or land at a suitable swimming hole. Always tie your canoe to an obstacle on land or pull it out of the water when going ashore so the current can't carry it away. Losing a canoe because you didn't secure it to the bank will surely tarnish your canoeing reputation and lighten your wallet.

2) Your downstream route away from a landing site should be well defined and free from threatening obstacles. Landing immediately above a rapids to scout them is rather foolish because you'll have a hard time positioning your canoe in a proper channel when you resume your trip.

3) On a windy day avoid landing at a beach because its sand will infiltrate your gear, lunch, hair, eyes, and clothes. In windy weather, seek sheltered landing areas behind landforms like peninsulas and islands.

4) Before beginning a river trip, remember a landmark like a bridge abutment or prominent beach upstream from your take-out location. Paddling back upstream to a take-out you ignorantly passed is tiring and embarrassing.

Odds and Ends

1) If an unpredictable current spins you around in a rapids, continue negotiating them backwards until you can enter a calm section or eddy and turn around again. Avoid turning around in the middle of a rapids to reduce the chance of broadsiding into an obstacle.

2) Both you and your partner may have to wade your canoe in shallow water, only one of you might wade while the other rides in slightly deeper water, or both of you can ride but will have to push off the bottom with your legs or paddles when there's enough water to float the canoe but not to paddle in it.

3) For safety, detour around low, overhanging tree limbs and brush near shore instead of paddling underneath them.

4) Never grab shoreline bushes to stop a moving canoe. Its momentum could pull you out of the boat and into the water. When pausing along the shore, feel free to hold onto bushes to keep your immobile canoe from drifting downstream though.

5) Always keep the inside of your canoe as dry as possible by cautiously paddling through large waves and emptying splashed water from it as soon as possible in or after a rapids. Water sloshing around in a boat makes it hard to maneuver, throws it off-balance when you lean or brace it, exaggerates its draft which increases the chance that you'll hit an obstacle, and threatens to soak your (hopefully waterproofed) gear.

6) Teamwork is extremely important when tandem canoeing on a river. Partners who don't coordinate their efforts require far more time and energy to navigate a section of river than people who do. The bowman must remember that the sternman is responsible for steering the boat, and he must refrain from altering its heading unless directed to do so. He may think the boat is drifting off-course but lacks the sternman's better reference position to know for sure. Likewise, the sternman must keep the boat on as safe and efficient a course as possible. It's frustrating to be a bowman in a boat that's zigzagging all over the water.

As soon as you begin a canoe trip in the stern, discuss what kind of verbal signals you will use to tell your bowman which way to turn in an emergency. For example, if you want to detour around a rock to your bowman's paddling side, you can either say "draw" or "right" ("left" if he's paddling on the left side of the boat). To go to the other side, you can either say "pry" or "left" ("right" if he's paddling on the left side of the boat). Beginners generally prefer the simpler direction signals, while experienced paddlers usually use the more instinctive "draw" or "pry" commands.

7) When approaching downstream fishermen, ask if it's okay to paddle through. When they wave you on, stay away from them so you don't scare their fish away. If they're in the middle of the stream, ask which way you should go around them before proceeding. Blindly charging downstream through a group of fishermen is one of the most inconsiderate things you can do in a canoe.

8) Paddle aggressively and with confidence in whitewater. Maneuvers like braces, eddy turns, and ferrying require a great deal of gusto to complete effectively. Leaning hard on a brace means extending your upper body *far* out over the water and putting *a lot* of weight on it.

9) If you're in a hurry, eat your lunch while floating down the river and not on shore. Let the current work for you while you relax.

RIVER RUNNING EXAMPLES

The next several pages illustrate true-life problems to help you develop your whitewater skills before actually going on a river. The first part of each example contains a sketch map of a set of rapids. Then descriptions explaining what to do in each case follow. Cases #4 and #5 illustrate how you can use various maneuvers to navigate a section of difficult whitewater and are included here without narrative comment. The symbols used throughout this problem section are described on page 126.

As you approach a river bend, you should observe how sharp the bend is, how great the current differential is between the inside and the outside of it, how steep the outside shoreline drops into the water, and the degree of vertical elevation loss in the river ahead. The greater each of these factors are, the greater the possibility that major rapids exist ahead, and the more you should position your canoe on the inside of the bend for safety. To simplify the following examples, let's assume you did this preliminary scouting from your canoe, actually scouted each rapids from shore first, are completely aware of every danger illustrated in the drawings, and are just beginning to journey through the rapids.

Case #1

In Position 1 you are entering the water after scouting the rapids from shore. At this point you should back-ferry your canoe in line with the channel you choose on your scouting trip before the current picks up speed.

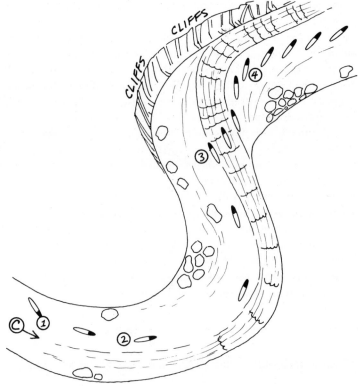

Example 9-15: River running problem—Case #1.

In general, it's best to position a canoe between the calm, shallow water inside the bend and the violent, swift water along its outer bank so you can either head into the faster, more dangerous current around the outside of the bend or retreat to the shallow water on its inside, as needed. In this case, however, it's best to completely avoid the large waves on the outside of the bend and stay in the calmer water inside it (Position 2), especially since no easily accessible landing area exists between this first bend and the dangerous second one.

The best thing to do when your boat is in Position 3 is to back-ferry across the main channel so you can hug the inside of the second bend and avoid the strong current driving into the steep cliff there. In cases like this, it's best to err on the cautious side by maneuvering to the inside of the bend fairly quickly after rounding the first turn and by positioning your canoe far to the inside of it.

In Position 4 you backpaddle to maintain your location on the inside of the bend. Remember, it's better to ground there than to get swept into the dangerous main channel and bash into the cliff.

You can position your canoe in the main channel again fairly quickly after the river straightens out to take advantage of the fast current and deep water there (Position 5). Be wary of standing waves in it for some distance downstream though.

Case #2

In Position 1 in this second example, you should be in a channel that you selected on your scouting trip. In this case the best initial channel is close to the right shore because of the dangerous sweeper tree on the left. If you landed on the left side of the river to scout for downstream obstacles, you should have ferried hard to move the canoe across most of the river. If, however, you landed on the right side of the river, you can simply hug that shore all the way around the bend for the greatest safety.

At Position 2 you should back-ferry as needed to maintain your position far to the right of the sweeper tree.

If you're paddling in warm weather, you can let your boat gradually slip into the main channel and enjoy the ride through the standing waves after passing the sweeper tree (Position 3a). If you're paddling in less optimum conditions where you can't risk a capsize, position your canoe more to the inside of the bend (Position 3b) where the water is calmer.

Finally, pick up the main current again (Position 4) as soon as you feel it's safe to do so to make use of its greater depth and speed.

Case #3

Again, maneuver into an appropriate channel (Position 1) after scouting the rapids, as described earlier. In this case, you must be careful not to pin a boat to one of the obstacles in the river, use extreme caution near the chute at the end of the rapids, and avoid grounding in the shallow region inside the bend.

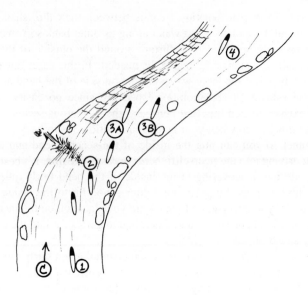

Example 9-16: River running problem—Case #2.

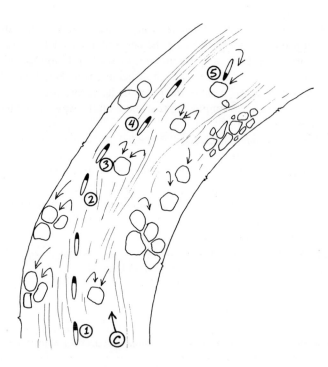

Example 9-17: River running problem—Case #3.

Assuming you're canoeing in ideal conditions and prefer a challenging route, position your canoe (Position 2) so you can follow the predominant current all the way through the rapids. Eddy-turn as often as necessary when doing this to maintain control of your canoe, plan your downstream route, and empty splashed water out of the boat.

Position 3 is your last chance to eddy in to rest, bail splashed water out of your boat, or realign your canoe with the current.

Keep your canoe as parallel as possible to the current when immediately upstream, in Position 4, and downstream from the chute to prevent being swept into the obstacles forming it and to keep from broaching in the standing waves there.

Eddy out below the chute (Position 5) to bail out your canoe, to wait for the rest of your group, and to offer assistance to anyone in trouble in the rapids.

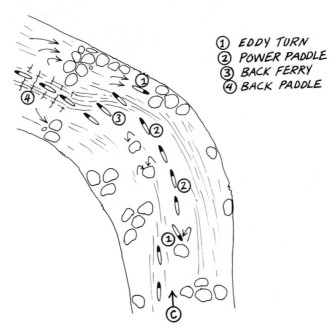

Example 9-18: River running problem—Case #4.

A WORD OF CAUTION FOR THE CAREFREE BOATER

A river is a beautiful and magical thing, especially when you're floating down it through pretty countryside, but it can quickly turn into a ruthless monster eager to devour your equipment and your life. If you're the kind of canoeist who paddles through rapids without scouting them first, if you're mesmerized by the thrill of running whitewater, or if you leave your life jacket in the bottom of your canoe because you don't like its confining feeling, then this short footnote is for you. The three most common canoeing mistakes you can make are overestimating your ability, underestimating the power of moving water, and not being prepared for potentially dangerous weather conditions. Any one of these things can kill you. If, despite this pointed warning, you continue to paddle on a river with carefree abandon, may the fortune of the lucky be your fate.

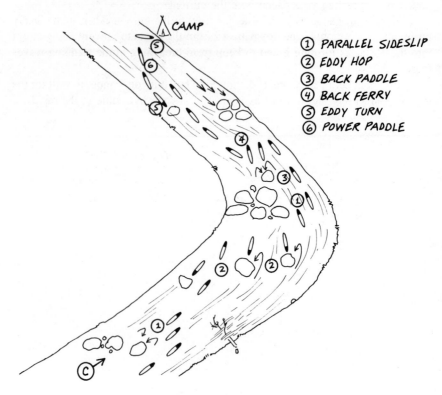

① PARALLEL SIDESLIP
② EDDY HOP
③ BACK PADDLE
④ BACK FERRY
⑤ EDDY TURN
⑥ POWER PADDLE

Example 9-19: River running problem—Case #5.

10

RELATED SPORTS

CANOE RACING

Canoe racing is such a specialized sport that only a brief discussion of it is possible here. If you're interested in it, racers in your local canoe club are your best source of the specific information you'll need. Also, the United States Canoe Association, American Canoe Association, and Canadian Canoe Association (see the Appendix for their addresses) can provide a schedule of upcoming races and information on general racing procedures, whereas local race sponsors can best supply information about regulations for a specific race. Pay close attention to these regulations, since they govern what kind of canoe you can legally use in a race, and they vary considerably with each one.

Canoe races are either sanctioned or unsanctioned. *Sanctioned races* meet the criteria and standards of prominent organizations like the United States Canoe Association, whereas qualifying regulations vary widely for *unsanctioned races*. Of course, the quality of a race depends on the quality of its promotion and organization. Both sanctioned and unsanctioned races are of high and low quality.

Slalom races involve maneuvering around and through poles called *gates* strung across a river. In a slalom race, you're judged on your time through the course and on how well you negotiate between and around the gates. Slalom races usually occur on a section of whitewater less than a half mile long. Some canoe clubs permanently rig slalom gates on popular paddling rivers so their members can practice at any time of the year. These places are ideal for perfecting your maneuvering techniques and for meeting other racers.

Downriver races are a second major category of canoe race. In them paddlers travel a 1- to 5-mile course in as short a time as possible. Usually these races involve all flatwater paddling or a combination of flatwater and easy rapids. *Flatwater races*, in which paddlers sprint up to a mile or so in as little time as possible, are short variations of downstream ones.

Marathon races are downriver races up to several hundred miles in length. They can occur over a period of several days and can involve canoe camping and portaging as well. Sometimes the term marathon racing is used to describe all the races discussed in this paragraph and not just long distance ones.

Canoe triathlons are a third kind of race. These are typically a grueling combination of long distance bicycling, long distance running, and long distance canoeing. They're the popular form of the triathlon in northern regions, whereas triathlons involving swimming, running, and bicycling are more common in areas with warmer water.

Finally, *specialized canoe races*, such as sailing and poling contests, exist. Consult the organizations listed in the Appendix, your local canoe club, or your boating friends for more information about them.

POLING

When *poling*, you use a long pole to travel on shallow waterways. This is especially useful when journeying up a stream and in shallow rapids, because the pole is in contact with the river bottom much of the time for better control of the boat. Poling is best done solo, since a great deal of skill, coordination, and balance is needed to tandem pole effectively.

Stand slightly in front of the center thwart when solo poling downstream and slightly behind it when traveling upstream solo. This properly trims the canoe with its downstream end heavier than its upstream end so it remains lined up with the river's current. You can also achieve this proper trim by positioning your cargo and passengers at appropriate places. For example, move farther to the stern when poling with a passenger in the bow seat. When poling, stand with your knees bent and flexible and your upper body slightly facing your poling side. Position your feet at least shoulders' width apart straddling the keel line and with the one away from your poling side somewhat in front of the other.

When in this position and before beginning the poling technique described below, practice keeping your upper body as motionless as possible while moving the part of your body below your waist so the canoe rocks back and forth in the water (Example 10-1). Do this for a while until you have a feel for how the boat balances and have found its capsize points. Practice this with a friend nearby for assistance if needed and in water deep enough so you won't hurt yourself on the bottom when you fall in. Become really comfortable standing in this position with the canoe moving under you before proceeding any further with this sport.

After practicing standing in a canoe and balancing it for awhile, you should be ready to begin poling. A poling *pole* should be lightweight, durable, strong, and slightly flexible, and should be about 1 or 2 inches in diameter and fit comfortably in the palms of your hands. Modern canoe poles are usually 10- to 13-foot sections of fiberglass or aluminum tubing built specifically for this sport.

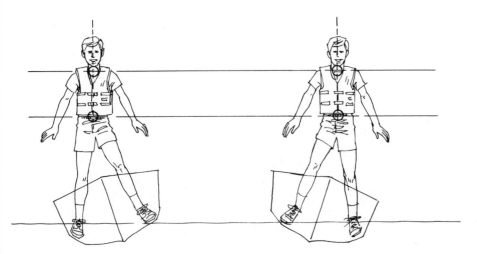

Example 10-1: Practice rocking the canoe to find its capsize points. Note that the upper body remains motionless throughout this procedure.

Some outdated canoeing books recommend cutting wood poles from the forest, but they are inferior to synthetic ones and cutting them can no longer be justified in these environmentally sensitive times. A *duck bill* shoe that fits on the bottom of a pole is helpful when poling on waterways with sandy or muddy bottoms. It opens when you push down on the pole and closes when you pull it back up through the water.

To pole a canoe, stand amidships as described above and hold the pole near its middle with both hands about shoulder-width apart on it (Example 10-2). Then plant the pole in the water close to the canoe and slightly behind you until it hits the bottom. Without removing it from the water, walk your hands up it crossing them over each other as you go until they near the end of it. Then push off with your arms, pull the pole out of the water, move it forward, plant the same end in the water on the same side of the boat again, and repeat the entire procedure outlined here as needed.

The *hand-over-hand switch stroke* is more powerful than the *standard poling stroke* detailed above, although it's somewhat more difficult to learn. To do it, plant your pole in the water and walk your hands up it until they are about 2 or 3 feet from its end. Then, instead of removing the pole from the water as described above, flip it out of the water and plant what was its upper end in the water on the opposite side of the canoe. Then hand-over-hand walk up the pole and repeat as needed.

Windmilling is a powerful stroke that involves moving the pole in a continuous, circular motion. After each pole plant and hand thrust, flip the pole completely around so the end of it resting on the bottom becomes the part that's

Example 10-2: The basic poling stance.

in the air for the next thrust. When doing this, the upper hand releases its grip on the pole just before it's windmilled around, the pole pivots in the lower hand much like a baton twirls in the controlling hand of a cheerleader, and then the upper hand regrips it again after the windmilling action ends. Note that when windmilling, the hands thrust once or twice in the middle of the pole instead of walking up it in a hand-over-hand pushing cycle, and the pole always remains on the same side of the canoe.

Upstream Travel

Because poling tends to turn a boat toward the poling side, you must angle your canoe into the current so it can travel straight upstream. Also, when poling upstream, you should plant your pole behind you towards the stern to get the most forward propulsion, close to the keel line for the smallest turning effect, and on the upstream side of the canoe so the boat doesn't snag on it and spin around out of control. If you broadside in the current, pushing your stern downstream so the boat lines up with the current again is easier than trying to correct your mistake by forcing the bow back in line with the current. Poling upstream is easiest when you avoid major currents and stay along the shore or in eddies as much as possible.

Downstream Travel

There are two ways to control a canoe's speed when traveling downstream. When *snubbing*, briefly place the pole in the water next to the canoe but several feet in front of your position. Your hands should remain in place on the pole and your arms and shoulders should act as shock absorbers that slow your forward momentum. *Dragging* the pole involves pressing down on it with your arms and body so its tip drags along the river bottom behind you. Dragging tends to turn the canoe towards the poling side and isn't as effective as snubbing in fast water.

Turning

To turn toward your poling side, plant the pole in the water about 3–4 feet away from the canoe and several feet behind you before proceeding with the regular hand-over-hand motion as described above. *To turn away from your poling side*, plant the pole in front of you and several feet away from the canoe before proceeding with the regular hand-over-hand poling motion. In both cases the farther away from the canoe you plant the pole, the more abrupt the turn will be. When making a major change in your course, always pole on the inside of your turn because its easier to turn toward your poling side than away from it.

11

CANOE REPAIRS

CANOE repairs can be classified as *temporary*, which make a boat seaworthy again so you can safely finish a trip, and *permanent* which make it function as if new. Usually permanent repairs are done at home when you have more time, materials, and tools available.

ALUMINUM

Aluminum canoes are generally quite easy to repair because of the nature of their construction and the properties of aluminum itself.

To repair a small dent in an aluminum hull, simply place the concave side of the damaged hull on a soft surface like a sandy beach and pound the dent out with your foot or a rubber mallet. *Fix a large dent* by drilling a small hole in the center of it and then pounding it back to its original shape by working slowly inward from its edges. Repair the hole you drilled as described below, if necessary. If a dent curves out from instead of into the boat, hold a sand-filled burlap bag against the inside of the boat and pound it out from the outside.

Often you can *permanently repair a leaking rivet* by placing the outside of the boat at the rivet on a large rock and hitting the part of the rivet on the inside of the hull with a hammer, rock, or other hard object.

Permanently replace leaking or lost rivets by removing any dirt or old rivet pieces from the rivet hole, applying waterproof caulking in the hole, sealing it with a riveting tool, and caulking around the new rivet if necessary. Refit the hole with a larger size rivet if the hole expanded with use or damage.

Temporarily *repair damaged aluminum gunwales, ribs, and thwarts* by bending them back to their original position as much as possible and lashing them in place with a log and some wire. Aluminum components with a T6 temper will occasionally crack further upon restraightening, so at times it may be better to proceed on your journey with bent T6 canoe parts instead of bending them back into their original shape and risk breaking them. Generally, aluminum trim parts must be replaced for a permanent repair, although you may be able to fix them by bolting or otherwise attaching reinforcing bars to them at critically damaged sections like cracks if they're only slightly damaged. When doing this be sure to use bars that run along the structural element for at least 3 or 4 inches beyond the damaged area in each direction.

Temporarily fix holes and cracks in an aluminum hull by bending any damaged ends back in place, drilling a hole (if possible) in the ends of cracks to keep them from lengthening, and sealing the area with chewing gum, duct tape, liquid metal, or quick-hardening marine epoxy. For best results, all these sealers should be applied to both the inside and the outside of a dry and warm boat, and liquid metal and epoxy should harden before use. If necessary, heat the aluminum with a candle or a camp stove on a cold day. For even greater protection, place sealer on both sides of the hull as just described, and then cover both the inside and the outside of the damaged area with duct tape. Simply sealing the damaged area with duct tape may be the best method of repair near the end of a trip or when you don't want to foul your boat with messy sealers before permanently repairing it.

Follow these steps to *permanently repair a hole or crack* in an aluminum canoe hull:

1) Remove debris from the damaged area. Drill a hole through the ends of each crack (if present) to keep it from spreading.

2) Bend deformed edges back into their original position. If the damaged area is badly torn, remove sections of it as necessary.

3) Cut a patch from a piece of aluminum so it overlaps the damaged area by at least 2 inches in all directions. This patch should be round or oval in shape and have beveled edges. Consider applying a patch on both the inside and the outside of the hull for greater strength.

4) Drill properly sized rivet holes about 1/2 inch from the edge of the patch and less than 1 inch apart all the way along its sides. File off any resulting burrs.

5) Hold the patch securely in position over the damaged area, mark each hole on the hull with a pencil, remove the patch, and drill the rivet holes through the canoe hull.

6) Remove burrs from the holes you just drilled with a file. Be sure the boat and the patch are free of dirt and grime.

7) Place a gasket material (like a piece of an old inner tube) between the patch and a wood block. Punch rivet holes in this material with a nail. Trim the gasket to the size of the patch.

8) Line the holes you drilled in the hull with caulking compound, sandwich the gasket between the patch and the hull, and rivet it in place with a riveting tool.

If you plan to extensively repair your canoe at home, you can buy special parts like thwarts, gunwales, and patch materials from your local boating dealer or from some of the companies listed in the Appendix. Notice that you should avoid welding an aluminum canoe, since this weakens the aluminum far more than it strengthens it.

PLASTIC AND ROYALEX

Bent plastic or Royalex canoe hulls are pitiful sights to those not familiar with their remarkable "memory." You can usually *repair minor dents in these materials* by letting them warm in the sun for a few minutes and can *fix major dents* in them by placing the damaged area on a soft meadow or sandy beach and stomping them back into shape. Even badly deformed plastic and Royalex hulls will reclaim their initial shape when their trim and structural components are bent back to their original position.

You can *permanently repair small cosmetic dents in a Royalex canoe* by blowing hot air (about 300°F) from a commercially available heat gun on them. Use caution when doing this, though, since heating the outer surface too fast, too hot, or with an open flame can severely damage it. In time, as the heat penetrates the Royalex material, it will expand and fill in the objectionable dent. You can encourage the removal of larger dents by manipulating one side of the hull with your fingers while applying heat as described above to the other side of it.

Repair damaged wood, aluminum, or plastic gunwales, seats, thwarts and related *trim items* as described for aluminum canoes whenever possible.

Temporarily repair holes and cracks in a plastic or Royalex canoe as described for aluminum canoes.

Permanently repairing holes or cracks in plastic materials is seldom necessary because of their durability. If however, you do need to fix a plastic canoe with a torn, cracked, or punctured hull, Coleman Company (the largest manufacturer of polyethylene canoes) recommends using a special repair kit available from their dealers or using a thermal welding process performed at selected nationwide repair stations.

You can *permanently repair small holes and tears in Royalex* canoe hulls by following these directions:

1) Thoroughly clean the damaged area.

2) Remove any pieces of loose material dangling near the damaged area.

3) If the interior foam is exposed, remove some of it from the damaged area, being sure to undercut the outer ABS material in the process.

4) Clean the damaged area with rubbing alcohol and let dry.

5) Thoroughly mix *epoxy-based* putty, resin, or adhesive (available in hardware stores) and completely plug the damaged area with it. Avoid polyester and vinyl-ester fillers.

6) Let dry for at least 8–10 hours.

7) Sand and paint if desired. Virtually any acrylic-based automotive or polyurethane-based marine paint works satisfactorily.

Permanently repair a severely torn, cracked, or punctured Royalex hull with fiberglass cloth and *epoxy* resin exactly as described below for fiberglass repairs. Note, though, that you should not sand away the outer vinyl covering before beginning, since epoxy adheres to it better than to the ABS material. If necessary, fill the damaged area with epoxy putty as described above before covering it with the fiberglass cloth/epoxy resin layers. You can begin this fiberglass repair process immediately after filling the hole with the putty since the epoxy resin and epoxy putty are compatible materials.

You can obtain special Royalex repair kits from your canoe dealer if you don't want to perform the "hardware store repairs" just described.

LAMINATES

To *remove a small dent* in a laminate boat, simply pop it out with a fist or foot.

Temporarily repair trim components like seats, thwarts, and gunwales as described for aluminum canoes, when possible. *Permanently repair laminate trim components and structural elements* by mixing a batch of resin, catalyst, and chopped fiberglass cloth in a container as described in step 8) below, applying it to the damaged area, and letting it harden. Fiberglass several layers of cloth over the damaged area as described below if needed for more support.

Temporarily repair holes or cracks in laminate canoe hulls as described for aluminum canoes.

Follow these steps to *permanently repair a damaged fiberglass or Kevlar hull:*

1) Position the boat outdoors at waist height on sawhorses, concrete blocks, or other strong supports. Cover any valuable floor or driveway areas under the boat with newspapers before beginning. Avoid extremes in temperatures and rainy, windy, dusty, or direct sunlight conditions.

2) Gather all the materials you'll need before proceeding further. These include:

    . . . resin (epoxy, polyester, or vinyl-ester to match your boat's construction)

    . . . catalyst

    . . . resin pigment that matches your boat's color (optional)

    . . . fiberglass or Kevlar cloth (8 to 10-ounce medium weave) Avoid mat materials. Note that Kevlar canoes are often repaired with fiberglass cloth

. . . an old pair of scissors to cut the cloth

. . . a disposable paintbrush

. . . a disposable can to mix the resin in

. . . a stirring stick

. . . gritty sandpaper

. . . a power sander (quite helpful for large repairs)

. . . disposable rubber dish gloves

. . . some kind of disposable scraper like an old putty knife

. . . acetone and rags for cleaning up

. . . goggles and a breathing mask for use when sanding

3) Put on old clothes and the rubber dish gloves to protect your skin.

4) Remove any torn fiberglass shreds from the damaged area. Remove any other obvious debris like mud and leaves.

5) Sand the damaged area to provide roughness for better adhesion. Be sure to remove the gel coat around the hole or crack.

6) Thoroughly clean the damaged area with rubbing alcohol and let dry.

7) Cut the patches you'll need to perform the necessary repairs. As a general rule, use 2–5 patches for each repair job, depending on the severity of the damage. Be sure the first patch overlaps the damaged area by at least 1 inch on every side, the second patch overlaps the damaged area by at least 2 inches on each side, and so forth.

Patching the outside of a canoe is easier than repairing it from its inside, though people who want to preserve its original outer appearance prefer working inside it. You may have to patch severely damaged areas on both sides of the boat, and may have to reinforce critically stressed areas like the lower bow with additional layers of fabric.

8) Plug a large hole with a resin and fiberglass mixture before patching it. Do this by taping one side of the hole with duct tape, mixing a batch of resin, catalyst, and finely cut fiberglass cloth in a container, and filling the hole with it.

Keep the shredded fiberglass-to-resin ratio as large as possible, since the glass provides the strength when cured.

Let this plug harden somewhat and remove the tape backing before proceeding.

9) Mix an appropriate amount of resin, catalyst, and resin pigment according to the directions on their containers. Now work fast to complete the repairs before the resin sets up.

10) Coat the damaged area with resin.

11) Place your first patch on the damaged area, saturate it with resin, remove excess resin with your scraper, and eliminate air bubbles in it.

Whitish cloth indicates a resin-weak area and resin running, dripping, or pooling anywhere indicates a resin-rich region.

Try to remove as much resin as possible without creating resin-weak areas, since the resin provides useless weight and no noticeable strength.

12) Repeat step 11) above until every patch is in place.

13) Let the patches harden for at least 10–15 hours before use.

14) Lightly sand the area to remove sharp spikes of hardened cloth. Finally, paint the patch with an acrylic-based automotive or polyurethane-based marine paint if desired.

Follow these safety precautions whenever fiberglassing a canoe as just described:

> . . . Work in a well-ventilated area.

> . . . Wear goggles and a breathing mask when sanding. Fiberglass particles are extremely dangerous in your lungs and eyes.

> . . . Wear rubber dishwashing gloves to protect your hands. Remember that fiberglass cloth is *glass* not *cloth*.

> . . . Don't touch your face, eyes, or other body parts during or after working with the fiberglass.

> . . . Shed your dirty clothes outside your house and shower thoroughly as soon as possible when done.

> . . . Wash your fiberglass-impregnated clothes separately from your regular laundry.

Retouch a canoe's gel coat by using a gel coat repair kit available from your dealer. Beware, though, that most of these kits should be used fairly soon after purchase, because they have a relatively short shelf life.

WOOD

No repair techniques are described here for wood canoes because they are made from a wide variety of materials (wood, fiberglass, canvas, etc.), and because listing a brief menu of common repairs would imply that you can easily fix a damaged wood boat. This, of course, is not the case. Skilled craftsmen labor endlessly with complicated construction techniques to build wood canoes and it would be a gross simplification to imply that you can perform quality repairs on them with casual woodworking knowledge and household tools. Consult specific wood canoe repair manuals for more information before attempting to permanently repair a damaged wood canoe.

CANOE REPAIR KITS

Lists of items typically included in complete canoe repair kits follow. You can pack a portable repair kit for use on the water by selecting the items you need from them.

aluminum canoes

1) several rolls of wide duct tape

2) liquid metal compound or quick-setting waterproof epoxy

3) a pop rivet tool

4) a generous supply of various-sized aluminum rivets similar to those on your boat

5) a small hand drill with metal-piercing bits sized to match your rivets. A power drill is, of course, more convenient for home use.

6) an assortment of rustproof bolts and nuts

7) several sheets of 6000 series aluminum alloy at least .03 inches thick

8) tin snips to cut the aluminum patches

9) caulking compound

10) rubber gaskets (pieces of old inner tube work fine)

11) pieces of strong, flexible stainless steel wire

12) miscellaneous tools including a screwdriver, pliers, wire cutters, hammer, metal file, and rubber mallet

13) several nails or punches slightly smaller than your canoe's rivet holes

14) a commercially available repair kit

plastic and Royalex canoes

items 1, 6, 9, 11, 12, and 14 listed above

laminate canoes

items 1, 6, 9, 11, 12, and 14 listed above
appropriate fiberglassing materials

wood canoes

items 1, 5, 6, 9, 10, 11, 12, and 14 listed above for starters. Also include canvas, fiberglass, and woodworking supplies and tools as needed.

PART
THREE

DANGER

12

CANOE RESCUES

THIS chapter details standard canoeing safety principles and rescue procedures. It's important that you're thoroughly familiar with this information before canoeing on moving water, alone, or in challenging situations.

RIVER RESCUES

The Power of Moving Water

Before proceeding further, you must have an understanding of the power of moving water. You can be swept off your feet when standing in knee-deep water with a fast current or when standing waist deep in slower water. When this happens, the downstream force of the current acting on your legs offsets the vertical pull of gravity holding you in place. What's important to understand here is how the exposed surface area of your legs (how deep you're standing in the water) and the river's current are interrelated. A large downstream force results from a large, exposed surface area in a fast current (when you're standing waist deep in fast water), a small downstream force results from a small surface area in a slow current (when you're standing ankle deep in slow water), and variations of both parameters produce a range of intermediate effects. The amount of this downstream force is what concerns us, since it's the force acting on you when trying to stand in a river, when swimming in it, and when canoeing in it.

If the current is fast and you're deep in the water, you could get pinned to an obstacle in the river and not be able to fight the large resulting downstream force and extricate yourself. Similarly, a capsized canoe floating in even a mild current can be pinned to a rock with such force that ten people can't remove it (because it has a large surface area exposed to the current), and a canoe drifting downstream can easily pin a person swimming in front of it to an obstacle and crush him against it as well. Thus, *it's extremely important that you never get downstream in front of a canoe in moving water*.

To make matters even worse, a canoe loaded with water or gear is much more dangerous than an empty one because the load in it—as well as the boat itself—is moving along with the current. Common sense tells us it takes far less energy to stop a bicycle traveling at 10 miles an hour than a truck moving at that same speed. Likewise, because much more energy is needed to stop a loaded canoe than an empty one, it exerts that much more pressure on anything trying to stop it or on anything—like a swimmer—that gets in its way. This explains why experienced paddlers use flotation devices to keep water out of their boats when canoeing in rapids.

Self-Rescue

If you're suddenly dumped into the water in a capsize or a collision with an obstacle, immediately concentrate on getting an adequate air supply and over-coming the shock from being wet and cold. Then locate the canoe and maneuver yourself upstream from it, sideways out of its way, or behind a safe, above-water rock *as quickly as possible*. The last place you want to be in moving water is downstream in front of a canoe. When doing this, check to be sure you're not tangled up in painter lines or in gear secured to the boat, and check to be sure your partner is not hurt, trapped under water, or ignorantly swimming downstream in front of the boat. If he needs assistance, help him as best you can—if you can.

Example 12-1 illustrates the proper way to float or swim in moving water. When doing this, keep your legs slightly bent, close to the water's surface, and pointing downstream so they can warn you about nearby rocks, so they're less likely to get stuck in underwater crevices, and so you can use them as shock absorbers to fend off obstacles. Use your hands to tread water at your sides and to maneuver sideways to avoid obstacles in your path. Always face downstream so you can see where you're going and can evade or brace for collisions with obstacles if necessary. When floating through rapids, be careful you don't bump into an obstacle and pivot around it out of this protective feet-first position, and be prepared for an occasional dunking in large waves.

It's extremely important that you keep your feet close to the surface when swimming through rapids in this fashion. If you try to stand up or if your legs hang low in the water, you'll end up in a dangerous head-first, stomach-down position because the strong downstream current at the surface will push your

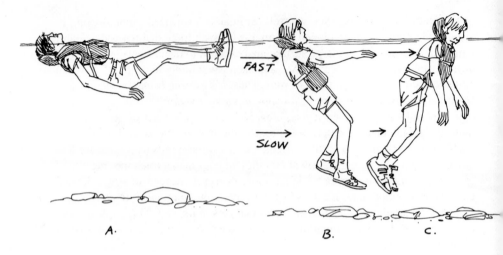

FAST

SLOW

A.   B.   C.

Figure A   **Figure B**   **Figure C**

Example 12-1: The proper way to float or swim in moving water (Figure A). What could happen if you get out of that safe position (Figures B and C). When your feet float low in the water or when you try to stand up in it, the current differential pushes you into a dangerous head-first position.

upper body along while your feet drag in the relatively slow current along the bottom. This problem is compounded if your dangling feet hit any rocks there.

Assess your situation as soon as you can after getting upstream away from your canoe and in the proper feet-first floating position. If the water is cold, head for shore. If the rapids are rough, seek shelter on shore, on an above-water obstacle, or in an eddy behind an obstruction. Make a conscious decision to continue swimming through rapids only if they're mild and short, if there's a calm section below them, and if other boaters know where you are and what you're going to do. Often it's best to wait for help to come to you rather than to try to swim to safety yourself.

When swimming to shore, maneuver yourself into calm, shallow water using the feet-first floating technique described above. Avoid trying to walk to shore in deep or fast water, since you could easily lose your balance and hurt yourself falling on an obstacle. Worse yet, you could get a leg stuck in a crack between two rocks and be pushed down and back by the current so your head is trapped underwater. When swimming to shore, it's far better to carefully work your way from eddy to eddy along a planned route than to blindly drift downstream at the mercy of the current.

If your canoe capsizes in rapids, try holding on to your paddle as you go overboard so you won't have to look for that later. If the rapids are fairly mild, position yourself at the upstream end of the canoe and try floating it upside down through the rapids so the air in it provides some buoyancy to lessen its impact with rocks. This is especially helpful if the canoe has no additional flotation devices in it. Also, try holding the far upstream end of the boat and keeping it parallel with the current so less of it is exposed to river obstacles, try keeping its open end away from the current if it hits an obstacle, and try pushing it into an eddy or swimming into an eddy and pulling the boat into it with its painter. While great in theory, all these things are difficult and potentially dangerous to do in the confusion of a rapids. Often the most prudent thing to do is leave the canoe alone while you concentrate on remaining upstream from it.

The best way to escape from inside a *hole* or *reversal* is by holding on to a rescue rope thrown to you from shore. If that's not available (it *always* should be), then you may have to escape by swimming perpendicular to shore along the obstacle causing it and out the end of it or by taking off your life jacket (its buoyancy keeps you at the surface of the recirculating water), diving deep underwater, and swimming out below the reversing current. These maneuvers are quite dangerous and should be used only as a last resort.

If your canoe is swept into a *strainer tree*, try leaning downstream into it and quickly climbing up on it as you hit it so you don't get trapped in its lower branches. Then work your way to shore along the top of the tree or wait where you are for help. Avoid the upstream side of the tree near the waterline at all costs, since the current can easily pin you underwater there. When rescuing anyone trapped in or on a strainer tree, always approach from the downstream side for the most safety.

If you're swimming in the water and the current is pushing you into a strainer tree, enter it face first. This way the tree will knock you on your back with your face above the water. If you turn around away from the tree to avoid scratching your face, it could knock you on your stomach and pin you face down in the water.

Rescuing Others

When a canoe in your party swamps, capsizes, or is pinned to a rock in a river, helping anyone trapped underwater is your highest priority. Your immediate goal is to get the victim's head above water so he can breathe. Then give CPR or mouth-to-mouth resuscitation if needed, give first aid for severe injuries in the water if necessary, and get him to shore. In this life-or-death situation, you must get to the victim the fastest safe way possible, including swimming down the rapids to him or eddy turning your canoe near him.

The next most dangerous situation occurs when someone is trapped in a river with their head above water. The victim could be stuck in a keeper hole, in a strainer tree, in a canoe wrapped around a rock, in a crevice between two submerged rocks, or between a pinned canoe and an obstruction. Depending on the situation, try throwing a rescue line, paddling a canoe, or swimming to him to help him get unstuck. Give first aid for severe injuries in the water as needed and get the victim to shore. In this case, you should free the victim as quickly as possible, since he could be pulled completely underwater at any moment. Rescuing people drifting downstream in the current is your third highest priority. Consider swimmers *accounted for* if you know where they are. If a canoe capsizes, first look for both swimmers to be sure they aren't trapped underwater. When you've observed them floating free or standing in the rapids, never take your eyes off them until you can classify them as *safe*. In mild weather and rapids swimmers can be considered safe when positioned on above-water obstructions in the river, in comfortable eddies, in shallow areas near shore, or in a calm pool at the bottom of a rapids. In cold weather or water, swimmers are considered safe only when completely out of the water. Finally, judge victims *secure* when they are out of the water and free from all danger, including hypothermia.

If you're canoeing in a small group, begin retrieving boating equipment when all your companions are secure from danger. Of course, if you have a large party, some people can collect floating gear or work to free any pinned canoes while others are helping overboard swimmers. The point here is that you should save people before worrying about their gear.

Boaters swimming through mild rapids are in no particular danger unless injured, the water or weather is cold, they're downstream in front of a canoe, or dangerous obstructions like a keeper hole await downstream. In nonthreatening situations, it's often easiest and safest to retrieve swimmers at the bottom of a set of mild rapids than risk confusing or compounding their situation by helping them as described below. In more dangerous cases, though, you must act quickly to rescue anyone in the water.

There are several ways to rescue a person floating through rapids from a canoe. You can position your boat in a downstream eddy and then throw a line to him as he drifts by. Similarly, people in a canoe downstream from a victim can quickly beach their boat and throw a rescue line to him from shore. Usually you can't help a victim from an upstream canoe, since you'll have to move it into a dangerous upstream position very close to him to help at all. Having a swimmer hang onto your stern painter as you travel past isn't recommended because there's a chance the person in the water will drift downstream ahead of the boat and get pinned to a rock by it. Hanging onto a rescue canoe's gunwales is even more foolish because the victim's legs can easily drift under the boat's hull and get crushed against an underwater obstacle.

To rescue someone swimming through rapids from shore, quickly get your rescue line or throw bag ready before he drifts downstream past you. Try to throw the line to the victim when he's as close to you as possible for the best accuracy, but don't forget to lead him to compensate for the current's force acting on him. If you missed the victim on your first toss, quickly reel in the line, run downstream, and try again. If he grabs the line, secure it around a tree or boulder to absorb the shock when the slack is used up, and then let the current slowly swing him in toward shore.

To rescue a person stranded on a rock or in an eddy, either throw a line to him from shore and *belay* him to shallow water as just described or paddle your canoe into the eddy behind the obstruction, let him get in, and transport him to shore or through the rest of the rapids.

Finally, after you're sure every overboard swimmer is secure, round up floating gear and free any pinned boats. This should be done quickly, since the longer a canoe is pinned to a rock, the greater the chance of it being destroyed, and the longer gear floats in the river the farther downstream you'll have to go to get it and the greater the possibility of its loss or damage. Hopefully your group is large enough so that several people can retrieve loose gear while others begin the chore of freeing pinned canoes. If not, you'll have to decide what your priorities are and how to allocate your resources for the tasks at hand.

You may face some rather uncomfortable decisions when dealing with a capsize in harsh weather or a remote area. For example, it may be best to rescue floating gear like sleeping bags and food containers before freeing a pinned canoe since you'll need those items for survival, even though delaying work on a boat greatly increases the chance of its destruction. Similarly, if you lose some gear or if a canoe is destroyed, you'll have to decide if it's feasible to continue your journey without that equipment or if you should set up camp and signal for help or send out a party of experienced boaters to contact the nearest rescue agency and then wait for assistance.

Retrieving a Drifting Canoe

You can either rescue a drifting, capsized canoe in the middle of a rapids or retrieve it at the bottom of them. If the rapids are mild, try pushing it in towards shore or into an eddy from or with your canoe, or try holding its painter and leading it through the rest of the rapids. Never tie two canoes together since this greatly increases the chance that both will get stuck or flip, and always be prepared to release the stranded canoe's line if either your canoe or the capsized one gets hung up on an obstacle. Usually, retrieving a swamped canoe at the bottom of a rapids is the best approach to use in rougher water when you must concentrate on remaining upright yourself.

Freeing a Pinned Canoe

As soon as you notice a canoe pinned to a rock, verify that its passengers are safely on shore and give first aid to them if needed before working to free the boat. Then gather as many people and as much rescue gear as possible and work fast to organize your efforts, devise a plan for removal, and free the canoe. While some people in your party are collecting rescue equipment, others should assess the situation to determine the best way to remove the boat.

If possible, get out to the pinned canoe as early in this planning stage as possible for a close view of its damage and another perspective of its predicament. You can do this by paddling a rescue canoe into an eddy near the pinned boat, by walking out to it in shallow water, or by belaying a swimmer down to it

on a rope. Don't forget that freeing a pinned canoe is often difficult and dangerous. Never risk anyone's safety during this or any other stage of the salvage
operation.

The general procedures you should follow to free a pinned canoe are:

1) *Estimate all the forces and moments acting on it.* Think of the canoe, the
current, and the obstacle in engineering terms of moments and forces (Example
12-2 and Chapter 6). When freeing a pinned canoe, your job is to unbalance
those forces and moments so the current can carry it downstream.

2) *Determine where you can get the most leverage* on the boat to offset the
current pinning it to the obstacle. For instance, in Example 12-2 notice that
pushing on the end of the boat farthest from the obstacle will have a much greater
effect than pushing on the end of it close to the obstruction.

3) *Find secure, convenient working locations* on shore or in the water near
the boat. Look for trees you can use to belay swimmers down to the canoe,
boulders you can secure the boat to so it won't drift down the rapids when freed,
and underwater obstacles you can use as fulcrums to pry the boat free with logs.

4) *Formulate a plan of action* based on the forces acting on the boat, the
working locations you found, and your available resources. You can pull, push,
lift, or pry a canoe off an obstruction horizontally to the left or right, at an angle
to the left or right, or vertically up over it with ropes, logs, or direct human
contact.

5) Finally, *execute your plans* and remove the boat.

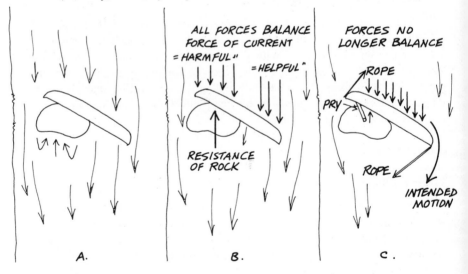

Figure A   Figure B   Figure C

Example 12-2: Thinking of a pinned canoe in terms of engineering forces. The actual situation (Figure A). The forces acting on
the pinned canoe (Figure B). Unbalancing those forces (Figure C).

You may have to repeat the steps outlined above several times until the boat is free. If you can't free it or if it's too dangerous to do so, leave the canoe where it is and return for it later. Often a several-inch drop in the water level will reduce the forces acting on it enough so you can easily remove it. When doing this, rig a line to the canoe and then secure that to a tree or boulder on shore so it can't drift downstream if it loosens before your return. Attach a prominent note with your address and phone number on it to this line so someone can contact you if the boat works itself free. There are still some honest people in the world who will help you as much as they can.

Several important principles to follow when freeing a pinned canoe are:

1) One of the first things you should do in long or difficult rapids is run a strong line between the pinned canoe and a shoreline obstacle so it won't drift down through the rest of the rapids when freed.

2) In almost any pin situation, some of the current is holding the canoe to the obstacle and some is actually trying to free it. Reduce the current pinning the canoe and encourage the current trying to free it by increasing the canoe's surface area exposed to the "helpful" current and reducing its area exposed to the "harmful" current.

3) Turn the canoe parallel to the current to lessen the forces acting on it.

4) Get as much of the canoe out of the water as possible to reduce its underwater surface area.

5) Roll the canoe so its hull (not its open end) faces upstream into the current. This way its bottom will deflect the current and reduce the amount of water acting as dead weight in it.

6) Work to get the upstream gunwale out of the water so the current can no longer pour into its open end.

7) When using a rope to free a pinned canoe, secure it around the entire hull and not just to a thwart or painter attachment that could easily rip out.

8) Everyone working in the water near the canoe should be safely upstream from it, positioned on an above-water obstruction, or in the eddy behind an above-water obstruction so the boat can't pin them to the obstacle when it works free.

9) At times, selectively removing gear from a pinned canoe will help free it. Usually, though, you should remove all the cargo from a pinned boat before freeing it.

There are several ways to remove gear from a pinned canoe. It's often easiest to paddle a rescue canoe into an eddy behind the pinned boat and load the salvaged gear directly into it. In shallow water you may be able to walk out to the pinned boat and carry its cargo to shore. To perform a more complicated method, first tightly secure a strong rope to a shoreline tree and to the pinned canoe. Then attach one end of a short rope to an item of gear and its other end around (not to) the first line you rigged. Finally, work your way to shore by holding on to the long line for support, letting the gear float in the water, and sliding the knot securing it around the main support rope along as you go. Repeat for each separate piece of equipment.

FLATWATER RESCUES

In general, always stay with a capsized canoe on flatwater, since an overturned boat indicates you're in trouble and anyone nearby will probably come to your aid. However, leave your canoe and swim to shore if it increases your safety. For example, remaining in a capsized canoe in cold, calm water is foolish if you're a good swimmer and the shore is only 30 yards away. Methods of righting and rescuing a capsized canoe are discussed in the rest of this chapter.

ENTERING AND LEAVING A CANOE

Entering the Water from a Canoe

Usually the best way to enter a lake or river from an upright canoe is to land it on shore first and then walk into the water. However, at times you may want to or have to leave a canoe without beaching it first. For example, you may want to cool off in the water when paddling on a large lake on a hot day, or you may have to quickly jump in the water to retrieve your eyeglasses that fell overboard.

Procedure:

1) Let your boating partner know what you intend to do so he can brace the canoe for you and so your actions don't surprise him.

2) Hold both gunwales with your hands, place some weight on them, and stand up with your feet on the keel line.

3) Jump up and swing your feet sideways over a gunwale into the water (Example 12-3). To avoid tipping the canoe, keep your weight on your hands on the gunwales as long as possible.

When doing this solo, hold on to your boat at all times so the wind can't blow it away from you.

Entering an Upright, Floating Canoe
With assistance from another canoe

Procedure:

1) Position the canoes parallel and touching each other.

2) If two paddlers are in the assisting canoe, they kneel at its bow and stern. If a solo paddler is helping (as illustrated here), he kneels amidships in his boat.

Example 12-3: Entering the water from an upright canoe.

The solo paddler or one of the tandem paddlers securely holds your boat's amidships gunwale while the other tandem paddler braces his boat for stability.

3) On signal, you grab your amidships gunwale across from your helper and pull yourself aboard (Example 12-4A). The assisting paddler should let the side of the canoe nearest you lower somewhat so you can climb in easier.

Figure A

Example 12-4: Entering a floating canoe with assistance from another canoe (Figure A), a swimmer (Figure B), and from a partner inside the canoe (Figure C).

With assistance from a swimmer

Procedure:

1) Position yourselves amidships at opposite gunwales.

2) On signal, your helper steadies the canoe while you climb in on your side. He should let your side of the canoe lower somewhat as you enter it (Example 12-4B).

Example 12-4 (Cont'd.)   **Figure B**

With assistance from inside the canoe

Procedure:

1) Position yourself in the water amidships. Your helper should be braced in position in the boat.

2) On signal, pull yourself in the canoe by hanging on the gunwale nearest you (Example 12-4C). Your helper should be prepared to counter sudden shifts in balance as you enter.

Example 12-4 (Cont'd.)   **Figure C**

With no assistance

Method #1—Procedure:

1) Position yourself amidships with your head near the center thwart.
2) Pull down on the closest gunwale with one hand, reach over the boat, and hold the far gunwale with the other (Example 12-5A).

   Don't be concerned if the canoe leans considerably and ships a little water while doing this.
3) Place your weight on your hands, kick hard with your feet, and propel yourself into the canoe.

Figure A

Example 12-5: Entering a canoe with no assistance, Method #1 (Figure A), and Method #2 (Figure B).

Method #2—Procedure:

1) Position yourself at the canoe's bow or stern with your hands on its deck plate.
2) Pull your chest up onto the deck plate (Example 12-5B).
3) Roll your body into the boat.

Example 12-5 (Cont'd.)   **Figure B**

Figure A

Example 12-6: Emptying a swamped canoe in shallow water (Figure A). Alone in deep water with Method #1 (Figure B), and Method #2 (Figure C).

EMPTYING A SWAMPED CANOE

In Shallow Water

Procedure:

1) Stand at opposite ends of the canoe.

2) Roll the boat on its side so some water pours out of it. Then continue rolling it upside down until it completely empties. Slightly lifting the canoe while rolling it helps empty it faster (Example 12-6A).

3) Lift the boat up so its lower gunwale clears the water and set it down upright in the water.

Alone in Deep Water

Method #1—Procedure:

1) Position yourself at the bow or stern.

2) Press down on the deck plate so the other end of the canoe rises and water drains from it (Example 12-6B).

3) While still pushing vertically down, push horizontally with a "down and out" motion so the canoe travels forward in the water. This forces additional water from it.

4) Repeat as needed.

Example 12-6 (Cont'd.)   **Figure B**

Method #2:

This fairly difficult technique is called the *shake-out* because you literally shake the water out of a swamped canoe. It's best done solo and with a canoe no more than half full of water.

Procedure:

1) Position yourself amidships with the swamped canoe floating upright in the water.

Example 12-6 (Cont'd.)   **Figure C**

2) Vigorously push down and out on the gunwale closest to you so water splashes out of the canoe (and into your face!) (Example 12-6C). As soon as the water stops flowing out of the boat, lift up on that gunwale so no more water can enter there.

3) Quickly repeat step 2 in a rocking rhythm until the canoe is empty.

Deep Water Group Techniques

Method #1

This method works best if a bunch of swimmers are nearby who can help.

Procedure:

1) Roll the canoe upside down.

2) The swimmers spread themselves out along the length of the boat, tread water in the air pocket under it, and coordinate plans.

3) On signal they hold the port and starboard gunwales with their left and right hands, kick hard, lift the canoe over their heads (as they sink underwater), and flip it over to a predetermined side. This lifting and flipping action must be done forcefully and simultaneously for greatest effect.

Method #2:

Use this *T-rescue* technique when an upright canoe can aid a swamped canoe or when two swamped canoes can aid each other. This method is described below for tandem canoes, though the principles are the same for solo ones. When emptying two swamped canoes, the "rescue canoe" described below is really the keel of an overturned, swamped canoe. Just pull the "swamped canoe" directly across the keel of the inverted "rescue canoe" and empty it as described. Then empty the remaining swamped boat as described below.

Procedure:

1) Position the swamped canoe upside down in the water, perpendicular to the upright one, and almost touching it amidships. One swimmer should be at the far end of the swamped canoe and the other swimmer (if tandem paddling) should stabilize the distant amidships gunwale on the upright boat.

   One person in the rescue canoe should be kneeling close to amidships, while his partner steadies the canoe from his normal bow or stern position.

2) The swimmer at the far end of the swamped canoe pushes down on his end of it to drain some water from it and forward on it to raise its distant end so the person kneeling in the rescue boat can lift it onto his canoe (Example 12-7A).

3) Both people handling the swamped canoe drag it across the gunwales of the rescue boat until it balances there completely out of the water (Example 12-7B).

Figure A

Example 12-7: Emptying a swamped canoe with a T-rescue.

Example 12-7 (Cont'd.)   Figure B

4) The person kneeling amidships in the rescue boat rolls the swamped canoe right side up and then slides it back into the water.

5) The "swamped canoe" is then pulled parallel alongside the rescue canoe and the swimmers board it.

SWIMMING AND LIFESAVING

Swimming and canoeing usually go hand in hand. However, swimming in a river or lake is far more dangerous than swimming in a supervised pool. For safety, never dive or jump into a waterway if you can't see its bottom and aren't sure exactly how deep it is, and never swim alone outdoors. Wear sneakers or boots to protect your feet from sharp rocks, broken glass, and fishhooks. Stay near shore where you can easily get out if you get cramps, are bitten by a poisonous creature (in the southeastern states and along the coasts), or get caught in an unpredictable current. Have someone in your group act as a lookout to watch for anyone in trouble when swimming, keep rescue equipment like throw lines nearby, and have everyone pair up with another person when in the water for safety. Children often exceed their physical limits when swimming. Be especially aware of them in and near the water.

If you plan to canoe extensively or in challenging situations, enroll in a college, Red Cross, Boy Scout, or community recreation *lifesaving course*. Because lifesaving techniques are complicated and highly dangerous unless performed properly, they're omitted from this book. However, because the reach-throw-row-go rule is so basic to lifesaving and summarizes the principles of water rescues, it's explained below. Simply stated, if you need to rescue someone in trouble in the water, follow these steps (in this order):

1) *Reach* something like a shirt, stick, belt, or canoe paddle out to the person in trouble.

2) *Throw* something out to the victim, like a rope or a life jacket.

3) *Row* a canoe out to him.

4) *Go* in the water to rescue the victim yourself *only if there's no other way to save him and only if you're an expert swimmer trained in lifesaving, water rescue techniques.* Newspapers are filled with stories of people who drowned while "saving" someone else.

13
SAFETY AND FIRST AID

AS you become more involved with canoeing, learn as much as you can about related sports like swimming, sailing, hiking, and orienteering because they'll give you a wide background that's comforting to have outdoors. In fact, learning some skills like technical rock climbing, outdoor survival, and first aid could even save your life in an emergency. If you plan to canoe alone, extensively, or in remote areas, it's imperative that you have a comprehensive background in and working knowledge of what to do in an emergency.

First aid is the temporary care you give an injured person when medical help is not available. Because the road to injury begins with the first careless step outdoors, it's important that solo paddlers and at least several people in every group of canoeists are trained in first aid techniques. While major disasters like being pinned between a canoe and a rock are exceedingly rare, they do occur and can challenge even the most highly trained outdoorsman. Even common minor problems like a cut foot or a sudden capsize can mushroom into dangerous life-or-death situations if dealt with carelessly or improperly.

Because first aid is a complicated subject, because it deals with a host of diverse problems, and because it requires extensive hands-on practice to master, it's not described in detail in this book. It's far better to direct you to the nearest Red Cross first aid class than to outline a handful of first aid concepts here and leave you with the illusion that you're trained in this exacting skill. Similarly, instead of lightly touching down in every area of the emergency rescue and outdoor survival fields, this chapter details a few safety topics especially useful when canoeing and stresses underlying principles that will help you prevent an emergency from occurring in the first place.

A thousand and one safety precautions are highlighted throughout this book to prepare you for the dangers out there in the canoeing world. Unfortunately, some of you had scoffed at those warnings as you journeyed through this book, and others of you will forget them as you gain confidence and experience on the water. If you're one of these people, may good fortune be in your hand of cards and countless suns light your path through life for years to come. Chances are, though, that some of you who ignored these warnings will not be so lucky. Indeed, some of you reading this book right now will die because the time you needed your life jacket for safety was the time you left it laying in your canoe, others of you will die because you laughed in the face of hypothermia, and still others of you will die because you didn't respect the power of moving water. Simply stated, *prevention* is doing things right the first time and every time. May all of you take the necessary precautions to prevent canoeing accidents from occurring, so that sometime in the future your friends won't have to look over their shoulders—in the direction you disappeared—with a tear of sadness in their eyes.

Always wear your life jacket when on the water, and especially when paddling in cold water, cold weather, moving water, and rapids. Never simply drape it over your shoulders without securing it properly around your chest. A life jacket that falls off in the water will do you no good. Children and nonswimmers should never get in a canoe without a life jacket on, and parents and more experienced swimmers should set a good example for their partners, family, and friends by never leaving theirs lay in the bottom of the boat. A life jacket, like a good insurance policy, should be there when you need it.

By now you should know that life jackets are no guarantee of safety. Nonswimmers and beginning swimmers not comfortable in water should never canoe through rapids, even with a life preserver on. They simply don't have the experience and confidence needed to survive a sudden float trip through rough water. Also, each nonswimmer, beginning swimmer, and young child should pair up with an experienced canoeist and skilled swimmer for the greatest safety. It's risky to allow two nonswimmers to paddle together, even if they wear their life jackets.

Know your limits. Never exceed your physical, mental, or spiritual capabilities when outdoors. Avoid water that's too cold, too rough, or too far from shore to swim in if you had to. Don't let other people talk you into traveling on a windy lake, through rough rapids, or in deep water if you personally cannot handle those situations. It's better to honestly announce your limitations to your boating partners than to force them to deal with an emergency situation because you canoed in conditions you couldn't handle.

Be prepared for all possible emergencies. Carry an adequate amount of clothing, food, purified drinking water, shelter, and boating supplies. Be especially ready to deal with an unexpected soaking, cold spell, or storm that could leave you with a dangerous case of hypothermia. Carry a spare paddle even when canoe sailing or motor canoeing, since you may have to paddle back to shore with it. Carry proper first aid and rescue equipment and know how to use everything you bring with you. Be sure your gear is in excellent working condition and repair any that's damaged before relying on it outdoors. Be prepared to deal with specific hazards like rough rapids, poisonous snakes, or voracious insects where you'll canoe.

Use common sense. Seek shelter from an approaching storm before it engulfs you. Avoid flooded, debris-choked rivers no matter how much you feel like canoeing on them. Never paddle alone unless you're able to deal with every possible emergency yourself. Don't hesitate to alter a trip if it's dangerous to proceed with your initial plans.

Finally, *always tell a reliable person where you're going, when you expect to return, and what they should do if you don't return by that time.* Be sure you tell them your exact put-in and take-out locations and where your vehicles are parked so rescuers can determine if you're still on the water or made it safely to the take-out but had problems on the way home. If at all possible, avoid changing your plans after finalizing them with your contacts at home. Allow plenty of time for the car shuttle, the drive to and from the waterway, the trip itself, and any obstacles like a headwind you could encounter on the water.

TEMPERATURE DANGERS

Hypothermia

Your body's *core* is its head and chest area containing vital organs like the brain, lungs, and heart. For it to function properly, its core temperature must be maintained at a constant level within a degree or two of 98°F. The *shell* is the outer layer of skin and the extremities. These noncritical areas of your body can become very cold or warm without affecting your body's overall operation or survival.

Hypothermia is the general cooling of the body's inner core. It occurs when the heat lost from your body is greater than the heat produced by it for long, gradual periods or for short, rapid periods of time. Hypothermia is fatal to people falling into cold water in as little as 15 minutes, but could take up to two or three days for someone stranded with no shelter in 50-degree weather. It can occur at any altitude from sea level to mountaintops, in any temperature, and during any time of the year. By far, *hypothermia is the greatest danger you'll face when canoeing.* Signs of hypothermia include shivering, slurred speech, cold hands and feet, amnesia, and poor overall coordination.

Hypothermia is caused by numerous compounding factors including inadequate protection from the wind, rain, and cold, fatigue from too much exercise, and insufficient food. You can prevent it by using a dependable shelter for protection from the wind and rain, eating quantities of high energy food to maintain an active metabolic rate, and carrying plenty of extra dry clothes. Guard against hypothermia by carefully securing your extra clothing in waterproof dry packs. Don't risk soaking your gear in a capsize. Dress for adequate protection from the elements by wearing synthetics or wool instead of cotton, a hat that reduces heat radiated from your head and neck areas, and windproof garments over your inner insulation layers. Be prepared for sudden capsizes by wearing appropriate gear like a wet suit in cooler weather.

Treat a hypothermia victim by preventing further heat loss and then gradually adding heat to warm him up. Get the victim out of the water as fast as possible; keep him sheltered from wind, rain, and snow; replace all his wet clothes with dry ones; and give him warm drinks and high energy foods (if and only if he's conscious). Additional methods for warming a hypothermia victim include placing him inside a sleeping bag with another person, having him sit by a fire, encircling him with a group of people, and placing hot water bottles at his neck, armpits, groin, and chest areas. Never put a person suffering from hypothermia in a cold sleeping bag alone though, since his body won't generate enough heat to warm it up. Also, never give cigarettes or alcohol to anyone suffering from hypothermia since these promote the transfer of body heat from the core.

Afterdrop is a dangerous lowering of a victim's core temperature that occurs when you accidentally confuse his body's heat regulating mechanism when treating hypothermia. For example, warming a hypothermia victim's extremities and skin too quickly can fool his body into thinking it's actually warmer than it is. To compensate for this perceived "excessive" warmth, his body transfers heat from its core, further cooling it. Similarly, issuing hot drinks to a severely hypothermic victim can cause a transfer of blood to his extremities where it cools and then returns and chills his core.

After a capsize never swim excessively in cold water unless you must avoid water dangers or are trying to reach shore or a nearby rescue craft, since this greatly increases your body's heat loss and encourages the onset of hypothermia. If you must wait in cold water for a period of time before rescuers can help you, assume an immobile, curled-up position as illustrated in Example 13-1. Don't put your head underwater and don't remove your clothing since it provides some insulation even when wet.

Example 13-1: Positions that reduce your body's heat loss in cold water.

Wind Chill

A *wind chill chart* (Example 13-2) tells you the temperature your bare skin feels at different thermometer readings and wind speeds. To use it, estimate the wind speed and air temperature. The *wind chill factor*, the temperature it feels like at that air temperature and wind speed, is where the lines intersect. For example, if a thermometer records a temperature of 40°F and a 10-mile-an-hour wind is blowing, your exposed skin feels a temperature of 28°F. You could be in serious trouble if you were paddling under these conditions and didn't carry clothes that could keep you warm below freezing.

				temperature			
wind speed	50	40	30	20	10	0	−10
0	50	40	30	20	10	10	−10
5	48	37	27	16	6	−5	−15
10	40	28	16	4	−9	−21	−33
15	36	22	9	−5	−18	−32	−45
20	32	18	4	−10	−25	−39	−53
25	30	16	0	−15	−29	−44	−59
30	28	13	−2	−18	−33	−48	−63

Example 13-2: The wind chill chart.

Water Chill

Since water conducts heat much faster than air, it's imperative that you stay as dry as possible in cool or cold weather. *Water chill*, especially when combined with a wind chill, can kill you in an incredibly short time. This warning cannot be stressed too much. The sport of canoeing requires that you are always close to and often immersed in the water. That, combined with a breeze and an even mild temperature, can sap your strength in a few short minutes. Hypothermia stalks everyone canoeing in anything less than hot weather, and the hand of death closely follows on its heels if those conditions are windy and cold as well.

Be especially careful to avoid going overboard into cold water, because a sudden immersion in it is physically painful, will probably knock the wind out of you, and will give you a helpless, panicky feeling. If you know you'll be canoeing in cold water, consider experiencing an immersion into frigid water in safe, controlled conditions with others nearby to assist you if needed before your trip.

GETTING HELP IN AN EMERGENCY

Before canoeing alone, be completely familiar with and comfortable in the outdoors and in a canoe, since you'll have to deal with problems ranging from a capsized boat to a hypothermia situation by yourself. Be thoroughly skilled in first aid, survival. swimming, camping, and all other skills you could possibly use for the kind of trip you're on. Also, be prepared to remain in place and signal others for help or to travel upstream, downstream, or cross-country to a community for assistance.

Fortunately, your options increase considerably when canoeing with a group of people. Depending on your situation, your group will either have to deal with its particular problem itself, transport a victim to help in a nearby community, or travel to a community and have trained medical help return to your victim. As examples, you should always be prepared to treat someone with hypothermia because it can be deadly in a very short time; you may decide to transport someone bitten by a poisonous snake to a town that's only an hour away; and you may need to travel to civilization and have rescuers return to your camp to aid someone mauled by a bear. When transporting a victim to a community for treatment, place him in the most experienced paddlers' canoe, have him wear a life preserver for safety, and position him in accordance with Red Cross methods that necessarily vary with the kind of injury he has. When you must bring rescuers to your victim, send one canoe with the two fastest, strongest, most experienced paddlers to civilization to make the necessary arrangements. Provision their boat with food, clothing, and shelter as necessary, but without burdening them with excess baggage that will slow them down. Always keep the person best trained in first aid with the victim, though, even if he's also the person most qualified to go for help.

EPILOGUE

. . . and so the world spun in its endless cycle of time. Winter, Spring, Summer, Fall—a thousand rising and dying suns, a thousand beautiful paintings in each and every one. Magicians' illusions. Reflections of campfires, cookouts, and carefree confusion. How the world changed with the passing years. How sad it seemed through countless tears. How much fun we've had despite our fears. I remember canoeing through the morning haze, eating blueberry feasts for days and days, watching the sun set the sky ablaze, and drifting asleep under a heavenly maze. A thousand times we laughed and cried, and danced and sang and touched the sky. Flocks of geese flew up high, and all the while, the Delaware flowed nigh. Golden memories sure can make you sigh, thinking of good times rolling on by . . .

"Remember the time a skunk got into Tom's tent at Skinner's Falls? He had to paddle all the way to Barryville by himself 'cause no one else could stand being with him in a canoe!"

"Yeah, and Ralph made him wash off with a couple gallons of tomato juice before he let him back in his car."

"Ralph was a riot to paddle with. I remember the time he capsized on the Delaware . . ."

". . . You mean the time he fell overboard 'cause he was laughing so hard at John's jokes?"

"No, I mean the time he flipped near Port Jervis! I can still see him standing in the water with that wet cigar sticking out of his mouth!"

"Bob, don't be so quick to laugh at Ralph. You and Lou capsized in that snowstorm!"

"The only time I ever capsized and it had to be in a blizzard . . ."

". . . and your dry clothes got soaked 'cause you didn't put them in plastic bags!"

"I remember the time Mark crashed into a huge rock on the Lehigh. He lost his radio in that one."

"Yeah, Mark was lost without that radio."

"Lost the boat, too."

"Ed, you're the only person I know who wrecked a boat on the upper Hudson. Seems like the rest of us made it through those rapids without a scratch."

"Wait a minute, John was my sternman. Blame that on him."

"John was the funniest person who ever went canoeing. He had to be the only one who could actually lose a paddle while fishing!"

"Yeah, and that wasn't the first time he lost one either!!"

"I remember when he stumbled into camp that night. He mumbled something about 'losing his paddle,' devoured half our dinner, and then fell asleep without even taking off his wet clothes!"

"Yeah, John, you never did explain the story about the wet clothes to us."

"Or why you disappeared early that next morning with *one* canoe and returned later with *two* of them!"

"You didn't have to swim back to camp that night, did you?"

"That sounds too much like work," John replied with a smile.

"Speaking of work, I'll never forget our first Canadian canoe trip. Two weeks of misery and total isolation."

"Almost total isolation. We had a billion hungry mosquitoes for company."

"That guide sure wasn't worth it on that trip. He didn't even know where we were. Ed and I found the river draining the lake we were lost in for three days. Then he had the nerve to scream at us for going too far down it before he scouted it for rapids."

"There are more rapids in a bathtub than there were on that entire trip."

"How many times did that guide make us paddle up and down that lake? It must 'of been at least three or four."

"I don't know for sure, but it wasn't easy in those waves. One capsize and it would have been all over. Ice cube city."

"Finally Mark came down with a sore throat that kept him from paddling, and Jeff couldn't paddle anymore because he stubbed his finger!"

"Here we are, two weeks and a hundred miles from civilization and Jeff couldn't paddle because he hurt his finger! . . ."

For a moment there was a pause in the conversation. With deliberation, Ed reached for another log and put it on the fire. The evening chill, like the uncertain future, was closing in.

"So have you guys heard from Jeff or Paul?"

"I haven't seen them for a month or so. The last I heard, they were still around Allentown."

"I heard Tom moved to Dayton, Ohio."

"What'd he ever do that for?"

"A job at GM, or something. Sure wasn't for the scenery."

"Kip joined the Navy. Said something about traveling and seeing the world."

"I got a letter from Carl a while ago. He's in California, and guess what he's doing there."

"Running rivers."

"Of course. How'd you know?"

"What else would someone like Carl be doing right now?"

"I really miss the days we paddled with Carl. He was good."

"Yeah, Carl had it together. That's more than I can say for the rest of us."

"Wait a minute! I had it together too!"

"Oh yeah! Who're you trying to kid, Bob? Remember the time the Coast Guard fished you out of Chesapeake Bay?"

"And remember when you fell into the Shenandoah trying to board your canoe and then tried to dry your clothes and burned them all in the campfire!"

"And remember when a bear stole our dinner and you chased it through the woods with your canoe paddle!!"

. . . From the east the lightening came, not so much as a flash or a glare, but as a faded black carpet being carefully unrolled across the pitch black Arizona sky. Gradually, and with deliberation, the heavens changed from a pale blackness to shades of dark purples, which in turn and in time became lighter purples, blues, maroons, and pinks. As the planet spun further eastward, those pinks became a collection of red colors creeping upward from beyond the distant horizon. Like all the colors that preceded it, the shades of red spread to the northeast and to the southeast, and eventually fanned out across the breadth of the sky. Then, with a thousand trumpeters of dawn rejoicing at the new day, the sun came charging above the desert skyline wearing her garments of red and riding her chariot of gold. As Orion marched from the east and Cassiopeia reigned high in the north sky, the orange disk of daylight—once again—began to spread its warmth across the land.

And now a cowboy returns to his office
Singing another river song
10,000 sunrises have come
10,000 sunsets have gone
And here in the western deserts
The coyotes still howl

Memories
And the joys the outdoors bring
Like the songs a sunrise sings
Keep rolling with the wind

Stay free

Bob Wirth

APPENDIX

The following lists of addresses are a sampling of companies and organizations that serve canoeists. They are by no means complete, and inclusion in them is not an indication of the quality of their products or services.

CANOEING EQUIPMENT SUPPLIERS AND MANUFACTURERS

The following companies either manufacture or market canoes, paddles, or miscellaneous boating gear like dry packs, knee pads, and life preservers.

Alumacraft Boat Company
315 W. St. Jullian St.
St. Peter, MN 56082

Bear Mountain Boat Shop
Box 1041
Bancroft, ONT KO1 1CO

Beaver Bark Canoes
Rt. 3 Box 2
Woodruff, WI 54568

Blackadar Boating Company
P.O. Box 1170
Highway 93 North
Salmon, ID 83467

Blackhawk Canoe Company
937 N. Washington St.
Jamesville, WI 53545

Blue Hole Canoes
Sunbright, TN 37872

Cascade Outfitters
P.O. Box 209
Springfield, OR 97477

Clement USA
Route 3 Box 422
Markesan, WI 53946

Coleman Canoes
250 N. St. Francis
Wichita, KS 67201

Colorado Kayak Supply
Box 291
Buena Vista, CO 81211

Curtis Canoes
4587 Clay St.
Hemlock, NY 14466

Grey Owl Paddles
101 Sheldon Drive
Cambridge, ONT N1R 6T6

Grumman Canoes
Marathon, NY 13803

Lincoln Canoes
RFD 1 Box 309 G
Waldoboro, ME 04572

Lotus Canoes
7005 N. 40th St.
Tampa, FL 33604

Mad River Canoe
P.O. Box 610 B
Waitsfield, VT 05673

Michi-Craft Canoes
20000 19-Mile Road
Big Rapids, MI 49307

Mohawk Canoes
P.O. Box 668-TP2
Longwood, FL 32750

Nimbus Paddles
2330 Tyner St.
Port Coquitlam, B.C. V3C 2Z1

Northwest River Supplies
P.O. Box 9186
Moscow, ID 83843

Old Town Canoes
P.O. Box 548
Old Town, ME 04468

Perception Canoes
P.O. Box 64
Liberty, SC 29657

Rainbow Boatworks
P.O. Box 159
Newport, VT 05855

Sawyer Canoes
Box 435
Oscoda, MI 48750

Seda Products
P.O. Box 997
Chula Vista, CA 92010

Voyageur Canoe Company
Dept. 102
3 King St.
Millbrook, ONT LOA 1GO

Voyageur's Canoe Supplies
P.O. Box 409
Gardner, KS 66030

We-no-nah Canoes
Box 247
Winona, MN 55987

Western Canoeing, Inc.
2142 W. Riverside Road
Box 115
Abbotsford, BC V25 4N8

CANOEING PUBLICATIONS

Adirondack Life
P.O. Box 6971
Syracuse, NY 13217

emphasizes the Adirondack Mountain region. Contains frequent canoeing articles

The American Canoeist
American Canoe Association
7217 Lockport Place
P.O. Box 248
Lorton, VA 22079

ACA newsletter
(address below)

American Rivers
American Rivers Conservation Council

stresses preserving free flowing rivers
(address below)

The Beaver
Hudson's Bay Company
77 Main St.
Winnipeg, MAN R3C 2R1

magazine of the Canadian frontier, frequent canoeing articles

Canoe Magazine
P.O. Box 10748
Des Moines, Iowa 50349

entire magazine for canoeists

Canoe News
U.S. Canoe Association

official publication of the USCA
(address below)

Currents
National Organization
for River Sports

legal river issues, races, safety, conservation, education
(address below)

Nastawgan
Wilderness Canoe Association

journal of the WCA
(address below)

National Outdoor Outfitters News
P.O. Box 2964
Clinton, Iowa 52735

covers all outdoor sports; free to all outdoor gear retailers

Outside Magazine
P.O. Box 2690
Boulder, CO 80321

articles cover all outdoor topics

Paddles Up
Canadian Canoe Association

official publication of the CCA
(address below)

River Runner Magazine
Powell Butte, OR 97753

slightly emphasizes kayaking and rafting whitewater

Sierra
Sierra Club
530 Bush St.
San Francisco, CA 94108

occasional canoeing articles; official Sierra Club publication

Small Boat Journal
P.O. Box 400
Bennington, VT 05201

emphasizes small sail and motor boats. Contains a few canoeing articles.

Wooden Boat Magazine
P.O. Box 78
Brooklin, ME 04616

information about all kinds of wooden boats, including wood canoes

Wooden Canoe
Wooden Canoe Heritage
Association

journal of the WCHA
(address below)

see also related sports magazines like *Outdoor Life*, *Sports Afield*, and *Field and Stream*.

ORGANIZATIONS

United States Government

U.S. Army Corps of Engineers
Recreation Resource Management Branch
Department of the Army
Washington, DC 20314

information on Refuse Act of 1899, dams, and water impoundments

Bureau of Reclamation
Department of the Interior
Washington, DC 20240

information on (mostly western) dams

Coast Guard
400 7th St. SW
Washington, DC 20590

for coastal information and boating regulations

U.S. Forest Service
Department of Agriculture
Washington, DC 20250

request Forest Service maps along your canoe route

Distribution Section
U.S. Geological Survey
1200 South Eads Street
Arlington, VA 22202

topographic maps, east of the Mississippi River

Distribution Section
U.S. Geological Survey
Box 25286
Denver Federal Center
Denver, CO 80225

topographic maps, west of the Mississippi River

National Park Service
Department of the Interior
Washington, DC 20240

information on wild and scenic rivers, national parks, and national recreation areas

State Governments

The National Marine Manufacturers Association has compiled an excellent guidebook that lists state, regional, and national addresses you can contact for canoeing information and describes the information you'll receive from each source. Request the free booklet "The Canoe Source Book" from either of these two addresses:

N.M.M.A.
P.O. Box 5555
Grand Central Station
New York, NY 10017

N.M.M.A.
401 N. Michigan Ave.
Chicago, Ill 60611

If the NMMA book is out of print you can get state and regional canoeing information by contacting the parks, recreation, tourism, or publicity offices for the state(s) you're interested in. Write them at this address:

State Office of Tourism, Department of Parks, Department of Information (or similar title)
State Capitol Building,
State Capital, State, Zip Code

Your letter will be funneled through bureaucratic channels to the appropriate office.

Canadian Governments

Canadian Map Office
Dept. of Energy, Mines, and
Resources
615 Booth Street
Ottawa, ONT KIA OE9

information about topographic maps

Office of Tourism
235 Queen Street O4E
Ottawa, Ontario K1A OH6

general tourist information

Parks, Canada
Ottawa, Ontario K1A 1G2

national parks information

Revenue Canada   customs information
Customs and Excise
Public Relations Branch
Ottawa, Ontario K1A OL5

Conservation/Private

American Red Cross   often offers local canoeing courses,
National Headquarters   films, etc.
Washington, DC 20006

American Rivers Conservation   emphasizes preserving free-
   Council   flowing rivers
323 Pennsylvania Ave. SE
Washington, DC 20003

Boy Scouts of America   organization for boys 8–17
P.O. Box 61030
Dallas/Fort Worth Airport, TX 75261

Environmental Defense Fund   seeks environmental protection in the
1525 18th St. NW   courts
Washington, DC 20003

Girl Scouts of America   organization for girls 8–17
830 Third Ave.
New York, NY 10022

GreenPeace   activist environmental organization
1700 Connecticut Ave. N.W.
Washington, DC 20070

National Audubon Society   powerful and respected environmental
950 Third Ave.   organization
New York, NY 10022

National Wildlife Federation   powerful and respected environmental
1412 16th Street NW   organization
Washington, DC 20036

Sierra Club   very active environmental organization
1050 Mills Tower   sponsors many outdoor trips
San Francisco, CA 94104

Wilderness Public Rights Fund   favors equitable recreational river ac-
P.O. Box 308   cess rights
Orinda, CA 94563

The Wilderness Society   favors wilderness protection
1901 Pennsylvania Ave. NW
Washington, DC 20006

Canoeing Associations

American Canoe Association
P.O. Box 248
Lorton, VA 22079

for people interested in canoeing,
canoe camping, and racing

Canadian Canoe Association
333 River Road
Vanier, ONT K1L 8H9

emphasizes competitive canoeing

Eastern Professional River
Outfitters
Box 119
Oak Hill, VA 25901

organization of professional guides on
eastern American rivers

National Association of Canoe
Liveries and Outfitters
221 N. LaSalle St.
Chicago, Ill 60601

publishes nationwide list of canoe
rental liveries

National Organization
for River Sports
314 N. 20th St.
Colorado Springs, CO 80904

represents river-running interests—
educational, legal, conservation

United States Canoe Association
2509 Kickapoo Drive
Lafayette, IN 47905

supports canoe races, canoe camping,
river conservation, and recreational
paddling

Western River Guide Association
994 Denver St.
Salt Lake City, UT 84111

organization of professional guides on
western American rivers

Wilderness Canoe Association
58 Eastborne Ave.
Toronto, ONT M5P 2G2

interested in wilderness canoeing

Wooden Canoe Heritage Association
P.O. Box 5634
Madison, WI 53705

emphasizes canoe heritage, wood
canoes, and wood canoe building

INDEX